WRITING ABOUT LEARNING AND TEACHING IN HIGHER EDUCATION

Center for Engaged Learning
Open Access Book Series

Series editors, Jessie L. Moore and Peter Felten

The Center for Engaged Learning (CEL) Open Access Book Series features concise, peer-reviewed books (both authored books and edited collections) for a multi-disciplinary, international, higher education audience interested in research-informed engaged learning practices.

The CEL Open Access Book Series offers an alternate publishing option for high-quality engaged learning books that align with the Center's mission, goals, and initiatives, and that experiment with genre or medium in ways that take advantage of an online and open access format.

CEL is committed to making these publications freely available to a global audience.

Pedagogical Partnerships: A How-To Guide for Faculty, Students, and Academic Developers in Higher Education
Alison Cook-Sather, Melanie Bahti, and Anita Ntem
https://doi.org/10.36284/celelon.oa1

The Power of Partnership: Students, Staff, and Faculty Revolutionizing Higher Education
Edited by Lucy Mercer-Mapstone and Sophia Abbot
https://doi.org/10.36284/celelon.oa2

Writing about Learning and Teaching

in Higher Education

Creating and Contributing to Scholarly Conversations across a Range of Genres

---

Mick Healey, Kelly E. Matthews, and Alison Cook-Sather

Elon University Center for Engaged Learning
Elon, North Carolina
www.CenterForEngagedLearning.org

This publication extends "Writing Scholarship of Teaching and Learning Articles
for Peer-Reviewed Journals" by Mick Healey, Kelly E. Matthews, and Alison
Cook-Sather (2019), originally published in *Teaching & Learning Inquiry* (*TLI*),
the official journal of the International Society for the Scholarship of Teaching
and Learning (ISSOTL). Articles published in *TLI* are licensed under a Creative
Commons Attribution-NonCommercial 4.0 International license. The original
article is available at https://doi.org/10.20343/teachlearninqu.7.2.3.

"Writing a draft paper" (Reflection 24.1) was originally published as a blog post
and is reproduced by permission of the author, Pat Thomson.

"What makes a good critical friend?" (Reflection 26.1) was originally published
as a blog post and is reproduced by permission of the author, Rebecca J. Hogue.

Series editors: Jessie L. Moore and Peter Felten
Copyeditor and designer: Jennie Goforth

Cataloging-in-Publication Data
Names: Healey, Mick | Matthews, Kelly E. | Cook-Sather, Alison
Title: Writing about Learning and Teaching in Higher Education / Mick Healey,
Kelly E. Matthews, and Alison Cook-Sather
Description: Elon, North Carolina : Elon University Center for Engaged
Learning, [2020] | Series: Center for engaged learning open access book series |
Includes bibliographical references and index.
Identifiers: LCCN 2020941985 | ISBN (PDF) 978-1-951414-04-7 | ISBN
(PBK) 978-1-951414-05-4 | DOI https://doi.org/10.36284/celelon.oa3
Subjects: LCSH: Academic writing handbooks, manuals, etc.; Education, Higher
Research; College teaching; College teachers as authors

ACKNOWLEDGEMENTS

We are deeply grateful to the colleagues listed below. They read drafts of part or all of the book, and they affirmed our efforts to both name and challenge conventions. They offered constructive feedback that helped clarify our argument, and they posed productively challenging questions that made us revisit assumptions. And they contributed reflections that enriched and animated the text. Their candor, generosity, and wisdom, all shared with both kindness and humor, significantly improved this text. Any remaining errors or oversights are ours.

> Sophia Abbot, graduate student in a Masters of Higher Education program and graduate apprentice in the Center for Engaged Learning at Elon University, US

> Ron Barnett, emeritus professor of higher education, University College London Institute of Education, UK

> Sally Brown, emerita professor, Leeds Beckett University, UK

> Jennifer Fraser, director of student partnership in the Centre for Teaching Innovation, Westminster University, UK

> Nattalia Godbold, doctoral student, University of Queensland, Australia

> Ruth Healey, associate professor in pedagogy in higher education, University of Chester, UK

> Pat Hutchings, senior associate, Carnegie Foundation, and senior scholar with the National Institute for Learning Outcomes Assessment, US

Amrita Kaur, senior lecturer, School of Education and Modern Language, Universiti Utara, Malaysia

John Lea, research director for the Scholarship Project, UK

Margy MacMillan, previously librarian at Mount Royal University, Calgary, Canada

Claire Simmons, academic developer, Coventry University, UK

Kathryn Sutherland, associate professor, Victoria University of Wellington, New Zealand

Pat Thomson, professor of education in the School of Education, University of Nottingham, UK

Preeti Vayada, doctoral student, University of Queensland, Australia

Nadya Yakovchuk, academic writing teaching fellow, Doctoral College, University of Surrey, UK

We are also grateful to our colleagues who enriched the book by writing and sharing their reflections. They are acknowledged in the text.

We wish to thank Jessie Moore and Peter Felten, founding editors of the Elon University Center for Engaged Learning Open Access Book Series, for their support and guidance; Jennie Goforth, for shepherding the book through production; Jasmine Huang and Preeti Vayada, for assisting with referencing and pre-production formatting; and Nicole Litvitskiy, for her work on the index.

Finally, we all want to acknowledge the encouraging support of our families—Mick to Chris; Kelly to Carlos, Alex, and Codi; and Alison to Scott and Morgan—as we juggled family time with writing and work.

TABLE OF CONTENTS

Part 5: Writing Efficiently, Effectively, and Energizingly

Part 6: Submitting, Responding to Reviewers, and Promoting Your Work

LIST OF FIGURES AND TABLES

FIGURES

TABLES

LIST OF GUIDING QUESTIONS

PART 1

UNDERSTANDING THE BOOK
AND MEETING THE AUTHORS

CHAPTER 1

ARTICULATING OUR GOALS

Origins, Audiences, and Structure

Many academics are surprised how little they know about writing and some are relieved finally to be able to admit it. (Murray 2009, 2-3)

For most academics, formal training on how to write "like a historian" or "like a biologist" begins and ends with the PhD, if it happens at all. (Sword 2012, 24)

How can a practice required of so many academics be so little understood and addressed? What are the implications of the lack of understanding and training that Rowena Murray and Helen Sword note in the quotes above for those new to the practice of academic writing, for those who have developed approaches that work for them, and for those in between?

While there may be a dearth of dialogue about writing in, about, and for the academy in general, the lack of guidance for writing about learning and teaching in particular is what inspired the three of us to compose an article entitled "Writing Scholarship of Teaching and Learning Articles for Peer-Reviewed Journals" (Healey, Matthews, and Cook-Sather 2019). Two things happened as we drafted that piece for publication. The first is that the critical friends we asked for feedback—some of whom were established scholars with extensive publication records and some of whom were new to academic writing—expressed enthusiastic appreciation for what we included (as well as offered useful suggestions for revision). The second thing that happened is that we realized there was so much more to say—and to learn. We decided to write this book to expand on what we addressed in that article and to build on the exchanges with colleagues it inspired.

Our goal with this book is to model and to support the creation of and contributions to scholarly conversations about learning and teaching in higher education across a wide range of genres. By "genre" we mean *the kind or form of writing* you select. For example, do you want to write an empirical research article, an opinion piece, a reflective essay, or a blog? As we discuss in part 2 of the book, approaches to creating and contributing to such exchanges in the academic community are inextricably linked to the ongoing processes of developing identities, clarifying your values, and learning through writing—processes in which all scholars of learning and teaching (faculty, academic staff, and students) must engage.

Who We Are as Learning and Teaching Scholars

Our purpose and focus are shaped by who we are and what we value. As the co-authors of this book, we share an interest in researching learning and teaching in higher education and have participated extensively in the growing national and international interest in the scholarship of teaching and learning (SoTL). We have a particular interest in partnerships among students, faculty/academics, and others in learning and teaching, and we are three of the founding co-editors of the *International Journal for Students as Partners* (*IJSaP*). However, our formative experiences of inquiring into learning and teaching were influenced by having worked in three different disciplinary contexts and on three different continents. Moreover, we have worked in this arena for varied lengths of time and have distinct approaches to academic writing. We acknowledge that we share a Western perspective, we all come from English-speaking countries, and we are all white, cisgender scholars, and that our cultural backgrounds and personal identities have shaped who we are as scholars and how we see the world. We include some background on our development as learning and teaching scholars in Our Perspectives 1.1.

Our Perspectives 1.1

How have you developed as a learning and teaching scholar and writer?

Mick: I come from a disciplinary approach to teaching. After more than fifteen years researching and writing about economic geography, my first learning and teaching publication developed from a reorganization of our first-year practical classes in geography at Coventry University, UK, in the late 1980s. Shortly after, I joined the editorial board of the *Journal of Geography in Higher Education*. It was only after winning a National Teaching Fellowship in 2000 (through what is now known as Advance HE in the UK, which recognizes outstanding impacts on student outcomes and the teaching profession in higher education), more than a decade after my first pedagogic publication, that I began to write more generally about learning and teaching issues. I grew as a learning and teaching scholar through engagement with the International Society for the Scholarship of Teaching and Learning (ISSOTL), co-editing the *International Journal for Academic Development,* and more recently becoming the inaugural senior editor of the *International Journal for Students as Partners.* Despite being the author of many publications, including several books, and being an experienced reviewer and editor, I have learned so much in preparing this book.

Kelly: I grew up as a white, middle-class tomboy from a broken home in suburban New Orleans—classic latchkey kid. My parents were not academic types although my mom was (what was then called) a secretary for thirty years in a university. Somehow (still a mystery to me) I ended up in a paid undergraduate research role in Professor Hill's lab group at Louisiana State University, where I co-authored two papers on viral interactions with neurodegenerative diseases—my first foray in academic publishing. However, lab life was not for me, and I moved into science teaching in "failing schools" in New Orleans. Then along came Hurricane Katrina in 2005. I moved to Australia with no job prospects, newly liberated from all my worldly possessions, and cured of misguided beliefs about certainty or long-term planning. A large, comprehensive Australian research-intensive university, The University of Queensland (UQ), hired me on a contract to support students from low socio-economic status backgrounds. Academic colleagues encouraged me to pursue a PhD, and the timing was right for me as UQ created a new academic role: teaching-focused staff who conducted SoTL instead of (or as well as, depending on who you asked) disciplinary research. With my skills as a teacher and curiosity about learning in university, I found myself enrolled in a PhD, mentoring teaching-focused academics and then becoming a teaching-focused academic myself in 2010. UQ offered me tremendous opportunities to engage in research and academic writing. Two kids, a PhD, and two promotions later, I—still a weak but persistent writer—continue on with my brand of relentless stubbornness to figure this writing thing out. My development as a scholar has been haphazard yet enabled by the privilege I was born into and the sponsorship of key colleagues along the way.

Alison: I spent my childhood in a large, Victorian house in San Francisco filled with books that belonged to a mother who quoted Shakespeare at dinner. That early exposure may have contributed to my choice to major in English literature at college and to teach it at high school level for a number of years. My decision to complete a PhD in education was driven in part by my own desire to keep learning and in part by my desire to pursue a career focused on creating meaningful learning experiences for others. When I assumed leadership of the secondary teacher certification program at Bryn Mawr and Haverford Colleges in the United States in 1994, my priority was to create opportunities for secondary students to inform the preparation of future teachers—and a teacher colleague and I designed a program to do just that, which continues to this day (Cook-Sather 2002; Cook-Sather and Curl 2014). In the early 2000s, I started to assume more responsibility for supporting the educational development of faculty at Bryn Mawr and Haverford Colleges, and I brought the focus of student-teacher partnership to that work, particularly as it affirmed the experiences and perspectives of underrepresented students (Cook-Sather 2018a). The Students as Learners and Teachers program I developed became internationally known and emulated, and as I started publishing work on that program (Cook-Sather 2008, 2011), I came into contact with learning and teaching scholars and practitioners who were also interested in students' voices and roles in educational development. These multiple forms of privilege and a fairly single-minded commitment made my development as a learning and teaching scholar a fairly smooth process.

Source: Based in part on Healey, Matthews, and Cook-Sather (2019, 29-30)

Your perspective: What influenced your development as a learning and teaching scholar?

Since both our shared and our diverse learning and teaching identities inform our arguments, we use a collective "we" throughout most of the book but also integrate several "Our Perspectives" text boxes like the one above that include all three of our experiences and perspectives. Our intent is for our respective "voices" to surface our different experiences and views to illustrate our argument that there is no one way to write about learning and teaching or to be a "learning and teaching scholar." For that reason and as an attempt to be, as best we can in a book format, in dialogue, we invite you—all of you—to address some of the same questions we tackle, as in the "Our Perspectives" text boxes.

We also include across the chapters stories from more than twenty colleagues, both experienced and relatively new to writing, in "Reflection" boxes. Our goal in doing so is to reveal the array of lived experiences of writing—the joys, vulnerabilities, fears, risks, surprises, and excitement that go hand-in-hand with this hard, yet rewarding, emotional and intellectual work. To create, as best we can, a sense of ongoing dialogue, we include discussion questions in the introductions to each part of the book and at the end of each chapter.

Finally, we weave into our discussion personal communications we received from critical friends in response to drafts of the book. In this we model the importance of critical friends and show the way they offered insights, based on their experiences and viewpoints, that changed our thinking and the shape of a text. Citing these personal communications also models another form of conversation among scholars that is typically invisible labor (what Sword [2017a] refers to as the generous work of being in a scholarly writing community—work that can burn people out). Conventional Western practices tell us to cite scholars in published outlets, which we do, but our integration of personal communications is our attempt to recognize people and the knowledge that they bring that moves us beyond our own, necessarily limited experiences and perspectives.

Intended Audiences and Our Terminology

How, what, when, and where students are learning are everyday discussions across campuses in North and South America, Europe, Africa, Asia, and Australasia. Therefore, the scholarship on such engagement needs to be broad and inclusive of a diversity of scholars. In this book we address members of several, sometimes overlapping groups:

- *academics*—members of faculty (a term commonly used in North America), academic staff (common outside of North America), instructors, lecturers, librarians (who are considered faculty in some contexts), higher education researchers, and educational developers or those in similar roles that typically involve teaching and research responsibilities;
- *professional staff*—learning designers, educational technologists, educational developers in non-academic/non-faculty positions, librarians (who are considered staff in some contexts), student services and student life staff, and non-teaching staff with essential roles to play in supporting teaching and student learning; and
- *students*—graduate students, whom we consider to be emerging practitioners within higher education, and undergraduates, who

are increasingly engaging in learning and teaching inquiry in higher education.

We anticipate that you will find the book useful if one or more of the following applies to you:

- you are knowledgeable about your disciplinary field but have had little opportunity to develop knowledge and write about higher education or engage in academic writing about learning and teaching;
- you strive to facilitate not only the work of developing teaching practices that support engaged learning but also wish to write about this work;
- you already publish about learning and teaching in higher education in your discipline and want to revise some of your established practices and expand your identities as a writer;
- you already publish about learning and teaching in higher education generally and want to review your writing practices and explore new ones;
- you want to write about learning and teaching and seek detailed guidance in navigating multiple forms of writing and conceptualizing your identity in ways that might be quite new and unfamiliar;
- you are pursuing a graduate certificate, master's, or PhD in learning and teaching;
- you are enrolled in undergraduate courses or graduate studies and are working in partnership with scholars on learning and teaching projects; or
- you are an applicant for institutional, national, or international teaching fellowship or award, or you are making a case for promotion based at least in part on the excellence of your teaching.

The diversity of roles in higher education and the different language used internationally to name such roles complicate how we talk about each other and the work in which we are engaged. For the sake of clarity and inclusion, in the rest of this book we adopt the broad term *scholar* to refer to all three groups named above (academics, professional staff, and students). This term aims to reflect our conviction that all of you can be *learning and teaching scholars* when you investigate and communicate about learning and teaching in a scholarly way. Sometimes, for the sake of simplicity, when it comes to you publishing your work, we refer to you simply as *writers* or *authors*.

Our Approach to Writing this Book

To be transparent about our own writing process as we offer guidance on writing, we want to share something of our approach to writing this book. We started by drafting the book proposal, including brief synopses and approximate word limits for each chapter. Though we had provisional discussions with our eventual publisher, we decided not to submit the formal proposal until we had drafted about one-third of the text. This proved to be an important decision, as we revised the content and structure in our initial proposal in several ways as a result of drafting the initial chapters.

We allocated the task of writing the first draft of each chapter among the three of us based on our interests, previous experiences, and workloads. As we completed each draft, we sent it around to the others for critical comment. Sometimes we rewrote sections or added or deleted sections; in other cases, the changes were mostly minor edits or alterations to sentence construction to enhance readability. On a few occasions, one or another of us had a writing block and passed the chapter over to one of the others to complete the first draft.

As we progressed to a first draft, the realities of our different workloads and lives reshaped our plan, prompting us to reframe our approach yet again. So, while we offer frameworks and guidance for writing, we also model through "Our Perspectives" boxes the messy, lived realities of the process, whether completed alone or in collaboration, that writers navigate with differing levels of comfort, joy, excitement, and disappointment. Our existing relationships and flexibility allowed us to accept these realties even though we hold different preferences for setting deadlines and making firm plans.

What to say and how to say it best are always questions in writing. As we drafted, we found that we wanted to say more than we had initially allowed the space for—a case of learning as we wrote! Sometimes we had to be strict with ourselves and cut whole sections, or exclude discussion of some topic areas, or simply point to other sources where readers would find the topic discussed.

We are fortunate to have extensive established networks that we drew on to find people to comment on our draft manuscript, and we were also fortunate to have worked with editors who welcomed dialogue during the composing process. In total, fourteen colleagues plus our three editors provided helpful suggestions for enhancing all or parts of the text (for a full list, see the acknowledgments). As a result of this feedback and our own reflections, we merged two chapters, split another one in two, redistributed the material from a further chapter, and added two more chapters, as well as rearranging, clarifying, adding, and deleting text within each chapter.

Structure and Organization of the Book

The above process resulted in the following structure and organization of the book. Depending on your experience with writing about learning and teaching for a scholarly audience, you might want to focus on some parts of the book and skip others entirely. In addition to the two introductory chapters that make up this part of the book, we think you will find that chapter 11 provides a useful introduction to the eleven different genres we discuss.

Part 1 is our effort to locate ourselves as people, scholars, and writers and to locate this book as part of larger, ongoing conversations. It explains the origins, audiences, and structure of the book followed by an explanation of our scope (what we do and do not focus on in the book). Why might you want to write about learning and teaching? We answer that question as we also locate the book at the intersection of higher education research and SoTL.

Part 2 provides the conceptual framework for the book. We offer this framework to make explicit our own values as participants in various formal discussions and analyses of learning and teaching and to suggest that scholarly writing is, ideally, at once dialogic and reflective—part both of a larger dialogue and of individual, ongoing learning. In this part of the book we argue for writing as:

- a way to create and contribute to scholarly conversations about learning and teaching,
- a method for fostering identities and clarifying values, and
- a medium for engaging in ongoing learning.

Part 3 invites you as writers to clarify your purpose and address some preliminary questions in preparation for drafting: What is motivating you to write about learning and teaching? Do you write alone or with others? How do you select an outlet to share your writing? Should you draft the title and, where relevant, an abstract or summary, before starting the substantive text? This part of the book aims to help you think about how you put your own version of the dialogue and reflective processes we discuss in part 2 into practice in your writing.

Part 4, by far the longest section of the book, provides guidelines for writing in eleven different genres (empirical research articles, theoretical and conceptual articles, literature reviews, case studies, books and edited collections, conference and workshop presentations, reflective essays, opinion pieces, stories, social media, and applications for teaching fellowships, awards, and promotions). In this part of the book we examine established practices in each of these genres, offer questions to consider as you write within each, and recommend ways in which you might both attend to existing practices and complicate or push beyond them. We offer this part of the book to both experienced and new scholars to support thinking through what is established within scholarly writing communities, what can evolve from those norms, and what might be developed anew.

Part 5 focuses on writing efficiently, effectively, and energizingly. This part of the book summarizes some of the advice about writing that can be found in general writing guides and advice for doctoral students. We offer it with the understanding that writing about learning and teaching may be a familiar, different, or new experience for differently positioned scholars. This advice therefore warrants revisiting (for some) and clarifying for the first time (for others) how to:

allot time and choose space to write; write and rewrite your draft; become an engaging writer; and develop a network of critical friends.

Part 6 focuses on the final stages of sending your writing into the public sphere to contribute to or create scholarly conversations about learning and teaching, including the processes of submitting your manuscript, responding to reviewers, and promoting your work.

The book's website (www.CenterForEngagedLearning.org/books/writing-about-learning) contains many online resources that offer activities, templates, and examples to give greater depth to selected topics in the book and engage you more actively in the writing process. Where these are provided, they are mentioned in the book. In addition, if you are reading the PDF version on screen, you may use the hyperlinks to external resources throughout the book to further support your writing.

Over to You

As a new or experienced academic, professional staff member, or student in the growing scholarly community committed to the improvement of learning and teaching in higher education, you have choices about the genres you write in, the aspects of learning and teaching you focus on, and who you are and want to be in the scholarly community—although the kind and extent of your choices will vary. Most people learn how to be an academic writer on the job, and for many it is a sink or swim experience. As Rowena Murray (2009, 1) observes, "The dominant characteristic of academic writers is their persistence." Reflecting on twenty years of publishing, Helen Sword (2017a, 7) also captures the role of persistence in writing: "I still find academic writing to be a frustrating, exhilarating, endlessly challenging process that never seems to get any easier—but that I wouldn't give up for the world." Our purpose in writing this book is to offer encouragement and guidance for all those who persist, whether in the context of SoTL, educational research, or as part of other discussions of learning and teaching in higher education.

As you contemplate who you are and who you want to become as a scholar of learning and teaching, consider how your choices about genre and focus might help you persist and experience the exhilaration as well as work through the challenges that Sword notes above. We offer the following questions for you to address before reading chapter 2 to help you clarify who you hope to become as a scholar of learning and teaching:

- What is your identity—or what are your identities—as a learning and teaching scholar? What experiences do you already have of writing about learning and teaching in higher education?
- What key questions do you have about writing about learning and teaching in higher education? What areas are you most interested in developing and enhancing?
- How will you go about reading this text? Which chapters interest you most? In what order will you read them?

Each introduction and chapter in the book includes reflection and discussion questions, like the ones above. We have gathered all these questions in the online resources as well.

CHAPTER 2

SITUATING OUR WORK

*Focus, Motivation, Educational Research,
and Scholarship of Teaching and Learning*

*Disciplines constitute a system of control in the production
of discourse, fixing its limits through the action of an identity taking the form of a permanent reactivation of the rules.
(Foucault 1972, 224)*

We describe in chapter 1 the ways in which we want both to illuminate
discourses associated with writing about learning and teaching and
to complicate those. We wish to acknowledge and also work against
the reproduction and reactivation of rules that limit and exclude, as
Michel Foucault highlights in the quote above. We focus on eleven
genres in which many scholars need or want to publish: empirical
research articles, theoretical and conceptual articles, literature reviews,
case studies, books and edited collections, conference and workshop
presentations, reflective essays, opinion pieces, stories, social media,
and applications for teaching fellowships, awards, and promotions.
We include communicating orally, such as by making a conference
presentation or giving a workshop, because such presentations
typically involve working with text and often are an important stage
in writing or promoting something that has already been or will be
written. Furthermore, by including writing applications for teaching
fellowships, awards, and promotions we recognize that not all writing
results in publication, although it is important to be aware of how

much gets "published" by virtue of being available electronically—a contemporary reality all writers should keep in mind.

At the same time, we cannot unpack every discourse or form of writing. Therefore, while we argue in this book for writing about learning and teaching in higher education across a wide range of genres, we do not discuss every genre of writing or associated form of production. For instance, we do not discuss theses, book reviews, or applications for educational grants. We also do not address video as a venue for dissemination, and we do not focus on writing for audiences beyond other scholars of learning and teaching—knowledge mobilization beyond the academy. Nor do we address the mechanics of grammar. Finally, we do not delve into *how* to conduct learning and teaching research. Rather, we focus on writing about such inquiries (usually for publication) in various genres, not only those that rely on dominant, distanced (and largely Western) constructs of data collection but also those that privilege personal, sometimes complicated and messy, lived experiences.

While conventional academic wisdom typically privileges data- or theory-driven research, and for good reasons, there are also good reasons to question dominant assumptions regarding what "counts" as research on learning and teaching, what is "publishable," and where we might publish our writing. Some of the genres we explore in this book are well established, some are more recently recognized, and all are always evolving. Furthermore, the divisions among the genres and the language used to distinguish them may be helpful in illuminating the current norms of any given approach, but our goal is also, to borrow Jennifer Fraser's (personal communication, August 4, 2019) phrase, "to trouble these divides." As they point out, for instance, "conceptual and theoretical pieces are also research articles."

We argue that creating and contributing to scholarly conversations about learning and teaching in higher education include, but also move beyond, traditional journal or book chapter outlets. While these may be required and appropriate venues for some scholarly work, we argue for complicating established genres and for publishing in outlets that welcome the rich, messy, and relational practices of learning and teaching in higher education institutions around the world. We advocate not only writing in a diversity of established and evolving genres but also blurring the divisions among those genres and embracing exploration, experimentation, and enjoyment as much as intentional adherence to expectations in writing. We see these efforts as part of pursing the larger goal of capturing and valuing the wide variety of learning and teaching practices that exist and the diversity of the perspectives of the many, differently positioned people engaged in such work.

We acknowledge, in advocating this expansion both of writing genres and of writing processes, the difficulty that many scholars experience when coming into learning and teaching as a scholarly field from different disciplinary contexts and institutional cultures and the extent to which identities affect and inform choices. You may be an accomplished academic who is an expert in your field but who also wants to write about learning and teaching; you might be in a teaching-focused role with little experience with academic writing; you may be an undergraduate or graduate student altogether new to academic writing. And regardless of your role, you may or may not be a confident academic writer, and how you experience yourself and how others perceive you will also have an impact on your choices. If writing about learning and teaching projects and experiences is new to you, you are simultaneously forging your identity as a learning and teaching scholar, striving to clarify your values as both a scholar and a practitioner, and continually learning through writing—hence the importance of understanding the fostering of identities as an ongoing process. This book aims to support all scholars, across roles and contexts, in their respective processes of creating and contributing to scholarly conversations about learning and teaching, and also of developing identities, clarifying values, and learning through writing.

Why Write about Learning and Teaching?

When Helen Sword (2012, 159) writes about writing, she uses the words "passion, commitment, pleasure, playfulness, humor, elegance, lyricism, originality, imagination, creativity, and undisciplined thinking." When Pat Hutchings (personal communication, June 11, 2019) reflected on her motivation for writing, as she read through a draft of this book, she mused: "When I'm working on a piece of writing, suddenly everything becomes more interesting, more connected, ideas get sparked. It brings thinking to life, so to speak." These reflections offer several of the best reasons we can think of to write. Writing can capture and convey what makes us human, what makes us connected, what keeps us alive; it allows us to express and to perceive the joyful feeling and clarified understanding of which humans are capable. And when, as Robin Wall Kimmerer (2014) argues, we use language that resonates for the people we address, we deepen understanding, catalyze learning, and foster connection.

These reflections on writing in general apply in particular ways to writing about learning and teaching. In the last two decades, quality in learning and teaching has become a priority for most institutions, governments, and professional bodies at state/province, national, and international levels. In keeping with this prioritization, we see increased professionalization of staff engaged in teaching and supporting learning, and we see increased demand to provide evidence of the beneficial impact of learning and teaching research, practices, and policies at individual, program, institutional, and national levels. These increases have led to expanded calls for and increased interest in writing about learning and teaching. We are at a moment when the ways that many of us in higher education spend our time—in engaging in or supporting learning and teaching—can become the focus of academic writing, allowing us to bring the personal, human potential of writing into dialogue with the professional, institutional work we do.

Like the language used to name the various genres for writing, the terms "learning" and "teaching" signal a far greater diversity of practices and subjects of inquiry than any single term can capture. When the terms are linked, as they are in our title and much of our discussion, they might seem to refer to a single, undifferentiated phenomenon, but our goal in linking them parallels our goal in at once naming and striving to complicate genres. Writing about teachers' teaching and about students' learning might, in some ways, as Ronald Barnett (personal communication, July 28, 2019) notes, "call for different stances on the part of the writer given the different considerations that come into view." At the same time, we suggest that learning and teaching are always happening in more than one direction and on more than one level. There are certainly instances of teachers learning from and teaching each other, students learning from and teaching each other, and, as our own work emphasizes, teachers and learners working in pedagogical partnerships in which typical roles are complicated and sometimes reversed. We therefore use "learning and teaching" not to conflate the multiple, multi-directional, multi-layered work each term signals but rather to offer a reminder of that multiplicity.

As we discuss across the chapters in this book, different genres of writing weave the personal and professional together in different ways, and each invites a foregrounding of and a focus on different aspects of the work of learning and teaching. Furthermore, writing can focus on theory- and research-led approaches or on practical applications. Whether you write in the more formal language typical of most empirical research articles, theoretical and conceptual articles, and literature reviews or the more informal language typical of reflective essays, opinion pieces, social media, and stories, you are conveying the phenomena, insights, and possibilities that affect us as human beings who engage in and reflect on learning and teaching. How all the genres for writing about learning and teaching evolve depends on how those who write and read shape those genres. This is the excitement of creating and contributing to scholarly conversations, developing identities, clarifying values, and learning through writing.

There are many excellent general guides to academic writing (e.g., Belcher 2009; Day 2016; Stevens 2019; Sword 2012, 2017a) that are packed with useful advice. However, few texts include discussion of writing about learning and teaching in higher education or examine the wide range of genres that we explore in this book. While many writing guides target PhD students publishing from their dissertations (e.g., Kamler and Thomson 2014), there are distinct issues in writing and publishing about learning and teaching that "remain unaddressed in generic or disciplinary publication materials" (Chick et al. 2014, 4). These issues include the need to analyze general processes of learning and teaching and go beyond discipline-specific phenomena, and the need to address a wider audience with a greater diversity of experiences and perspectives than you might find within particular disciplines. While you may find some sections of the text clearly focused on writing about learning and teaching, it may seem that other parts of the book discuss writing more generally. We have endeavored to strike a balance among the following:

- arguing for writing as creating and contributing to scholarly conversations, developing identities and affirming and expanding values, and engaging in ongoing learning;
- illuminating and complicating established genres and legitimating newer and evolving ones; and
- offering advice about writing that might be familiar for some and can be found elsewhere but might be new to others and feel different as one approaches writing about learning and teaching.

Linking Higher Education Research and the Scholarship of Teaching and Learning

Since this book is concerned with writing about learning and teaching in higher education, it is relevant to authors contributing to higher education research conversations and to scholarship of teaching and learning (SoTL) conversations. The similarities and differences between higher education research and SoTL have been widely debated over the last two decades (e.g., Brew 2011; Case 2015; Geertsema 2016; Larsson et al. 2017; Potter and Kustra 2011; Tight 2018a; Trigwell and Shale 2004). Perhaps the key distinction centers on the purposes of the scholarly inquiry being conducted; in educational research, the fundamental goal is generalizable knowledge, and in SoTL the core purpose is to improve teaching and learning for the particular students being studied (Geertsema 2016). This primary difference often leads to divergence in the research methods and the audiences for educational research and SoTL (Ashwin and Trigwell

2004, 122), and positions SoTL as a form of both scholarly inquiry and academic development (Felten and Chick 2018).

This distinction also has implications for how scholars and practitioners write about learning and teaching. The essential genre of educational research is the scholarly article, while SoTL is open to a far wider range of "going public" with processes and findings. These include not only articles in journals but also approaches such as presenting at university learning and teaching conferences, writing reflective essays, and applying for learning and teaching fellowships (Fanghanel 2013; Geertsema 2016). Keith Trigwell and Susan Shale (2004, 534) suggest that publication is one way, but not the only way, to communicate about learning and teaching:

> We have publication of research on teaching as a component in making scholarly teaching activity public, but as there are many other ways of making public how learning has been made possible, we believe it not to be essential and that the scholarship of teaching could be happening without it.

Paul Ashwin and Keith Trigwell (2004) offer different levels of pedagogic investigation to show a range of ways of communicating the outcomes of learning and teaching investigations (Table 2.1). All three levels involve scholarship and are interrelated, in that personal knowledge underpins contributions to local and public knowledge, and contributions to local knowledge may be a stepping-stone to contributing to public knowledge. Public knowledge, in turn, is "read by others to inform themselves, . . . build local, institutional knowledge, and thus the cycle of knowledge building continues" (Geertsema 2016, 129).

Since many scholars come to SoTL or discipline-based educational research from a different disciplinary location than education, producing educational research outputs will be a different challenge for them than it is for those trained in education (see also chapter 22). Kerri-Lee Krause (2019) outlines a spectrum of education research paradigms, from positivist through to supercomplexity—with neo-positivist, pragmatic, interpretivist, and transformative in between—that offers another way for writers to make sense of learning and teaching in a supercomplex higher education environment. Regardless of which paradigm you write in, however, we recognize, as Ronald Barnett (2019a, 239) argues, that "writing is at once a communicative act and a creative act."

Table 2.1: Levels of pedagogic investigation

Level	Purpose of investigation	Evidence gathering methods and conclusions will be	Investigation results in
1	To inform oneself	Verified by self	Personal knowledge
2	To inform a group within a shared context	Verified by those within same context	Local knowledge
3	To inform a wider audience	Verified by those within same context	Public knowledge

Source: Ashwin and Trigwell (2004, 122)

Over to You

The argument that runs throughout this book is twofold. First, we argue that writing for publication is a complex process of creating and contributing to conversations, forging identities, and embracing opportunities for ongoing learning. Second, we argue that we should recognize and value writing about learning and teaching through many different writing genres. Much of what we argue goes well beyond learning and teaching, but this is our area of expertise that we are passionate about and applying our arguments to this area is the focus of this book.

How do you see yourself starting or continuing to engage in scholarly conversations about learning and teaching in higher education across a wide range of genres? Answering the following questions may help you address that larger query and position yourself to realize the potential of writing about learning and teaching:

- Why are you interested in writing about learning and teaching?
- Which genres of writing have you experienced, and which would you like to try out?
- In writing about learning and teaching, do you see yourself as contributing to higher education research or SoTL, or both?

PART 2

EMBRACING THE POTENTIAL OF WRITING ABOUT LEARNING AND TEACHING

Introduction to Part 2

In this section of the book we begin by sharing how we think about writing about learning and teaching before we discuss how to go about writing across a range of genres. Woven across all the chapters of this book are three key threads that stitch together how we make sense of writing as a subjective and complex human experience. To us, writing is:

- a way to create and contribute to scholarly conversations about learning and teaching,
- a method for fostering identities and clarifying values, and
- a medium for engaging in ongoing learning.

How we experience the writing process and the decisions we make about writing—what we write about; whom we write with, about, and for; what genres we prefer to write in—shape the writers we are and will become. Our aim in this book is to offer practical and helpful guidance for writing about learning and teaching that is firmly grounded in an understanding of the writer as a person within the scholarly learning and teaching community. We hope our guidance supports you as you consider *how* you want to write and publish and *who* you want to be as a member of the growing community of people committed to learning and teaching as important and scholarly work in higher education.

Before you embark on reading part 2, we recommend that you address these questions for yourself, and then keep them in mind as you read:

- With which learning and teaching communities do you want to be in dialogue?
- How do you see yourself as a writer? How do other people see you as a writer?
- What matters to you about writing?
- How are you learning as you write?

You might want to return to these questions and think about how your answers change, if at all, when you consider your purposes for writing, as you prepare to start drafting (part 3), and as you clarify your preferences for a particular writing genre (part 4).

CHAPTER 3

CREATING AND CONTRIBUTING TO SCHOLARLY CONVERSATIONS THROUGH WRITING

Done well, writing SoTL [scholarship of teaching and learning] puts our work in conversation with prior scholarship and opens up portals with others to respond to our research, add to it, and continue the dialogue for years to come. (Moore 2018, 125-6)

Choosing a scholarly conversation involves two interacting decisions: the kind of scholar you want to be, and the kind of knowledge you believe is worth developing. (Huff 2008, 5)

To write is to compose—to put words together in ways that strive both to constitute and to invite particular understandings. It is, therefore, inherently expressive and communicative: it is used to capture and convey ideas, feelings, arguments, and more. In this book we are focused on writing as a process of communication to share and further develop ideas, to exchange experiences and insights, and to contribute new understandings about and suggest new practices in learning and teaching in higher education. As the subtitle of our book suggests, we think of writing about learning and teaching as creating and contributing to scholarly conversations—an ongoing dialogue, as Jessie Moore describes, that, as Anne Huff suggests, involves people and our construction of knowledge.

Communicating with Learning and Teaching Communities

The learning and teaching community in higher education is many communities. This multiplicity is evident in chapter 8 where we explore publication outlets that have distinct themes (e.g., active learning, critical pedagogies) or are organized by discipline. When we think about writing as communication, we have to consider with whom we are communicating about our practices and inquiries. Unless we come from the interdisciplinary realm of education, we likely come as scholars to learning and teaching from an academic discipline not related to pedagogy. Where we come from matters not only because it shapes our identities as writers (see chapter 4) but also because it means we have been trained in certain ways of writing as a form of scholarly communication.

Thus, for some of us, writing to communicate about learning and teaching with other scholars means unlearning disciplinary norms or stretching our thinking about written communication. For those of us who need to engage in such unlearning, this is the exciting opportunity that writing about learning and teaching offers—learning new ways of writing and communicating that reach into new and different communities of scholars as part of a wider dialogue. Regardless of our disciplinary backgrounds, writing about learning and teaching is about people either directly or indirectly. Whether you are writing about the practices of teachers, the learning of students, policies written by people, ideas shaping the practices of university communities, or the intersection of any of these or other topics we have not listed, people are involved in every aspect of learning and teaching scholarship.

First, there are the people we write about, typically students, teachers, and staff supporting the learning and teaching endeavor, including ourselves. Second, there are the people with whom we write when we collaborate and with whom we are literally in dialogue through the co-authoring process. Third, there are the fellow scholars whose work we draw and build on as we develop our scholarship in public conversation with others (through citing other people's published work). Next, there are editors and reviewers who will inform our work and play a crucial role in determining where it is published, especially in the case of peer-reviewed writing outlets. Fifth, there are the people who will read our written work, perhaps draw and expand on it in their writing, and use it to inform their learning and teaching. These groups may overlap or be distinct.

Depending on whom you write about, with, to, and for, you will need to communicate in different ways. Perhaps you will want to demonstrate the technical use of particular learning and teaching terms specific to a niche community or engage in conversations that are more accessible to a broader group—or you may wish to complicate such dichotomies.

Creating and Contributing to Scholarly Conversations: A Metaphor for Writing

The metaphor of writing as contributing to and creating public conversations resonates with us, as we discuss in our *Teaching & Learning Inquiry* article (Healey, Matthews, and Cook-Sather 2019), and we are encouraged to see it deeply incorporated in a relatively new framework for information literacy (ACRL 2016).

This metaphor resonates primarily because it reminds us that writing is about people communicating with one another, either within an existing community or by creating a new one. For instance, Ronald Barnett's 1990 publication, *The Idea of Higher Education*, was an explicit attempt to create a new conversation around a new sub-discipline in the educational studies community. Gerardo Patriotta (2016, 2017), an editor for the *Journal of Management Studies*, also describes writing as a conversation through which written works are not created by authors but by other works that speak to each other—a way of thinking about writing inspired by Umberto Eco (1984). Drawing on the metaphor of being in conversation with another scholar, Patriotta (2017, 753) writes:

> Anne Huff (1998) has used the metaphor of the conversation to characterize interactions among scholars. She believes that writing for scholarly publication is about

joining conversations within a particular field of interest in order to improve understanding of a particular
phenomenon. Some conversations are well established
and easier to join, but they tend to take place within
a crowded space, and thereby constrain the scope of a
contribution. Newer conversations offer greater scope for
contribution, but authors will need to spend more time
legitimizing their chosen focus. Starting new conversations is a challenging endeavour, but if it is successful, it
can lead to ground breaking contributions.

Anne Huff's distinction between joining existing conversations
and starting new ones is an important one to keep in mind when
choosing to write in a particular genre for a particular purpose and
to a particular audience. Legitimizing a focus, especially if it is novel
or challenges established understandings, and embracing a form of
writing that might not conform to traditional expectations are hard
for anyone, but even more so for those striving to establish themselves
as scholars. Hence the inclusion of both "creating" and "contributing
to" in the subtitle of our book.

The metaphor of writing as scholarly conversation especially
matters now in the era of "publish or perish." Publications are academic
currency that carry symbolic and material power linked to status and
hierarchy in most universities and disciplinary communities. In this
drive to publish, we appreciate how easily writing for publication
can become a product and outcome, a necessity for entering into
the academy and securing academic positions. If we also appreciate
writing as a process of being in dialogue—sometimes comfortable,
sometimes difficult—with fellow scholars, then writing becomes part
of being in a scholarly community (Lave and Wenger 1991) that builds
connection and commitment to one another as people as well as to
the practice and scholarship of learning and teaching.

Pat Thomson and Barbara Kamler discuss writing journal articles as a way to be in the conversation of a particular community of
practice. In a literal sense, they describe the conversation of a journal
article between writers and readers.

> If the writer invites conversation through their journal article, and the reader enters that conversation through their reading, and then responds in their own piece of writing, we can begin to see how journals make possible conversation via articles. And if we understand that both the readers and writers around a journal belong to a particular discourse community, we can see how the conversation constitutes a social dialogue. We can thus think of the journal itself as an ongoing set of conversations between writers and readers in a scholarly discourse community. And if each article makes a contribution, then the conversation in the journal can be seen as a collaborative process of knowledge building. (Thomson and Kamler 2013, 57)

By characterizing writing about learning and teaching as a scholarly conversation that is about people within a given community contributing to a shared process of knowledge generation, we argue for seeing writing as a human experience through which people bring diverse perspectives to bear on the practice of learning and teaching. This approach to writing matters to us because we understand the focus of scholarship and inquiry in learning and teaching to be about pedagogies, about students, about the pedagogical relationship, about relationships between academics as teachers and their managers, and about institutional policies and priorities across educational contexts. We also recognize that not everyone has the same standing or the same voice in any given context or discourse community, and we understand that writing about this host of learning- and teaching-related phenomena carries different stakes for different people.

There Are Many Communities Having Different Conversations about Learning and Teaching

Another key factor influencing scholarly conversations about learning and teaching is culture, and many of those conversations privilege Western experiences and perspectives. As Huang Hoon Chng and Peter Looker (2013, 140) note: "The scholarship of teaching and learning is not neutral territory. As it has been formulated so far, it decontextualizes teaching and learning from deeper cultural practices and particular socioeconomic conditions." Chng describes the sense that scholarship of teaching and learning (SoTL) was "an alien territory" she entered with "mixed feelings" (Chng and Looker 2013, 132). Looker reflects on the importance of acknowledging our lack of cultural awareness as we strive to ensure that writing about learning and teaching connects globally in Reflection 3.1.

Reflection 3.1

Cultural contexts of conversations and communities

If writing about learning and teaching is to be global, then writers need to recognize their current biases, or perhaps blindness. I am a white, Western-educated male scholar, and as I spend more time in South Africa combined with living in Singapore, I have come to see the "scholarship of teaching and learning" (SoTL) movement differently. I now see how deeply biased writers from Western and anglophone countries writing about teaching and learning can be. The conversations in South Africa about decolonialisation of teaching, learning, and curriculum are a very different conversation than the ones I am aware of in the North American SoTL communities. Acknowledging the influence of our culture on how we understand learning and teaching, and then situating ourselves within the global conversations is critical for truly international SoTL conversations. (See also Looker 2018.)

Peter Looker is chief learning officer at EON Reality.

The "place"—geopolitical and cultural context—in which learning and teaching unfold fundamentally shapes how we learn and affects our experience of learning (Ruitenberg 2005). Connecting with Claudia Ruitenberg's thinking about "place," Catherine Manathunga (2018, 102) argues for seeing the learning and teaching process in new ways that allow for "transgressive and messy research that moves beyond Western/Northern Enlightenment notions of knowledge as universal, rational, secular and homogenous to include forms of knowing, being and doing that are evident in Southern/Eastern and Indigenous cultures." The scholarly conversation about learning and teaching is a global one with much to be learned by connecting across different forums for dialogue. But even in connecting across these forums, we need to be cognizant of biases and prejudices, recognize that some voices are heard as more legitimate than others, and understand that those of us who engage in these exchanges, therefore, always need to be attentive to who is speaking and who is listening, who is writing and who is reading.

Over to You

We are framing writing about learning and teaching as more than joining an ongoing conversation. It is, we argue, a means of creating as well as contributing to conversations. In making that argument, we are bringing the social and relational aspects of writing that we experience as complex human beings to the forefront, exploring writing as an act of creation and communication. Take a moment to reflect on the chapter and think though the following questions:

- How do your personal, cultural, and institutional identities inform the choices you might make about creating and communicating within a scholarly community?
- What are the taken-for-granted writing norms in your discipline? How does writing about your learning and teaching allow you to communicate in new ways?
- Who are the scholars you want to be in dialogue with?
- What is the cultural context for your learning and teaching? How does that context influence the scholarly conversation you are in, seek to contribute to, or hope to create?

CHAPTER 4

FOSTERING IDENTITY THROUGH A VALUES-BASED APPROACH TO WRITING

Engaging in the Scholarship of Teaching and Learning requires instructors to critically reflect on aspects of their practice, examine their beliefs about teaching, consider their sense of self in relation to their practice, and even question and challenge institutional and social norms related to teaching (Cranton 2011; Kreber 2013; Manarin and Abrahamson, 2016). (Miller-Young, Yeo, and Manarin 2018, 1)

Writing is an important medium of expression in most disciplines in higher education, and the range of intersecting practices that inform such writing, as Janice Miller-Young, Michelle Yeo, and Karen Manarin note above, involve our whole beings. Research findings, insights from experiences, opinions, stories, and more are typically shared through written formats, mainly academic journals, books, chapters, or conference proceedings and, increasingly, in various forms of digital media. In the process of selecting and organizing the new knowledge created, the academy relies on peer review through which established scholars evaluate the quality and importance of submitted work and offer reasons for their assessments. While we regularly write about what we discover through our research and teaching, compose new curricular content, or offer written feedback on student work, many of us would not identify ourselves as *writers*. Instead, we are teachers, or students, or researchers, or scholars along with being family members, friends, caregivers, and members of non-work-related communities. One of the reasons we have written this book is to encourage more academics to consider themselves writers. Writing of a wide variety of kinds is indeed one of our responsibilities as academics, and to embrace that responsibility as an expression and further development of identity and values can be an empowering experience.

Building on chapter 3, in which we framed writing as creating and contributing to a scholarly conversation, we therefore assert that writing is a relational communication process that is informed by and shapes our identities as writers and scholars in learning and teaching in higher education in ways that are intertwined with our values. Our values become clear when we interrogate our assumptions. We all hold assumptions about what constitutes good quality and important scholarly publications, for example. These assumptions influence our writing and how we understand ourselves as writers—our identity. In the introduction to part 2, we wrote: "How we experience the writing process and the decisions we make about writing—what we write about; whom we write with, about, and for; what genres we prefer to write in—shape the writers we are and will become." These decisions that shape us as writers are driven by what we value in writing and as writers. Exploring the values informing your writing can uncover assumptions, provoke new insights into your identities as a learning and teaching scholar, and enable a more purposeful approach to writing, including possibly writing in new genres.

In this chapter, we outline this central thread in the book—that writing is a process of identity formation that enacts and clarifies our values and, therefore, affects us intellectually, socially, and emotionally. By exploring the ways writing about learning and teaching both draws on and can complicate, shape, and reshape our academic identities, we reveal writing as more than something we do in some mechanical, one-off way; it is an intellectual, social, and emotional activity that requires deep engagement in a series of thoughtful, iterative steps. We discuss how writing affects us, why writing about learning and teaching can be easier for some and more difficult for others, and why the writing process can provoke a range of emotions. In doing so, we offer a set of questions to illuminate the benefits and the challenges of embracing writing about learning and teaching.

Writing as "Values Work"

Barbara Kamler and Pat Thomson (2014) view writing as work that requires physical and mental effort. They also discuss writing as "identity work." This physical, mental, and identity work is all guided by values, whether explicit or tacit. By values, we are referring to what matters to you, what you believe is worthy of writing about, what you see as important in the process of writing, and what you strive for in terms of outcomes of the work of writing. These values take the form of principles or personal standards that influence how you judge your writing and the writing of others. Your values inform decisions about what writing genres you prefer to read and write in because of what those different genres privilege and make possible.

For example, do you prefer reading or writing empirical research articles over opinion pieces? Why? How do you feel about writing award applications focused on your own practices? Why do you feel that way? Do you believe writing about learning and teaching is more rigorous when it claims to be presenting objective facts? Why or why not? Can undergraduate students contribute to knowledge generation by writing about learning and teaching? Why or why not? Are written works about learning and teaching only scholarly if they cite other published works? Why or why not? How you answer these questions reveals what you value about writing along with beliefs about research, what counts as scholarly writing, and who is able to contribute to and create conversations about learning and teaching in higher education (see chapter 3).

Our values are inextricably linked with our identities as writers. Our values about writing tend to arise from our disciplinary or "home base" communities and only reveal themselves when we start to write in new ways. Some of our disciplinary backgrounds align more closely with writing about learning and teaching than others. Mick, coming into learning and teaching from geography, had a different experience from Alison, who came from education, who, in turn, had a different experience from Kelly, who navigated from early publications in biomedical sciences to higher education. In each case our disciplinary training is grounded in specific ways of seeing the world and in certain understandings of knowledge that also reveal what we value in writing. In practice, these can translate in subtle ways. For example, whether we use the first person or not speaks to how we value the position of the writer—whether they distance themselves from the written work or claim their agency in authoring it.

Embracing writing as values-based work further affirms how our unique positionality shapes us as writers and helps us identify our motivations for writing about learning and teaching (see chapter 6). Knowing what matters to you about writing also shapes your identity as a writer, a process in continuous formation.

What Do We Mean by "Identity"?

We think of "identity" as the way in which "individuals define and experience themselves and are defined by others—how an individual/personal sense of sociocultural location and character intersects with how that individual is constructed in many different ways within any given culture and society" (Cook-Sather 2015, 2). We all have values and commitments as well as backgrounds and experiences that inform our identities, and as Jennifer Fraser (personal communication, August 8, 2019) reiterated when reading a draft of this book, "our identities are also constructed/imposed depending on the structural privileges and oppressions that we experience in the academy." Pat Thomson and Barbara Kamler's (2013, 2016) thinking about "identity work" in their texts focuses on getting published in the social sciences and conveys the idea that, as writers, we are enacting an imagined view of who we are and want to be. That means the whole writing process is a personal experience that affects us as people and is affected by the people with whom we interact.

Our identities as writers in higher education are complex and dynamic. As three white academics who have been in full-time positions in institutions of higher education in Australia, the UK, and the United States, we have benefited from the privileges afforded people with our ethnic and institutional identities. This means we have not had to negotiate certain practices of exclusion, bias, and other forms of discrimination and harm that some of our colleagues with different identities have had to navigate. We have also endeavored to use our privileged positions to create new spaces and opportunities, such as through the students-as-partners work we all do. Furthermore, Alison has focused on culturally responsive practice (Cook-Sather and Agu 2013; Cook-Sather and Des-Ogugua 2018) and epistemic justice (de Bie et al. 2019), while Mick has explored how disabled students may be better included in higher education (Fuller et al. 2009; Healey et al. 2006; Healey, Jenkins, and Leach 2006). With colleagues, Kelly has argued for the inclusion of subjective self-definition of social class in higher education research (Rubin et al. 2014) and offered approaches to inclusive practices in introductory science subjects (Matthews, Moni, and Moni 2007). Through our work as co-editors of *IJSaP*, we have created space for students historically marginalized in higher education to have a voice in the academic literature (Bindra et al. 2018; Yahlnaaw / Aaron Grant 2019). In this book, we use our privileged positions to argue for, model, and invite the creation of and contribution to scholarly conversations that support the development of identities, clarification of values, and learning through writing for a range of differently positioned scholars. In this chapter, we focus on how our disciplinary identities interact with our identities as writers in learning and teaching.

How We See Ourselves as Writers in Higher Education

Much of higher education is organized into disciplinary groups. Scholars have evoked the analogy of academic tribes and territories to describe the cultural norms engrained in most academic disciplines (Becher 1994; Becher and Trowler 2001). Most of us learn to write for publication through our disciplinary training, and we see the writing process as part of joining that disciplinary community—as fostering our identity as a scholar in a discipline. Writing in mathematics is a fundamentally different experience from writing in education, even mathematics education. Whether we are writing alone or in collaboration (see chapter 7), our views on authorship are shaped by our disciplinary location (see chapter 8). Our disciplinary identities shape the information context we work in—the discourses that flow around us, influencing what we see, read, hear—even before we go searching for material to draw from. They also influence whom we cite in our publications (Tight 2008).

As more and more universities embrace Lee Shulman's (1993) notion of teaching as community property that should be as public as research, there has been a surge in academics publishing about learning and teaching in higher education. Yet many of us are coming from a disciplinary background that did not train us in writing at all, let alone in writing about learning and teaching, and it can often be profoundly destabilizing to become a beginner in a discourse again and cause scholars to question at once two activities they may be expert in—teaching and research (Weller 2011). Indeed, trying to learn to write about learning and teaching can disrupt our sense of identity as scholars and raise uncomfortable questions about ourselves (Miller-Young, Yeo, and Manarin 2018). In particular, if we view writing as only a technical activity, then the assumptions from our discipline might come into unproductive conflict with assumptions that underpin the learning and teaching scholarship field, which is rich in context, subjectivity, and messy human relationships. If embraced, however, the "troublesome conflict" of coming into learning and teaching scholarship that some people experience can be transformative, particularly when the struggles are shared with others in a supportive learning process that nurtures our identities as writers in learning and teaching (Simmons et al. 2013).

While a small yet growing number of students are studying learning and teaching in higher education through graduate programs and PhD studies in disciplines beyond education, many of you will come to this form of writing from an academic discipline other than education. The process of writing according to the conventions and norms of your discipline shaped or are shaping your identity as a scholar, and learning to write about learning and teaching is also a process of identity formation. Acknowledging this is important because it creates space to recognize the worldviews and assumptions you bring from your discipline. Regardless of your disciplinary pathway into writing about learning and teaching, your identity plays a role in how you become a learning and teaching scholar, as illuminated in Reflection 4.1.

Reflection 4.1

How engaging in a pedagogic research project changed my identity

My conversion to a discipline-based pedagogic researcher was an unintended outcome of participating in an early 2000s project to improve the educational effectiveness of fieldwork in geography and the earth and environmental sciences. Initially, I was skeptical, even dismissive about the rigor of the pedagogical research component, due in part to my own shortcomings and my science background. I could only see quantitative research and large data sets. However, what interested me was the fieldwork element, and how I could possibly enhance the quality of my own fieldwork teaching. So I thought I would give it go. Over the course of a residential training event and subsequent national research project with like-minded colleagues, I was able to try out qualitative research for the first time, and realising it has value, I had a road-to-Damascus moment. Subsequently, I have focused my research almost entirely on writing about learning and teaching. So, what happened to me? I think it was an exposure to, and the better understanding of the value of, pedagogic research approaches, and how they can be used to make direct impact on day-to-day teaching with students.

Derek France is professor of pedagogy in geographical sciences at the University of Chester, UK.

Becoming a Learning and Teaching Scholar through Writing

We become scholars of learning and teaching through writing as our identities evolve from either another disciplinary location or through direct preparation in the field of higher education. We encourage you to be conscious and intentional about developing your identities as a learning and teaching scholar through experimenting with multiple genres (see part 4) that both conform to and diverge from writing norms and conventions typically privileged in Western academic contexts (see chapter 11). Because this range of genres enables more people, and a greater diversity of people, to create and contribute to conversations about learning and teaching, we urge you not only to develop your own voice but also to learn to read the voices of those differently positioned from yourself. This will allow you to forge identities for yourself in dialogue and collaboration with others who are forming their—possibly very different—identities. A community like this will only thrive when scholars with differing identities reflect on their experiences of learning and teaching to tell "true" stories (see chapter 20), as advocated by Nancy Chick and Peter Felten (2018). These stories can reflect how learning and teaching unfold across and within different countries and contexts for scholars in an array of social locations. To tell such true stories—and there is never only a single such story (Adichie 2009)—it is essential to reflect on the values shaping our writing about learning and teaching.

The Opportunity to Embrace and Expand Your Values in Writing about Learning and Teaching

In asserting that writing is a values-based practice, we encourage all of you as writers to intentionally live the values that matter to you. This could mean embracing new possibilities as a writer that may at first cause discomfort and perhaps even angst. This could equally mean affirming values that lead you to embrace another way of writing about learning and teaching. We are exploring values not to reach consensus about what the values informing your writing about learning and teaching should be, but rather to demonstrate how a diversity of writers with different values can be in conversation to construct richer understandings of learning and teaching in higher education across contexts, countries, and cultures.

To that end, we come back to a set of interrelated questions published in our *Teaching & Learning Inquiry* article (Healey, Matthews, and Cook-Sather 2019).

Guiding Questions to Reflect on Your Values as a Learning and Teaching Writer

1. **How can you use writing in learning and teaching in higher education to:**
   - shape your identities and nurture your sense of belonging within the learning and teaching discourse community?
   - bring yourself to your writing and express yourself with a clear voice?
   - engage both emotionally and intellectually?

2. **What opportunities does writing about learning and teaching afford you to:**
   - inquire into the complexities of teaching (and learning) and of students' experiences of learning (and teaching)?
   - participate in an ongoing conversation with the learning and teaching in higher education discourse community?
   - push "conventional boundaries" within the discourse community by drawing on your disciplinary expertise or embracing a methodological pluralism?

3. **How might you embrace the potential of learning and teaching writing to:**
   - acknowledge, affirm, and constructively critique rather than attack or undermine?
   - illuminate and expand, rather than obscure or diminish?
   - represent context-specific complexity well, rather than reduce to generalizable simplicity? (Poole 2013)

Source: Adapted from Healey, Matthews, and Cook-Sather (2019, 34).

Our values can shift and wobble in ways that are both liberating and exhausting. As Nicola Simmons illustrates in Reflection 4.2, what we value about writing speaks to our motivations to write and can come into conflict with how we work in, and what we understand to be the purpose of, higher education. If we value collaborative writing, as Nicola Simmons does, then writing is a process of shared learning and sense making with others. How we approach writing if we value collaboration is far different from how we approach writing alone. Nicola Simmons' reflection names the entangled messiness of our fluid identities as writers as those identities embody and enact what matters to us and intersect with other aspects of our lives.

Reflection 4.2

How values shape our motivation to write

To be honest, although it would be simple to say that I write because of academic expectations, that is not my main driver. I write because writing helps me make my thinking explicit and lets me see it from outside, and I often write collaboratively because I am hoping to support others' work or gather multiple perspectives to enhance my own. I love writing with diverse groups and am always excited at helping stitch together a transdisciplinary and transnational space. That building of bridges and smoothing of edges is an inherent part of me; editing diverse group perspectives lets me express it in written form. When I was asked to reflect for this book, I was also reminded of how writing can be a lovely form of escapism: by working with people from around the world, I get a chance to travel and to leave behind some of the work challenges one too often encounters. The intellectual play of the collaborative writing craft offers a wonderful holiday from the daily angst.

Nicola Simmons is assistant professor in the Department of Educational Studies at Brock University, Canada.

Our culture also shapes what we value. Peter Looker, in chapter 3, reflected on the importance of acknowledging our "cultural blindness" to ensure that writing about learning and teaching connects globally (see Reflection 3.1). We can extend his reflection to encompass the importance of acknowledging how our culture shapes our values. By reflecting on our values as writers, we can become more aware of what others value and create space for richer conversations informed by multiple perspectives and differing values about learning and teaching.

Over to You

We understand writing to be a form of communication, a relational process, that brings us into conversations with a community of scholars. A thread weaving throughout this book is writing as a process of identity formation—a process that intersects with our values and affects us intellectually, socially, and emotionally. For this reason, we include "Our Perspectives" and "Reflections" from colleagues throughout the book to show the varied experience of writing about learning and teaching in higher education. Here are some questions to consider about fostering your identities through a values-based process of writing:

- How do you see yourself as a writer, and how do you want others to see you as a writer?
- What matters to you about writing?
- Which of these priorities relate to discipline-specific work and might be a benefit or a barrier to writing in a different field?
- What does dialogue with differently positioned people reveal to you about your identities? In what ways have you used or could you use writing to develop your identities and support the development of others' identities?

CHAPTER 5

CONCEPTUALIZING WRITING AS A LEARNING PROCESS

It is uncontested that writing enhances learning. (Silva and Limongi 2019, 213)

Expert writing is a process of discovery or invention. (Baaijen and Galbraith 2018, 199)

The first two chapters in part 2 of this book emphasize the deeply inter- and intra-personal work of writing: thinking about your writing as a way of creating and contributing to scholarly conversations (chapter 3), and fostering your identities as a writer within those conversations and for yourself in ways that intersect with your values (chapter 4). This chapter focuses on writing as a learning process—as a way of learning about the scholarly conversations you might want to create or contribute to, about yourself and your values, and about what you already know and do not yet know or understand about learning and teaching. It embraces a concept, writing to learn, that was developed during the 1970s and 1980s in relation to teaching higher education students to write (Writing Across the Curriculum Clearinghouse) and that has come to be accepted as a given among writing scholars, as the assertions above from Silva and Limongi (2019) and Baaijen and Galbraith (2018) attest. In this chapter we cite some of the foundational thinkers of the writing-to-learn movement and discuss this widely accepted concept in relation to the writing that you as experienced scholars, new scholars, or student scholars can use both as a mode of exploration and discovery and as a form of publication in and of itself.

Writing to Learn: Origins and Applications

Two of the early proponents of writing to learn, Toby Fulwiler and Art Young (1982), explain that writing to learn is focused on writing "to order and represent experience to our own understanding." By writing for ourselves as learners and audience, we can benefit from writing to learn because the language we generate "provides us with a unique way of knowing and becomes a tool for discovering, for shaping meaning, and for reaching understanding" (Fulwiler and Young 1982, x). William Zinsser (1988) wrote a book with the title *Writing to Learn* to ease the fear people feel regarding writing in general and the particular fear people have of writing about topics for which they assume they have no aptitude. Like Toby Fulwiler and Art Young, William Zinsser made the argument that writing can be understood as a form of thinking, and that by writing through your thoughts you clarify and gain confidence in them.

Writing to learn is used most often in pedagogical contexts as a strategy employed by teachers across the disciplines to help support student writing (see, for example, advice from the Center for Teaching Excellence at Duquesne University). It is one of several categories of writing typically emphasized in higher education, which include:

- writing in the disciplines (developing the language and discourse practices of particular areas of study),
- writing to engage (which focuses on promoting critical thinking), and
- writing to learn (typically short, impromptu or otherwise informal and low-stakes writing tasks).

Writing to learn is often juxtaposed to "transactional writing" that aims "to accomplish something, to inform, instruct, or persuade" (Writing Across the Curriculum Clearinghouse, n.d.).

In short, what distinguishes writing to learn from writing for other purposes is its focus on the process of coming to understanding and its emphasis on the benefit to the person doing the writing as a form of learning.

Using Writing to Learn for Yourself

Using writing to learn requires seeing your writing as a space in which you learn for and by yourself. Many people, especially those who do not think of themselves as writers, have trouble believing that writing can be helpful to clarify thinking. In *Becoming a Writer*, Dorothea Brande (1934) offers advice that still resonates nearly a century after she wrote it: develop a mindset or attitude that makes possible the productive generation of words to name insights and experiences. If you are one of those people who does not see yourself as a writer or who doubts the benefit of writing to clarify thinking, ask yourself what kind of shift in mindset (perhaps created by making time to free write, reading books on writing, or participating in a writing workshop) and what kind of encouragement (e.g., collaborating with an experienced colleague in writing a blog) you might need to embrace writing as a generative process of learning.

Once you embrace a mindset conducive to this approach, you can use writing to learn as an experienced scholar, a new scholar, or a student scholar to help you figure out what you are thinking and to keep track of your thoughts. Perhaps you will want to keep a journal, a kind of ongoing dialogue with yourself through which you clarify both your questions and your evolving understandings of learning and teaching. Naming those insights for yourself helps you not only clarify them but also find language to capture and represent them. You might focus on naming for yourself what scholarly conversations you want to contribute to, or create, and why. The understandings you develop through this focus and the language you develop to name those understandings will help you clarify with whom you want to be in dialogue and perhaps what you want to talk about. You might focus on writing to yourself about your identities, how you define yourself and are defined by others—how your "individual/personal sense of sociocultural location and character intersects with how [you are] constructed in many different ways within any given culture and society" (Cook-Sather 2015, 2)—to develop who you want to be through your writing. Finally, you might consider writing to learn about your assumptions, to uncover and explore them through reflection, which can provoke new insights into your identities as a learning and teaching scholar and enable more purposeful approaches to writing across genres.

If you experience fear of writing, you can use writing to learn to work through it. Such fear manifests itself in many forms, and Our Perspectives 5.1 offers some glimpses of our own experiences to open up the conversation about fear. The anxiety, fear, and relentless discomfort of expressing yourself through written text is common to many, but not all, writers. Accepting that writing is a process and that it does not have to be perfect before others can see it can be difficult when you feel the fear of rejection, humiliation, and failure (see chapter 28). Talking about our fears as writers and what shapes these fears is a first step in addressing them. Reframing writing as a learning process, instead of a technical right/wrong task or only a performance for others, is another way to overcome fear. Fear may also dissipate if you give yourself permission to dwell, explore, ponder, imagine, and experiment. Many people find a form of free writing—continuous writing for a set amount of time, such as five or fifteen minutes, without stopping, censoring, or editing—especially helpful to access and express what they are thinking (Brande 1934; Elbow 1975). Technology today allows for countless drafts that can remain private or be shared as needed.

Our Perspectives 5.1

Opening up about our fears of writing

Kelly: Writing is a daily act of courage for me. My fear of writing dates back to first grade when my identity as a reader, writer, and student took shape. I was labelled a slow reader by the teacher (Ms. Claudia, who is forever burnt into my memory). My mother viewed the problem as a school problem, so I was given special tutoring at school but no reading or writing support at home. I spent countless weekends writing spelling words over and over as a result of failing the weekly spelling tests. When I started to show improvement, Ms. Claudia assumed I was copying off the boy next to me. To address the issue, she literally caged me off from the class by surrounding my desk with a large, cut-out box so I could not see anyone during test time. Of course I have a complicated relationship with writing marked by anxiety and fear. It was not until my undergraduate research experience that I learned that writing is never perfect, spelling errors are easy to fix, and writing is an iterative process. Dr. Hill, the lab leader, would send me draft manuscripts to edit, which seemed crazy to me, yet I would not have dared to decline his requests. Imagine my surprise to find his writing was filled with the little errors that used to get me in trouble in English classes. I would fix them, and he would be grateful I had. He was not embarrassed or bothered in any visible way about his errors. Through that experience, I realized writing is a learning and thinking process, which addressed some of my fears of being humiliated (thank you, Ms. Claudia) and gave me courage to face my writing fears.

Alison: I have never had any fear of writing, and I actually look forward to the few minutes here and there as well as to the entire days I can devote to working through draft after draft of any piece. This easy relationship with writing has meant, though, that I need regularly to remind myself how difficult, challenging, and even torturous writing is for many people. When I forget that fact, I can be less than empathetic and even impatient (with colleagues, never with those I am teaching to write)—responses I recognize as profoundly ungenerous and inequitable. It's also the case that, although I don't struggle with writing, I do worry that what I write might not make sense to others—and sometimes, in fact, it doesn't, if I haven't spent enough time translating what is clear to me into terms that might resonate for—or at least make sense to—others. But perhaps because my identity as a writer has woven itself through every phase of my life and virtually every role I have had, from teaching high school English through teaching college composition through embracing writing as an integral and ener-gizing aspect of my identity as an academic, I do not have fear around it.

Mick: Fear of writing for me revolves around lack of confidence in what others will think of what I have written. Have I misunderstood some of the arguments? Have I expressed my ideas poorly? I cope with these fears through redrafting what I have written several times before asking generous colleagues for their comments. Hence, through self-evaluation and by responding to the feedback from my critical friends, I use my writing as a learning experience. However, I have a residual fear about how much I have learnt and whether I continue to make the same mistakes, especially in the quality of the writing.

Your perspective: What fears, if any, are shaping your writing and how can reframing writing as a learning process change your relationship to those fears?

Moving from Writing to Learn for Yourself to Sharing Your Writing to Learn with Others

The audience for writing to learn is, initially at least, yourself. If you want to move from writing to learn for yourself to writing to learn to share with others, you will want to shift from what Linda Flower (1979) called "writer-based prose" to what she called "reader-based prose." Shifting from an audience of yourself to an audience outside yourself and likely outside your context requires thinking about how to translate what you have represented to your own understanding, to use Fulwiler and Young's (1982) terms, into a representation accessible to others' understanding. Reflective essays (see chapter 16) and stories (see chapter 20) are genres particularly conducive to the products of writing to learn, focusing as they do on lived experiences and day-to-day practicalities of the work of learning and teaching in higher education. An undergraduate student author explains how such reflective writing supports a "manner of inquiry" through which you can "make sense of things and find patterns without being tunnel focused on arriving at conclusions" (quoted in Cook-Sather, Abbot, and Felten 2019, 19). And, as Pat Hutchings, Mary Tyler Huber, and Anthony Ciccone (2011, 37-38) argue, "The writing process not only focuses one's attention on one's own work but has a marvelous way of lighting up the work of others, bringing what might otherwise go unnoticed into one's sphere of interest and analysis."

Over to You

In this chapter we extend to all writers the concept and practice of writing to learn as it has been used to teach university students. We see this as part of our larger project in this book to expand who can be seen as writers about learning and teaching, how we write, and what we write about. We invite you to pause to reflect on yourself as a learner and a writer by answering these questions:

- What do you want to learn more about regarding learning and teaching in higher education, and how can you use writing to explore that?
- What insights that you generate for yourself through writing might be usefully shared with a wider audience?
- How can you imagine using writing to clarify your understandings of ongoing and potential scholarly conversations about learning and teaching, your own identities and possible roles in those conversations, and your values as a writer?

CLARIFYING YOUR PURPOSE AND PREPARING TO DRAFT

Introduction to Part 3

This part of the book explores some of the topics that we argue can be precursors to starting to write and engage in productive dialogue with potential co-authors, editors, reviewers, and readers. We begin with a discussion of motivations for writing, because clarifying your purpose will help you identify how and for whom you write. Your motivations are closely related to your ever-evolving identity as a learning and teaching scholar, which we discussed in part 2. Also related to your motivations is the question of whether you write on your own or in collaboration with colleagues or students. Exploration of this topic raises issues of ethical authorship.

If you are the kind of person who writes better within clear parameters, there are several key questions you may want to address before you start writing, including: Who can benefit from reading what I plan to write? In which outlet should I seek to publish? What is an appropriate working title for the piece of writing I am working on? What might a short summary of the piece include? Whatever you write will, of course, only be initial drafts, and you should expect to keep returning to and revising them as you write.

We recognize, however, that people vary in how helpful they find this type of planning before starting to write. If you are the kind of person who writes better with fewer parameters to start with, you may want to leave these questions until after you have drafted your piece, or at least are well down the writing road. Others find it helpful to draft their answers to these questions early for some writing, but later for other kinds of writing. Our approach varies. Mick and Kelly tend to favor the early planning route, while Alison varies in which strategy she follows. These approaches are not mutually exclusive, of course. Regardless of what approach you take, what is crucial is that any position or argument that you adopt early on is modifiable as the writing proceeds. All should be open to change, including the title, until the moment of submission. Otherwise, the learning opportunities are going to be severely diminished.

One other topic that is important to consider before starting to write is what publishing genre is appropriate. This question is so central to this book that the whole of part 4 is dedicated to exploring it. You may find reading chapter 11, which discusses the main features of eleven different genres, helpful at an early stage in your planning.

Key questions you might want to address before you read part 3 and then keep in mind while you are reading include:

- What is your motivation for writing?
- What kind of approach or structure—following guiding questions or exploring through the writing itself—works best for you as a writing process?
- Which genre are you preparing to write for and how might that influence your writing?

CHAPTER 6

REFLECTING ON MOTIVATIONS

*Clarifying Your Identity as a
Learning and Teaching Scholar*

*For me, the purpose of writing was first to secure a faculty
position, then tenure, and then promotion. After that was accomplished, I engaged in writing projects to clarify ideas, explore
areas, and contribute to the profession. (Rocco 2011, 4)*

*In the last twenty years, educators who have dared to study
and learn new ways of thinking and teaching so that the work
we do does not reinforce systems of domination, of imperialism,
racism, sexism or class elitism have created a pedagogy of hope.
(hooks 2003, xiv)*

Motivations for writing are as various as the scholars driven by them.
They can be informed by practical needs (getting a job), passionate
interests (clarifying ideas, exploring new areas), and personal and
political commitments (combating systems of domination). They can
change over time, across contexts and circumstances, and depend on
your identities. Those of us who write about learning and teaching in
higher education have the opportunity to affect learning and teaching
practices, making the work we do, as well as the ways we write about
it, uniquely animating. Lori Breslow and her colleagues (2004, 84)
suggest that, "One of the key ways in which to engage colleagues
in their development as critical and reflective teachers . . . is . . . to
stimulate their intellectual curiosity." If, as they contend, "the asking
of questions is at the heart of intellectual curiosity and engaging staff

in the scholarship of teaching and learning" (Breslow et al. 2004, 84), we would also suggest that motivation, while sometimes of necessity practical, can also be a kind of life force—what bell hooks (2003, x) describes as a "sense of organic necessity that often drives me to passionate writing." The statements offered by Tonette Rocco, bell hooks, and Lori Breslow and colleagues may or may not resemble your own reasons for writing, but they throw into relief the importance of considering your motivations (Black et al. 1998).

The Nature of Motivations

In a discussion of various dimensions of writing development at different ages, Charles Bazerman and colleagues (2017, 352) note the growing body of research on "psychological processes, social situations, motivations, and self-perceptions of writers." They offer eight principles that constitute what they call "taking the long view of writing development." Most relevant to our discussion are the following five: writing can develop across the lifespan as part of changing contexts; writing development is complex because writing is complex; writing development is variable—there is no single path and no single endpoint; writers develop in relation to the changing social needs, opportunities, resources, and technologies of their time and place; and writing and other forms of development have reciprocal and mutually supporting relationships. We urge you to keep these in mind as you consider your motivations for writing about learning and teaching.

Like the motivations of the scholars quoted in the opening section of this chapter, our own motivations to write about learning and teaching have varied across our circumstances and over time, as reflected in our different experiences (Our Perspectives 6.1).

Our Perspectives 6.1

What were our motivations to start writing about learning and teaching and how have they shifted over time?

Alison: I have always been motivated to write about what effectively supports engaged learning for both students and teachers and to do so in ways that are fun for me as a writer and accessible to readers. This motivation, focused on both content and process, has remained consistent regardless of publication purpose and venue, including writing to meet requirements for tenure and promotion, writing to share ideas and practices, writing to explore and discover, and writing to combat systems of domination. I am motivated to write about what I care about, and letting passion and commitment drive my writing projects is part of what has allowed me to be so prolific. As the pedagogical partnership approach that I developed has gained recognition, I have used that recognition to make space for and offer support to others who want to engage in dialogue about and pursue such work. I have been motivated to offer not only inspiration and insights from research but also practical guidance for how to support both prospective and practicing teachers in reflecting on, affirming, and further refining learning and teaching in dialogue and collaboration with students, particularly those who have been underserved and often harmed by higher education.

Kelly: At this stage in my career, in response to the question, "Why write about learning and teaching?", I initially thought: because I have something I want to say about teaching and learning (and clearly an identity that gives me confidence to say it). For the purposes of this book and the thread of creating and contributing to scholarly conversation, I would say: I want to engage in a scholarly conversation about learning and teaching with like-minded peers. In doing so, I am reflecting on practice and becoming a better teacher while also becoming a better writer, which is generally important in the academy. At the start of my career, I would have 100% agreed about the importance of "the external drivers" and answered the questions with: I *need* to publish to gain credibility within the academy in a university that values scholarship of teaching and learning (SoTL) through publication. I *need* to publish in my role as an early-career academic in a centralized teaching and learning unit. I *need* to publish so I can influence my colleagues and impact teaching practices because my colleagues value publications. My motivation has shifted toward the intrinsic yet is balanced with extrinsic drivers.

Mick: When I began writing about my teaching in the late 1980s, my main motivation was to share with my geography colleagues the initiatives and experiences that appeared to enhance the quality of learning of our students. Hence, it was very much embedded in the practice of teaching, and the main genres I pursued were papers and posters for conferences and empirical research articles and case studies published in journals. As I became more experienced, my focus shifted more toward review papers and reports summarizing interesting practices in geography in higher education from around the world, but then shifted after 10-15 years toward higher education generally, regardless of discipline. However, my motivation continued to be an interest in trying to enhance the quality of student learning. This is not to argue that the motivation was purely intrinsic or altruistic, as these drivers were reinforced by peer-recognition and success in attracting grants and awards, to the extent that in 2010, I was able to become an independent higher education consultant and researcher.

Your perspective: What are your motivations to write about learning and teaching and have they shifted over time?

Your motivations for engaging in writing about learning and teaching will be influenced by larger questions of why write about learning and teaching, as we discussed in chapter 2, and will also be closely related to your identities as a person and a professional and your identity—or identities—as a learning and teaching scholar, as discussed in chapter 4. Many SoTL scholars have as a primary motivation to enhance the quality of student learning through inquiry. As we argued in chapter 2, this may, or may not, mean engaging in higher education research, as there are many different ways of creating and contributing to conversations about learning and teaching (Fanghanel 2013; Trigwell and Shale 2004). Some of these may be local institution-based exchanges, while others may involve going public in wider national and international outlets (Ashwin and Trigwell 2004; Geertsema 2016).

Joelle Fanghanel (2013, 63) points out that: "The aim in SoTL is not to publish but to uncover the complexity of academic practice through reflection and engagement with relevant partners (colleagues, students) and to draw lessons that are subjected to debate and contradiction. Change emerges from inquiry." Writing and making presentations about learning and teaching are key ways of going public, but they are the means to an end not the end in itself. Based on your context, your position, and your identity as a learning and teaching scholar, you will need to decide for yourself what motivations for writing to embrace. Remember Pat Hutchings' reflection from chapter 2 in which she described the way writing can bring thinking to life.

Reflecting on Your Motivations

Reflecting on your motivations can make required writing joyful and fulfilling; allow you to clarify for yourself particular questions about learning and teaching; facilitate your contributions to evolving and new conversations about learning and teaching; and bring you into dialogue with colleagues that both capture and generate insights.

Making Required Writing Joyful and Fulfilling

In many higher education contexts, writing for publication is required for review, promotion, and job-seeking. Much of this work is expected to be disciplinary. More than a decade ago Paul Witman and Laurie Richlin (2007) found that SoTL had achieved varying levels of acceptance across the disciplines. Offering a recent example from the field of art history that suggests these conditions persist in some fields at least, Denise Baxter and Kelly Donohue-Wallace (2016) cautioned those on the job market and those not yet tenured to "assess cautiously whether engaging in this type of research puts them in a position" to be hired or promoted because "some institutions will embrace it, but some will not."

What kind of writing is expected or accepted in your discipline given where you are in your trajectory as a scholar is an important consideration as you assess what might motivate you to write. If you are an academic in a traditional discipline, does your discipline in general (and in the context in which you work, or hope to work) value writing about learning and teaching in higher education? If publication is required or expected in your role, have you published enough in the required/expected forms of writing, whether discipline focused or teaching-and-learning focused, that you can invest time in writing for the first time or in new ways about learning and teaching? If you are a graduate or an undergraduate student, would such writing be beneficial to you as you navigate academia?

If you conclude that writing about learning and teaching would be valued or beneficial, ask yourself what could make that writing most joyful and fulfilling. If you enjoy and feel good about what you are writing, it will contribute to sustaining you, as well as be more appealing to others. Some scholars, like Alison, experience writing to be a joy. But if that is not your experience, remind yourself, as we noted in chapter 2, to evoke Helen Sword's (2012, 159) terms as inspiration: "passion, commitment, pleasure, playfulness, humor, elegance, lyricism, originality, imagination, creativity, and undisciplined thinking." Also try to remind yourself that if you embrace writing and let it follow or lead your thinking, "suddenly everything becomes more interesting, more connected, ideas get sparked" (Hutchings, personal communication, June 11, 2019). In short, remind yourself, as we argue in chapter 2, that writing can capture and convey what makes us human, what makes us connected, what keeps us alive—and, as bell hooks (2003) notes, what is of necessity.

If you experience writing as hard work, you may need to seek joy and fulfilment in acknowledging that work. Kelly, commenting on a draft of this chapter, observed that:

While I appreciate the talk of writing as joyful and awesome, I never felt that when I started academic writing because I was never a strong writer, so that discourse (typically espoused by friends in writing disciplines) left me feeling more sure I was not a writer (because I was not enjoying it). For me, the acknowledgment that writing is hard work and that we get better through practice, and even playing with writing, spoke to me.

External factors may also affect motivations, both positively and negatively, and finding joy and fulfilment in managing those may require yet a different mindset and approach. Kelly commented above (in Our Perspectives 6.1) how institutional policies were an important factor motivating her to publish as an early-career academic. In contrast, Alison labors under similar institutional policies but has focused on writing about what excites her and what feels important, and she has managed both to stay true to her commitments and to meet external requirements.

Writing for Yourself to Clarify Particular Questions about Learning and Teaching

As we discuss in chapter 5, William Zinnser (1988) made the argument that writing can be understood as a form of thinking and that by writing through your thoughts you clarify them. You can use writing to learn to work through fear, if you have it, or to give yourself permission to dwell, explore, ponder, imagine, and experiment.

When you prepare to produce a version of your writing for others to read, ensure that you shift from your own exploration for an audience of yourself to a consideration of how you might represent key insights from that exploration for an external audience (see chapters 8, 23, 24, and 25). In chapter 18 on reflective essays, we suggest that informal, first-person accounts that focus on analyses of lived experiences and illuminate the day-to-day practicalities of the work of learning and teaching in higher education might be particularly well suited to writing for yourself to clarify particular questions about that work—a particularly generative "manner of inquiry," as one student author asserted (quoted in Cook-Sather, Abbot, and Felten 2019, 19). Considering the benefits to readers of reflective writing to clarify thinking and practice, one faculty member suggests that such writing "tends to let readers in on the writer's experiences and thinking/feeling in a way that's invitational, inclusive" (quoted in Cook-Sather, Abbot, and Felten 2019, 21).

Finding Inspiration to Contribute to Evolving and New Conversations about Learning and Teaching

Whether you are required by external expectations, inspired by an internal drive, or moved by an intersection of the personal and the political, consider how you might generate or harness inspiration to contribute to established and evolving conversations about learning and teaching or create new ones. We suggest in chapter 8 that choosing an outlet for your work is about choosing whom you want to be in dialogue with. An important dimension of that decision is identifying what you can contribute to an existing discussion or why you might start a new one. Do you have a unique experience based on your position or perspective? Do you have a strong opinion that might help the field expand and further develop? Do you have data that can inform evolving theories? Do you have a case study that illustrates or contradicts some of the continuing conversations? Part 4 of this book can help you decide what genre makes most sense for any given piece of your work. But before you think about genre, think about motivation.

For instance, Natasha Daviduke (2018) made an important contribution to the debate on whether undergraduate students who participate in pedagogical partnerships focused on classroom practices need to have disciplinary knowledge. Based on her own experience and her analysis of it, she argued that, rather than being a deficit, as many fear, a student partner who is not in the discipline of the faculty partner can be a benefit. In her words, "My disciplinary differences with my partners made for rich, supportive, and innovative collaborations and exciting educational insights" (156).

Students and faculty alike often doubt that their contributions will be significant, but keep in mind Lee Shulman's (1993, 6) argument that the status of teaching depends on shifting it from private to "community property" (see also chapter 22). Something you might think is obvious, insignificant, or irrelevant might be the very thing that can change the way people think. It is also important to acknowledge and address the de-motivating forces some people experience, as Preeti Vayada suggests in Reflection 6.1.

Reflection 6.1

Considering de-motivating forces

As important as the motivations for writing mentioned here are, discussion of de-motivating forces is equally important as it resonates with the scholar who wants to write but is unable to do so. Reasons can be numerous, including writing anxiety, limited understanding of writing and the publication process, and coming from a non-Anglophonic background. However, from my personal experience as an early writer, I found that professional support and encouragement are immensely helpful. So, whenever Kelly says, "Don't underestimate your contributions," it not only feels good but also provides a strong motivating dose to introspect one's strengths.

Preeti Vayada is a PhD student at The University of Queensland, Australia.

Letting Dialogue with Colleagues Increase and Help Direct Your Motivation

Is your image of writing that of the solitary person toiling away in the ivory tower, local public library, or noisy café? While allotting time and choosing space for yourself to write is a topic we take up in chapter 23, engaging in dialogue about learning and teaching in higher education with scholars can inspire you and help you find the motivation to write. In chapter 26 we discuss the importance of seeking feedback from critical friends before you submit a piece for publication. Equally important, though, is the dialogue with critical friends and thought partners as you are seeking motivation for beginning or continuing to write.

Sometimes you might have an idea that seems clear in your head but as soon as you try to express it to someone, out loud or in an email, you realize it was not so clear after all. Conversely, you might think your idea is murky and unformed, but as you explain it to a friend or colleague, you realize that it's clearer than you thought, and you feel quite strongly about sharing it. In both cases your critical friends can help you further clarify and substantiate the idea, and they can affirm its worth and your excitement about it or help you refine and further develop it. As we discuss in chapter 7, if you choose to co-author with others, they can provide this kind of support as well as motivate you through the task, offering a usefully different perspective.

Over to You

Dimensions of motivation highlight both reason and feeling, both internal and external factors and forces, both inward- and outward-focused attention. For you, does motivation (wanting to communicate) come before inspiration (having something to communicate)? Inspiration involves your head and your heart and listening to your own voice and to the voices of others. Keep in mind that, "Once published, you begin to meet people who know you through your writing" (Day 2016, 14) and "seeing your name in print gives a satisfying frisson of excitement" (Day 2016, 15). Consider addressing the following questions to explore your motivations to write about learning and teaching:

- How does your motivation relate to your identity or identities as a learning and teaching scholar?
- If you are writing about learning and teaching only because it is required or expected by your department or institution, how can you make such required activity joyful and fulfilling?
- What kind of writing is best suited to clarify your own questions about learning and teaching?

- How might you inspire yourself to contribute insights, approaches, challenges, and recommendations to any given evolving discussion or new dialogue about learning and teaching?
- In what ways might dialogue with colleagues increase and help direct your motivation?

CHAPTER 7

WRITING ALONE OR WITH OTHERS

Solitude, Writing Groups, and the
Role of Collaboration in Writing

Sole-authored articles are the most highly prized by [higher education institutions] due to neoliberal imperatives such as funding formulae for research incentives and rewards. (Bozalek et al. 2017, 2)

What I learned through . . . [writing partnerships] is that I am more likely to "get stuff done" when I work with someone else. It is not always straight forward nor painless, but in most cases, work written in this way seems to proceed more quickly to publication. (Simmons and Singh 2019, xxix)

Whether you write alone or co-author in collaboration with others is in part dictated by institutional expectations, as Vivienne Bozalek and her colleagues note above, and in part by personal decisions, though opportunities often arise that affect these choices. We have all written on our own and in partnership with co-authors, and we see benefits and challenges in relation to both, as Nicola Simmons and Ann Singh's quote above suggests. In this chapter we first consider writing alone and then address how to maximize the benefits and reduce or overcome the challenges of working with others to produce a scholarly writing output.

Writing Alone

Many appreciate the independence of writing on their own, and single-authored publications are expected in some disciplines, particularly within the humanities, and can be a boost to your curriculum vitae (CV). To succeed as a sole author, it is critical that you have something worth saying and a powerful desire to communicate it (Black et al. 1998; Sadler 2006). If you do, you can set your own schedule, write at your own pace, and use your own voice. These are all benefits.

While most authors will write alone some of the time, producing your first piece of writing for publication can be a scary experience. You have to be very determined and self-motivated to complete the task. As we discuss in chapter 23, allotting time and choosing space to write involves self-awareness and intentionality, and that is also the case for writing alone, whether you are just starting out or have a good deal of experience.

If you are introverted or appreciate solitude, writing alone can be energizing and efficient. If you are more extroverted and thrive in the company of others, then writing on your own can be a lonely business. One way to both write alone and benefit from others' insights is to join a writing group or attend a writing retreat.

Writing as a Sole Author in a Writing Group

Writing groups, or "publication syndicates" (Sadler 1999), can be a supportive way for both experienced and inexperienced writers to set aside dedicated time to write. Here we focus on the writing group model in which members are working on their own pieces of writing and generate critical feedback for other participants. Writing groups may meet at a formal writing retreat (at a local or distant destination for differing lengths of time), a café, the library, or online (Simmons and Singh 2019), and a range of evidence suggests involvement in any model of supported writing enhances productivity (Geller and Eodice 2013). Writing retreats may be held over several consecutive days, or at a regular time weekly, fortnightly, or monthly (Moore 2018). Most meet face to face, but online versions have also been developed (see, for example, Laura Pasquini's (2016) online summer writing group).

Some writing groups are designed for particular groups, e.g., doctoral students (Wilmot 2018), faculty of color (Rockquemore and Laszloffy 2008), or women (Grant 2008). A few are aimed specifically at people who want to write about their scholarship of teaching and learning (SoTL) projects (Chick et al. 2014; Felten, Moore, and Strickland 2009; Moore 2018). One group followed Wendy Belcher's (2009) book *Writing Your Journal Article in 12 Weeks* to structure a SoTL writing program (Weaver, Robbie, and Radloff 2014). Less formal writing groups may be established by two or three colleagues willing to support each other. Participants in such approaches might be better described as "writing partners."

Rowena Murray (2009, 170-71) proposes five benefits of a writers' group: making time for writing, getting feedback on writing, discussing writing practices, developing productive practices, and sharing information about journals, editors, and reviewers. Of these, the first two are probably the most important, the next two are discussed in chapters 23-25, and the last one applies if the writing group is based around a specific topic, such as SoTL, and is discussed briefly in chapter 8. Many of the questions we have included at the end of each chapter and posted in the online resources of this book could be useful for discussion by a writing group or with a writing partner. The critical thing, though, is to agree on the purpose of the group and to share with one another what your writing goals are. Writing as a dialogue with critical friends is discussed in chapter 26.

Writing retreats can be designed to maximize publication outputs. One study found that:

> The five key elements of writing retreats conducive to increasing publication output were protected time and space; community of practice; development of academic writing competence; intra-personal benefits; and organisational investment. Participants involved achieved greater publication outputs, particularly when provided ongoing support. (Kornhaber et al. 2016, 1210)

Moreover, writing retreats may contribute to the well-being of participants, as Rowena Murray (2009, 175) notes:

> Perhaps the greatest benefit of attending writers' group meetings is that people often report that they arrive at the meeting "in a frenzy, but leave on a high." Some turn up with very low feelings about their writing and about academic life in general, and leave with a sense of satisfaction at having, in spite of everything, progressed their writing project. This facility for turning around very negative feelings is perhaps one of the healthiest outcomes of a professional activity.

Collaborative Writing

Writing with others offers different benefits and challenges from writing alone. If you have not co-authored before, you might consider trying a shorter piece of writing, such as a case study, reflective essay, or blog post before trying a research article or chapter, or co-editing a book. Pat Thomson and Barbara Kamler (2013, 146) distinguish among three types of collaborative writing:

1. Type-talk: where two or more people sit side by side at the computer and work together
2. Cut it up and put it back together: where two or more people divide the paper into sections and write these separately, then one person puts the draft together
3. First cut: where one person takes the lead and writes the first draft in its entirety and the others add, subtract, and amend.

As we pointed out in chapter 1, our strategy for writing this book falls somewhere between the last two types. In Reflection 7.1, Kathryn Sutherland reflects on her experience of using all three strategies at different times.

Reflection 7.1

The experience of using Thomson and Kamler's (2013) three types of collaborative writing

I'm a talker and can rattle off ideas eloquently (mostly!) in discussion, but I sometimes struggle to commit them as easily to the page. So, all three of these techniques work really well for me.

I used the "type-talk" technique with a Canadian colleague when I was on sabbatical: we holed up for three days in my hotel room and I talked while he typed (and also talked and questioned and challenged). We churned out a decent first draft this way. Distance then got in the way, and it took a couple of years—and a call for a special issue with a close fit to our manuscript—before we finally transformed that first draft into a publishable article (Holmes and Sutherland 2015).

I often use the "cut it up and put it back together" technique when writing with students, to make sure that everyone's voices are incorporated. It does require some effort to bring different narrative styles together coherently, but that work pays off when everyone can see how they've contributed (Sutherland, Lenihan-Ikin, and Rushforth 2019).

The "first cut" method, where one person produces the first draft which others add to and amend, is probably the "easiest" form of collaborative writing but also the least collaborative. To alleviate this, we often turn the tables for the next piece of work and swap the responsibility around, so a different person takes the lead each time (Hall and Sutherland 2013, 2018).

Kathryn Sutherland is associate professor at Victoria University of Wellington, New Zealand.

The Advantages and Challenges of Writing in Partnership

Collaborative writing involves "pooling strengths, skills and contacts" (Murray 2009, 33). The multiple perspectives brought to bear can lead to a higher quality output as you clarify or complicate understanding, deepen analyses, shape and reshape arguments, and edit each other's contributions. More can be achieved in a shorter time period, and there is also evidence, at least in the sciences, that the higher the number of authors of a paper, the greater the probability of publication and the more citations it receives (Weller, 2001). It's also worth considering long-term writing partners. As Pat Hutchings (personal communication, June 11, 2019) notes: "Many of us, over the years, find one or two authors we write really well with, and that becomes an ongoing partnership that is incredibly rewarding." Indeed, when writing partnerships work, they can be highly enjoyable and energizing and help build the confidence of all the participants (see chapter 26).

A challenge, however, is that when you have multiple authors, the process often takes longer as the tendency is to go at the speed of the slowest. We recently celebrated the publication of a paper that we began two years previously and involved nine authors, six faculty and three students (Matthews et al. 2018). Although there were periods of inactivity as other commitments intervened, we felt the project needed that time to ensure everyone contributed and felt part of the team. Another challenge is that tensions can arise if the co-authors have strongly held contrasting viewpoints or, as Mick notes in Our Perspectives 7.1, they have different attitudes toward keeping to deadlines and responding in a timely manner to queries and drafts.

To write together effectively requires that all parties be open to discussion and willing to accept feedback and to compromise. It is also important to spend time ensuring that there is a common style of writing throughout the piece. Sometimes one of the co-authors may be given the role of checking for style consistency. This does not mean that differences of opinion should be glossed over. In this book we use the "Our Perspectives" sections to highlight where we have different approaches to writing.

Our Perspectives 7.1

Collaboration versus writing solo

Kelly: I collaborate a lot—90% of my publications are co-authored. The collaborative process is a rich learning process that offers collegiality, connection, and mentorship. However, collaboration can be slower than solo writing, and different voices can get lost or overpower others in the process. Increasingly, I co-author with undergraduate students, which has inspired my writing and thinking in new ways. To keep collaborators on the same page and create space for everyone to contribute meaningfully, I usually start new writing projects by outlining some key points (journal, aim, contribution) using one-page plans (Matthews 2018a, 2018b; see online resources: "Simple Publication Plan for Getting Started" and "Project Plan for Research").

Alison: I experience collaborative writing as a form of dialogue in practice, and I find that it can invite further dialogue. Although I am profoundly introverted, I am energized by most co-authorship, and I am smarter in collaboration than I am alone. Through writing with others, I am forced to wrestle, grow, reconsider, and compromise as well as to learn new things and to make explicit what I think I already know. To my mind, co-authoring has a better chance of capturing the multiplicity of perspectives that is virtually always relevant.

Mick: When I wrote as an economic geographer, I usually wrote by myself. When I moved into writing about geography in higher education and then about SoTL and higher education research more generally, I more commonly co-wrote with colleagues. Collaborating generally made the writing process a much more enjoyable experience and improved the clarity and quality of our writing. I usually learn a tremendous amount from my co-authors, as has happened, for example, in writing this book. The only times collaboration has not worked quite so well was when my co-authors had different attitudes than me toward keeping to deadlines and responding in a timely manner to queries. So, choose your co-authors with care!

Source: Based on Healey, Matthews, and Cook-Sather (2019, 40)

Your perspective: What are your experiences of and thoughts on collaborating versus writing solo?

Similar benefits and challenges have been noted regarding the experience of participating in international collaborative writing groups, which have become a signature pedagogy of the International Society for the Scholarship of Teaching (ISSOTL). These are discussed in the online resource "The Experience of International Collaborative Writing Groups."

Ethical Authorship

Who should be credited as an author and in what order is another area where there is potential for disagreement and ill feeling. These questions may arise from different practices in different disciplines but are also open to potential abuse when there are power differences between team members. For instance, in some disciplines, graduate students at some institutions are required to add their supervisors as co-authors on papers, whether those supervisors were supportive and contributed in meaningful and productive ways or not.

There are guidelines on ethical authorship. However, the Committee on Publication Ethics (COPE), whose membership includes more than 4,000 journals from all research fields, acknowledges that "there is no universally agreed definition of authorship" (White 2004, 70). Many journals, particularly in the sciences, have adopted the definition of the International Committee of Medical Journal Editors (ICMJE 2017, 2), which identifies four criteria for authorship, the first three of which may have some relevance to learning and teaching journals:

- Substantial contributions to the conception or design of the work; or the acquisition, analysis, or interpretation of data for the work;
- Drafting the work or revising it critically for important intellectual content; and

- Final approval of the version to be published.

One of the issues these guidelines were designed to address is "gift authorship," i.e., including names of those who took little or no part in the research and who may be better listed in the acknowledgments.

As for the order of authors' names, there is again a variety of practices in different disciplines (Tscharntke et al. 2007), although in the education field it is most common to list authors in order of their contribution and to put authors in alphabetical order where the contribution is similar. Applying these guidelines to writing about learning and teaching can, however, be problematic. As Trent Maurer (2017, 1) points out, "The collaborative interdisciplinary nature of much SoTL work, along with the increasing focus of SoTL on students as co-inquirers into SoTL research, creates unique issues and challenges in ethically assigning authorship credit on SoTL projects." He further suggests that "if authorship credit is reserved for idea generation, research design, and manuscript writing, many students, especially undergraduate students, would be ineligible for significant credit even in fairly collaborative projects" (3). He goes on to propose a process-focused approach to determining authorship based on the Research Skill Development framework (Willison 2009), in which we find ways to value, in Angela Brew's (2006, 136) words, "the contributions of each person no matter what their level of prior understanding and knowledge."

For the reasons cited above, the ethics of authorship is a complex and sometimes controversial area. We advise teams to discuss the issues involved early on but also be flexible and open to amendment should the assumptions on which the initial decisions are based change during the writing process.

Writing in collaboration is intellectual and emotional work in which the participants undergo a learning journey and develop their identities (see chapters 3–5). This is apparent in the reflections of three co-authors who collaborated on thirty-five publications over two decades: "In any one session, we learned to expect the unexpected—to be exhilarated and confused, surprised and displeased, praised and pained—sometimes at the same time" (Nevin, Thousand, and Villa

2011, 290). Clearly, positive experiences of co-authoring can lead to long-term and rewarding writing partnerships.

Academics and Students Writing Together

Academics and students co-authoring offers particular challenges and rewards. One challenge is that there are different expectations for faculty/academic staff and students regarding where they need to put their time and energy. While writing for publication is an expectation for many scholars in higher education and therefore factored into how faculty spend their time and energy, most students, particularly undergraduates, may not have the time, interest, or confidence to author traditional scholarly texts, given their commitments to their courses, jobs, and extracurricular activities, as well as their academic goals (Cook-Sather, Abbot, and Felten 2019; see also Maurer 2017, for some of the structural barriers to students as co-authors in SoTL).

While some faculty might not be compelled by the idea of writing with students, others who are might not be able to do so because of the pressures those faculty feel due to tenure expectations, requirements to seek funding, and workload. For undergraduate students, writing for publication is often an add-on for which there is not necessarily any benefit beyond the experience and satisfaction of co-authoring with a faculty member. Furthermore, because of the demands on their time and their own priorities, students may not have the time to familiarize themselves with the literature that constitutes any given conversation in the field, unless the writing project is part of a course or research project conducted in collaboration with faculty. Finally, many of the genres of writing typically expected and valued in academia consist of what one student author described as "clear logic and air-tight assertions" that many students find "stuffy" and uninteresting (student authors quoted in Cook-Sather, Abbot, and Felten 2019, 19, 21). This type of writing may also exacerbate the imposter syndrome so many students feel, as Sophia Abbot notes in Reflection 7.2. Some genres we discuss (such as reflective essays and stories) and others we do not delve into (including feminist and queer autoethnography, collective writing approaches, and critical social work) enact alternative modes of analysis and reject some traditional norms of academic writing.

Reflection 7.2

Acknowledging imposter syndrome

I certainly had a strong feeling of imposter syndrome as an undergraduate writing for publication: How could I be so bold as to believe that *I*—a 20-year-old with very little life or scholarly experience—have something worth saying and sharing with the world!? Even now, despite my experience writing, publishing, and being a scholar, I feel those uncertainties. My imposter syndrome has been exacerbated by the "air-tight assertions" expectation, because it is easy as a newer scholar, still getting to know a body of scholarship, to wonder whether my assertions really are airtight. Writing in other genres has given me space to explore my ideas and get affirmation on the value of them.

Sophia Abbot is a graduate student at Elon University, US.

For academics and professional staff, the rewards of co-authoring with students include the opportunity to learn from the perspectives that students bring and, in some cases, the conceptual frames they introduce (Cook-Sather 2018b). For students, co-authoring with academics and professional staff affords opportunities to affirm their identities and perspectives and contribute their knowledge to wider discussions—a form of epistemic justice—a concept, by the way, introduced by a (then) graduate student author, Alise de Bie, to Alise's faculty and undergraduate co-authors (de Bie et al. 2019).

Over to You

Writing on your own affords independence, and sole-authored publications are often expected in many higher education contexts. Co-authoring in collaboration with others can be enormously satisfying and the benefits usually far outweigh any challenges.

Alone or together? Take a moment to reflect on your preferences and assumptions:

- Do you prefer writing alone or in partnership? What do you see as the benefits and challenges of each?
- If you are new to writing, do you have someone you think you could work with in collaboration?
- How can you best promote a culture of ethical authorship?
- How might you go about joining a writing group or setting one up with colleagues? How might this benefit you?

CHAPTER 8

CHOOSING AN OUTLET

*Whom Do You Want to Talk to
about Learning and Teaching?*

*For most academics, developing the scholarship of teaching and
learning will only bring about change in their priorities if it
is embedded in disciplines and departments. (Healey 2000,
172-3)*

*There is a great deal more in common [between disciplines]
than many teachers normally perceive or acknowledge. Many
teaching methods described as discipline-specific are used widely
across the disciplines and take much the same form regardless
of context. (Gibbs 2000, 41)*

*Choosing a journal is in reality choosing a reader, a reader who
is a member of a specific discourse community. (Thomson and
Kamler 2013, 36)*

In choosing a journal, publisher, or conference to which to submit
your work, there are many factors to consider. As the above quotes
suggest, a key decision for scholars writing about learning and
teaching is whether to join a discipline-specific exchange or a
cross-disciplinary one. Other considerations include the timing of
selecting an outlet, whether or not the outlet is peer-reviewed, the
prestige factor (including the possibility of later submitting the piece
of writing to a national research assessment exercise, such as occurs
in the UK and Australia), and the research norms of specific outlets.

Selecting an outlet is not simple. It depends on your context, your personal and professional identities, your career aspirations, and your preferences, as well as consideration of the difficulty of getting published in some of the most competitive outlets or accepted to present at conferences that have a limited number of slots. Regarding the latter, Barbara Grant (2017) prefers small conferences, and Pat Thomson (2017a) advises: "You only conference when you have good cause." We focus mainly on publishing in journals in this chapter, but we also include a section on writing book chapters. The principles we discuss apply to choosing between many other types of outlets (see also Thomson 2013a). We make some specific comments about choosing book publishers in chapter 16, and in chapter 21 we discuss writing on various social media platforms.

Start by Considering the Audience and the Conversation You Are Joining or Trying to Create

Here we argue that the first question you need to answer is: With whom do you want to be in conversation? As we point out in chapter 3, writing about learning and teaching means contributing to or creating a conversation. Hence, in choosing an outlet, ask yourself two questions:

- Is this the group (faculty/academic staff, students, public, etc.) that I want to be in dialogue with?
- Will this work contribute to a current conversation in this discourse community or create a necessary new one?

If you are aiming to submit to a journal, select one or two to target. Look at the journals in which the articles you cite are published and look at the articles' reference lists. Read the mission statements of these journals and scan what else they have published in the last few years that may relate to your topic. Editors appreciate citations to relevant work published in their own journals. Even better, rather than cherry-picking citations, show that you are listening to and engaging with current conversations. There is evidence that submitting to an inappropriate journal is the most common reason editors give for rejecting articles (Noble 1989). Though slightly dated, the finding resonates with our own experience of editing learning and teaching journals.

Publishing Within and Reaching Beyond Discipline-Specific Learning and Teaching Journals

Most authors approach publishing about learning and teaching from a disciplinary lens, as indicated in the quote from Mick at the beginning of this chapter. David Baume (1996, 4) similarly noted in the editorial of the first issue of the *International Journal for Academic Development:* "Many academics derive most of their professional identity from their discipline." This reality has been recognized in the last twenty years by academics in Australia (Neumann 2001), the UK (Cleaver, Lintern, and McLinden 2018; Healey and Jenkins 2003), and the United States (Huber 2000; McKinney 2012a). The best examples of putting this phenomenon into practice were the twenty-four Subject Centres, which were established in the UK (2000–2011) to promote discipline-based approaches to learning and teaching.

The Subject Centres, and other discipline-based initiatives, recognized that not only is the primary allegiance of most academics to their discipline or profession, but that some disciplines are characterized by distinctive forms of teaching, such as studio critiques in art and design, work-based learning in nursing and social work, laboratory classes in the sciences, and fieldwork in geography and earth and environmental sciences. If you are interested in writing about these pedagogies, a discipline-based outlet may be a suitable choice. Moreover, all disciplines have particular conceptions of knowledge, which are closely linked to the complexity of current research and scholarship in the discipline (Healey and Jenkins 2003; Kreber 2009). Denis Berthiaume (2008) contends that discipline-specific pedagogical knowledge is critical for understanding learning and teaching. The same may be argued for writing about learning and teaching.

Graham Gibbs (2000) notes that it is not just a matter of selecting a discipline-specific or generic higher education outlet. Instead, the question comes back to: *What conversations do you want to contribute to or create, which such exchanges are open to you, and which might not be and why?* Different outlets foster diverse, yet related, discussions, and different values and dimensions of identity will influence both what you want to say and how or whether it will be received. These considerations are relevant to chapter 4 on identity and writing as a values-based practice.

When we think about publishing as being *in conversation* with others, then new possibilities emerge for contributing to different yet related conversations that reach new and wider audiences. The critical point is to recognize that the interests and situations of different audiences vary. If you recognize your audience, the unique contributions of your work can be clearly linked to the ongoing conversation of the outlet. All too frequently authors make assumptions about their readers' knowledge and understanding of disciplinary practices and national education contexts. Providing sufficient explanations of these details is particularly important if you are writing for a transdisciplinary, international audience (Thomson 2017b). Martin Haigh (2012) provides a useful discussion about writing successfully for one discipline-based journal, and his advice applies to most learning and teaching journals, whether discipline based or otherwise.

Publishing in "High-Prestige," Open Access, and Institutional Outlets

In recent years, as research and teaching assessment exercises have grown in importance, scholars have come under pressure to publish in what are perceived as "high-prestige" journals and other outlets. Those scholars going for promotion or bidding for grants have felt similar pressures. Publication in such outlets does not, of course, mean that the papers are themselves high quality, or that high-quality papers are not published in other journals, but there is a basking-in-reflected-glory factor at work here, associating yourself, should you be published in a prestige journal, with well-known authors who have also been published there. The "top 10" higher education journals, based on Google Scholar citations, are shown in Table 8.1. One of the impacts of the pressures to publish in these journals is that they also have high rejection rates. *Higher Education Research & Development,* for example, rejects 80% of submissions (Grant 2016).

Table 8.1: The "top 10" higher education journals, 2019

Publication	h5-index
1. Studies in Higher Education	52
2. Higher Education	50
3. Research in Higher Education	37
4. Assessment & Evaluation in Higher Education	37
5. The Journal of Higher Education	36
6. Higher Education Research & Development	34
7. Journal of Studies in International Education	31
8. Journal of College Student Development	31
9. Teaching in Higher Education	30
10. Innovations in Education and Teaching International	29

Source: Google Scholar, July 2019

Citations for journals listed in Web of Science are widely used to provide rankings, though they are biased toward periodicals published in North America and have other issues as well (Rushforth and de Rijcke 2016). However, many journals concerned with learning and teaching in higher education are too new to have received a full listing, though some appear in the Emerging Sources Citation Index. Despite journal impact factors being widely criticized as a measure of individual academic performance, they continue to be used to underpin some institutions' academic review, promotion, and tenure policies (McKiernan, Alperin, and Fleerackers 2019).

Open access journals are becoming increasingly common as part of an ethos of open knowledge sharing in the digital age, and they are disrupting conventional academic publishing practices. For example,

Teaching & Learning Inquiry began life with a commercial university press publisher, but then transferred to become an open access journal. There are pressures from research funders for publications resulting from their grants to be made available instantly in open access depositories. Open access journals are free to read, although some have publishing fees to subsidize the costs of editing a journal. Most are supported by academic societies or higher education institutions. Like other journals, most have a rigorous peer-review system. Some depend on editorial review to ensure the quality of the publications. Many learning and teaching journals are published in open access format with no charges for submission or access—some examples are given in Table 8.2. These journals may be the most appropriate outlets for some of your work and link you to ongoing exchanges with colleagues interested in similar topics. We have each published in high-prestige journals and other learning and teaching journals in both print and open access formats, including many of the journals listed in Tables 8.1 and 8.2. We recommend seeking publication in a diversity of outlets.

Some commercial publishers also offer an open access option, but they will charge you to make your article available for free download. There is evidence that works published in open access are downloaded and cited more than those that are not (Hitchcock 2011; Piwowar et al. 2018). Pre-publication versions of papers may usually be uploaded to open access platforms (see chapter 28).

The pay-to-publish journals to be avoided are the predatory ones that promise very quick publication with virtually no quality checks (see Beall's List of Predatory Journals and Publishers). Be wary of unsolicited emails from journals that promise publication in a month or two. If you are unfamiliar with a journal, check to see if the authors publishing in the journal are leaders in their field and look on the journal website for the names of the editors or editorial board. You should also be wary of predatory conference invitations (see Rehm 2013 for a related discussion on ResearchGate).

Table 8.2: Ten selected open access learning and teaching in higher education journals

Asian Journal of the Scholarship of Teaching and Learning (AJSoTL)
The Canadian Journal for the Scholarship of Teaching and Learning (CJSoTL)
International Journal for Students as Partners (IJSaP)
International Journal for the Scholarship of Teaching & Learning (IJ-SoTL)
Online Learning Journal (OL)
SoTL in the South
Student Engagement in Higher Education Journal (SEHEJ)
Student Success
Teaching & Learning Inquiry (TLI)
Teaching and Learning Together in Higher Education (TLTHE)

When first seeking to have your scholarship published, you may lack confidence to submit to a national or international journal, whether open access or closed, high prestige or otherwise. For you, an institutional journal may be the place to start. In the UK about 10% of universities have their own in-house journals, some of which publish work from authors outside the institution (Mistry 2017, 2018). Some are only available for faculty/academic staff of the university to see (Robinson-Self 2018). Publishing in such journals is a useful way of gaining experience with the process of publication and making your institutional colleagues aware of your learning and teaching interests, but these journals' dependence on volunteers who may change institutions or roles within the institution means that many of them only last a few years and the number of issues published each year can vary. You should ask yourself, "If my writing is good enough to be published in an in-house journal, is it strong enough to be published in a national or even international journal?" By the time you have finished reading this book, you should be able to make an informed decision. Your choice of genre (for example, a research article or a case study, a reflective essay or a story) also affects your choice of outlet as some of the genres discussed in part 4 are not accepted by some journals.

When selecting an outlet, the likely time to publication may be a factor. The review process for many of the "high-prestige" higher education journals can take up to a year or more, and because these journals are inundated with submissions, many have a backlog of accepted submissions that delay assignment to a printed volume, though many are now making the accepted version of a paper available electronically before the print issue of the journal is published. However, the time question needs to be balanced with the reputation of the journal, especially if you are in the early stages of your academic career. It may be not only necessary but also wise to settle for a less prestigious outlet if you are just starting out or doing a PhD by publication of prior work or by portfolio (Smith 2015).

Writing a Book Chapter

Sometimes an alternative outlet for your writing may be as a book chapter. Writing a journal article and writing a book chapter about learning and teaching have much in common, though the latter generally gives you more flexibility in length and structure, as well as in what can be included. This difference is well articulated by Pat Thomson (2013a):

> For a start, you can assume with a book chapter that you don't have to convince readers that the topic you're writing about is important. The editors are going to do that in the foreword. They are also likely to do a pretty thorough survey of the field, and to cover its history. So you don't have to do that kind of literature work in a chapter, unless it is one about the literature. . . . You just have to situate your own position and indicate the literatures that you draw on and to which you are talking/ contributing.

It is essential, of course, that a book chapter fits into the theme of the edited collection. This may restrict the topics you can write about compared with writing journal articles, and it may increase the need to cross reference and avoid overlap with other chapters. However, if your chapter is part of a themed collection, you may reach readers who might not have looked at your article isolated in a journal, or whose institutions do not have access to the journal. Moreover, chapters may be easier to write if they do not involve undertaking primary research.

Two further differences between a book chapter and a journal article are that, first, book chapters do not always go through the anonymous review process that characterizes most academic journals. This can have the advantage, dependent on the book editor, that you need not make as many changes in the chapter. On the other hand, many promotion and tenure review committees and national research assessment exercises do not value chapters as highly as they value peer-reviewed journal articles. This may partially explain why book chapters traditionally receive fewer citations than journal articles. Discoverability and accessibility are also important factors to consider (Anderson 2012). Many publishers are now allocating DOIs (Digital Object Identifiers) to chapters in edited books and making most academic books available in e-book format, so chapters are becoming more discoverable and accessible. The cost of edited books varies widely, with some priced so high that only selected libraries can afford them. The emergence of open access book publishers is making these outlets an attractive option through which authors can disseminate their work. It remains to be seen whether these changes will have an impact on book chapters' citation patterns compared with journal articles.

A second difference between a book chapter and a journal article is that choosing to write a book chapter is not as simple as choosing to write a journal article. You usually have to be invited by the book editor or respond to a call for chapter proposals for a book project. Sometimes the idea for a learning and teaching book arises from a themed session at a conference, so looking out for such calls for papers can be a way of contributing to a book. Another way is to propose to edit such a book yourself (see chapter 18).

When to Select Your Outlet

Some academics leave the selection of a suitable outlet until after they have drafted their work, particularly if they are targeting general higher education journals, because there are many to choose from. Others start with a specific journal in mind, which might reflect a desire, or the pressure, to publish in the "top journals," or it might reflect a wish to write for a specific audience. Still other scholars decide as they are writing, taking account of the authors and publications they cite that link to the conversation with which they want to engage or that they want to start. Your decision depends on your situation. If you choose your outlet *before* you start writing, then you can write with a specific audience in mind and use the format and style appropriate to that outlet from the beginning. However, you might find the choice becomes constraining as you start writing. Perhaps you are citing more works from another journal, which might indicate that you should be speaking to a different audience. Or you find you need more space, so a journal with a higher word count might be a better option. On the other hand, having a journal identified from the start could keep you focused in a way that helps you complete the manuscript in a timely manner.

You may prefer to select two or three possible journals, so if you are rejected by your first choice you can amend your article for submission to your second choice quickly, though you will need to ensure that you are addressing their readership directly and you will, of course, need to reformat the manuscript to fit the journal's house style, including the format of references. Editors and reviewers are not impressed when they receive submissions that clearly—from the format—have been submitted to another outlet previously.

If you are struggling to identify an audience/outlet or are feeling overwhelmed by the writing task ahead, you might try searching keywords relevant to the piece you want to write in a general database like Google Scholar to see who is publishing similar work. Maybe, if you are struggling to identify a suitable outlet, you should consider writing in a different genre. You might also revisit your abstract, if the genre for which you are writing requires one; revising it along the lines suggested in chapter 10 may help you decide on an appropriate outlet. If you are still uncertain, consider shaping the work for a conference talk. This may present an opportunity to engage in dialogue with other scholars about your work by creating time for discussion, often after your formal presentation (see chapter 17). You might also consider summarizing your paper by writing it as a blog post (see chapter 21) or a contribution to a professional society newsletter before starting work on a full journal article. Just be careful not to share too much if you plan to write it up for submission to a peer-reviewed venue, since many publications have legitimate concerns about work that is already published.

The Focus and Research Norms of the Outlet

Selecting an outlet is related to selecting a genre, which we discuss in more depth in chapter 11. Whatever your preference for selecting a venue, it is important to ensure that your work is connected to the focus of the outlet *and* communicated in a way that makes sense for that journal. For example, if your work presents rich and in-depth narratives from a handful of colleagues to illuminate the complexities of pedagogical decision-making for new scholars in the health sciences, then your chosen journal should have a history of publishing rich qualitative studies or perhaps have new editors seeking to expand the methodological pluralism of the journal. In other words, your work needs to contribute to an ongoing conversation in a given discourse community, while also linking to the research norms of that community—or if it does not, you must find a way to productively challenge those norms and start a new discussion.

The importance of matching your article to the journal to which you are submitting is conveyed in the questions listed below, which were stimulated in part by an analysis of why sixty articles were rejected by the editors of the *Educational Action Research* journal (Convery and Townsend 2018).

1. Why do I want to submit to this journal?
2. Does the article focus on the stated aim of the journal?
3. Is your article written in a genre (e.g., empirical, conceptual, case study) which is acceptable to the journal? And, if not, have you contacted the editor to see whether they might accept something in a different genre (e.g., reflective essay, opinion piece, video)?
4. Have you read any articles from this journal? How does your submission fit alongside them?
5. Does it extend and challenge our knowledge and understanding?
6. Is the argument and contribution of your article explicit?

The key takeaway message from this chapter is that choosing an outlet means being explicit about who you want to be in conversation with and then checking that your article aligns with the outlet's aim and scope.

Over to You

Choosing a suitable outlet to submit to, especially when you may have spent several months writing the piece, is a key decision. Whether you choose a discipline-based journal or a generic one, a chapter in an edited book or an article in a refereed journal, and whether you make your selection before, during, or after you have written your piece, is a highly contextualized judgment. Some questions that you may wish to consider in choosing a suitable outlet include:

- Will the outlet put you into dialogue with the intended audience (general higher education/discipline/region)?
- Does publishing in "top journals" in your field matter for your career progression?
- Are you in a hurry to get the work published?
- Have you considered developing a publication plan that reaches varied audiences with different forms of scholarship (see chapter 29)?
- Do you have the opportunity to submit a chapter to an edited collection? If so, is this a more suitable outlet for you than submitting to a refereed journal?

CHAPTER 9

SELECTING A TITLE

*What You Decide Matters More
than You Might Realize*

Like a hat on the head or the front door to a house . . .
(Sword 2012, 63)

Because it is the first thing people will see, like a hat or a front door, the title of your written work has a big job to do. While it is small compared to what it introduces, its few words are immediately visible: they will appear in tables of contents, online news feeds, Google Scholar searches, reference lists, and your curriculum vitae (CV), and they affect how findable your work will be. Not only does a title offer "a powerful first impression," as Helen Sword (2012, 63) continues, it is the set of words that will carry your argument or perspective across scholarly exchanges. We therefore encourage you to consider and reconsider your title as you compose, keeping in mind whom you are talking with (audience), the form of your title (structure), and what your title captures and communicates (content) (see also chapter 27).

The Title Has a Big Job to Do

The title is the primary filter potential readers use to decide whether to read any further or to pursue access to the publication. Most people will not read beyond the title. So, your title needs to encourage people interested in your topic to read further.

There can be tension among writing eye-catching titles, avoiding giving readers misleading information, and attracting the readers interested in your subject. Helen Sword (2012, 67) notes that, "Among the many decisions faced by authors composing an academic title, the most basic choice is whether to *engage* the reader, *inform* the reader, or do both at once." Most titles used by academics fall into the inform category: "It could even be said, in the case of titles in the age of online publication, that boring and factual is good" (Thomson and Kamler 2013, 86). However, being informative is only one function of the title; another is clarifying the argument. What is your take-home message (Thomson 2016a)? We struggled for some time in devising a title for this book, for instance, to try to capture the arguments that underpin the text. We experimented with several different titles, which we rejected as they did not encapsulate all the main themes of the book. Although we quickly decided on the gist of the main title, *Writing about Teaching and Learning in Higher Education,* the subtitle went through many versions, such as:

> *Becoming a Scholar through Publishing*
>
> *Publishing and Disseminating Your Work while Nurturing Your Faculty Identity*
>
> *Publishing Your Pedagogical Scholarship and Nurturing Your Professional Identity*
>
> *Joining Scholarly Conversations, Fostering Identities, and Deepening Understanding through Publishing across a Range of Genres*
>
> *Joining Scholarly Conversations and Fostering Identities*

Through discussion among ourselves and with feedback and suggestions from critical friends and our publishers, we came up with an overall title that we were happy with: *Writing about Learning and Teaching in Higher Education: Creating and Contributing to Scholarly Conversations across a Range of Genres.*

It is not particularly eye-catching, but it is informative. Patrick Dunleavy (2014) recommends that authors list a minimum of ten possible titles and then "see if recombining words from different titles might work better." Eye-catching titles may be more important in social media posts because the audience is wider and the space for informative titles is generally less.

Consider, too, the relevance of title and keywords in terms of digital visibility and search engine optimization (Taylor & Francis, "A Researcher's Guide to Search Engine Optimization"). Try putting your initial chosen title through Google Scholar to see if anybody has used that title before. This may also help you find other reference material that might be useful. Michael Townsend (1983) suggests that having a colon in the middle of your title makes it more publishable—the first part acts as the "hat on the head," as Helen Sword suggests, and the second part unpacks it a little bit to make it easier for editors to select referees (if it is a peer-reviewed outlet) and for readers to get a sense of what to expect. An example of a title with an-eye catching "hat" and an informative post-colon description is: "'Writing My First Academic Article Feels Like Dancing Around Naked': Research Development for Higher Education Lecturers Working in Further Education Colleges" (Turner, Brown, and Edwards-Jones 2014, 87).

The Form of Your Title

James Hartley (2008, 23) argues that the title "needs to stand out in some way from the other thousands of titles that compete for the reader's attention, but it also needs to tell the reader what the paper is about." Madeline Haggan (2004) notes a trend toward increasing informativeness of titles and has referred to them as "texts in miniature," but there can be a danger in being too specific. In the context of devising titles for conference participants, Alice Cassidy (2018a, 55) warns: "The more you narrow down your title, the fewer potential participants will see it being relevant to them." One way to be both engaging and informative is to use the main title to stand out and the subtitle to inform. Nancy Chick provides a good example in her co-authored article, "Reconciling Apples & Oranges: A Constructivist

SoTL Writing Program" (Chick et al. 2014). Daniel Feldman (2004) coined the intriguing title for his editorial: "The Devil Is in the Details: Converting Good Research into Publishable Articles." Not that you want to use a colon in every case. Often you can summarize the content of your contribution in one phrase (Cassidy, 2018a). For example, *How to Get Research Published in Journals* (Day 2016) and "Addressing Feedback from Reviewers and Editors" (Brookfield 2011) both state clearly what the author intends to cover. Our own approaches to deciding on titles are outlined in Our Perspectives 9.1.

Our Perspectives 9.1

How do you decide on a title?

Mick: I lack the imagination to come up with many catchy titles. Most of mine are informative and in roughly half I use a colon.

Kelly: I appreciate catchy and clever titles. But I am not a wordsmith, so I struggle to come up with titles that grab attention while also communicating the essence of my work. I tend to stick to informative. Sometimes, I find a salient quote in qualitative data that captures a key point, and I include that in the title.

Alison: I enjoy unexpected juxtapositions of words and literary devices such as alliteration, but I can sometimes get carried away with what I consider to be the aesthetic appeal of the title and forget some of the points we make above (such as being direct in helping readers know what the piece is about!). I have received feedback from reviewers who sometimes ask for a more descriptive, less poetic, title, but I tend to persist in using titles that require some linguistic imagination.

Your perspective: How do you decide on a title?

Communicating with Your Audience

It is critical to consider your target audience when deciding on titles. For instance, if you are presenting at a higher education conference, it is unnecessary to include the words "higher education" in the title, as the participants should assume that is the case. And if you are presenting to a general audience, it's probably best not to include reference to a particular discipline. Mick learned this lesson the hard way when he presented a paper at the International Consortium for Educational Development conference in Austin, Texas, US, in 1998. Up to that point his research and development practice had primarily been within his discipline, and he submitted a paper entitled "Developing Good Educational Practices: Lessons from Geography." But when it came time for the session, nobody showed up! On reflection, that is hardly surprising as none of the other delegates were geographers. He later used much of the material from the presentation in an article accepted for publication in *Higher Education Research and Development,* but he changed the title to "Developing the Scholarship of Teaching through the Disciplines" (Healey 2000). With over 450 citations, it is in his top five most cited papers. The change of the title cannot explain its impact, but it probably contributed.

Over to You

Choosing a suitable title can be an enjoyable intellectual exercise, but it has a serious purpose as it is critical in attracting potential readers and making your work visible. Striving to achieve a balance among capturing potential readers' attention, being informative, ensuring that your publication will show up in digital searches, and being true to who you are as a scholar matter when selecting a title. These questions can support your efforts:

- What is the first impression your title gives?
- How have you balanced being catchy (maybe before the colon) with being informative (maybe after the colon)?
- Does it include terms readers will likely search for?
- How have critical friend responded to the title?

CHAPTER 10

PREPARING THE ABSTRACT

Planning and Clarifying the
Potential Structure of Your Writing

[A] well-prepared abstract can be the most important single paragraph in an article. . . . Most people will have their first contact with an article by seeing just the abstract. (American Psychological Association 2010, 26)

The number one problem with abstracts is too much approach, not enough arrival. (Feldman 2004, 2)

It is worth rewriting the abstract as many times as may be needed to make sure that it really does summarize the main thrust of your writing and your findings. (Black et al. 1998, 113)

If the genre in which you are writing requires an abstract, take time to write an effective one. Abstracts are a key way of telling editors, reviewers, and potential readers about your work and are very common in academic journals and conference programs. Along with the title, the abstract will be read by many more people than the rest of the publication. Hence, your abstract should tell the story of your paper, including, as Daniel Feldman and Dolores Black and colleagues advise above, the main findings. But it can also play other vital roles in the writing process: as a planning device and as a final check on clarity.

The Function of Abstracts

Titles and abstracts are often the only parts of your paper that are freely available online, unless you publish in an open access journal or book. Moreover, they are the first thing that journal editors and reviewers read. "While busy journal editors may use the abstract to decide whether to send a paper for peer review or reject it outright, reviewers will form their first impression about your paper on reading it" (Rodrigues 2013). The function of the abstract is not only to attract readers, but also to deter those whose interests are not addressed in the paper (Day 2016). Extended abstracts are often used by conference organizers to select papers for presentation, although shorter abstracts may be all that they publish in the program. Video abstracts are also growing in importance for promoting publications (see chapter 29).

What Should Your Abstract Contain?

The style of journal abstracts varies both between and within disciplines, and even sometimes within the same journal. In the social sciences and humanities, abstracts are typically descriptive, while in the sciences, they are commonly structured to describe the background, methods, results, and conclusions (Cerejo 2013). "Writing [an abstract] in a structured format (with or without the headings) ensures that it is informative and complete" (Hartley 2008, 34). Ian McNay (2010), who for many years edited *Higher Education Abstracts*, and Royce Sadler (2006), who wrote the influential Higher Education Research and Development Society of Australasia's Green Guide to publishing in scholarly journals, provide some useful advice on writing an abstract for an empirical learning and teaching article, which we synthesize here.

The abstract should:
- give a clear summary of the study, including a brief rationale and a concise description of the aim;
- summarize the methods used, including where and when the research took place and the number and type of sample or participants;
- state some specific results or findings; and

- discuss implications, recommendations, and limitations.

Depending on the length of the abstract, it may be challenging to include all their suggestions. The most important is to state clearly your main argument and what you are adding to the literature. They also advise avoiding using general statements such as "implications are considered" or "recommendations are listed."

Rowena Murray recommends analyzing the structure and style of abstracts in your target journal as a way to plan your abstract. Looking at these examples will guide you in deciding:

- how to write "uncontentious opener" sentences;
- how to make the case for your work;
- how to link what is known/not known and your work;
- how to write about your methodology;
- how much detail to give on your results; and
- how to define your contribution—options and specific terms to use.

(Murray 2009, 59)

This set of recommendations should help you build your confidence in contributing to or creating a conversation hosted by that journal. Murray (2009, 132-33, 146-50) also provides a checklist of prompt questions and active verbs that you may consider using.

When Should You Write the Abstract?

There are differences of opinion about when to write the abstract. Some people advise leaving it until after you have finished writing your paper (Black et al. 1998; Cerejo 2013; Kate, Kumar, and Subair 2017), when it can be used to clarify whether you have made the argument you intended and prompt you to revise as needed. Others make a case for starting by writing the first draft of your abstract (Belcher 2009; Healey, Matthews, and Cook-Sather 2019; Sadler 2006; Thomson and Kamler 2013). What all agree, though, as indicated in the final quote at the beginning of this chapter, is that getting it right requires meticulous attention.

We also have different views on this topic. Alison usually leaves writing the abstract until at least the first draft of the paper is completed. Mick and Kelly used to do this as well until they came across the argument put forward by Pat Thomson and Barbara Kamler (2013) that there are considerable benefits to writing the abstract first and using it as a planning tool to clarify the argument, contribution, and structure of the paper and revisiting it several times during the writing process (see chapter 24). This is how we approached writing our *Teaching & Learning Inquiry* article (Healey, Matthews, and Cook-Sather 2019). As we discussed there, we also have different approaches to using abstract templates, frameworks, or structures: Alison finds them constraining, while Mick and Kelly believe they help focus their thinking before they write. Again, there is no one way to go about writing an abstract or deciding when to write it.

Structuring Your Abstract

A straightforward structure for an abstract is to identify the purpose, the argument, and the conclusion (Day 2016). Thomson and Kamler (2013, 52) suggest that you should think of your whole abstract "as an argument—a text that makes its key point explicit and highlights its contribution to the field." They propose thinking of the abstract as a "tiny text" that has five "moves": locate, focus, anchor, report, and argue (Table 10.1). A version of this table with the last two columns left empty is available in the online resources: "A Planning Tool for Drafting Your Abstract." You may find it helpful in drafting your abstract. A possible mnemonic to help remember the five moves "L F A R A" is "**L**earning **F**rom **A**cademic **R**esearch **A**rticles."

While there are many templates and strategies for approaching the abstract, we find the Barbara Kamler and Pat Thomson (2013) model helpful because it positions the abstract as a planning tool while clearly indicating a framework to draft the abstract. New writers, like Joanne Bouma, have found this approach motivating (Reflection 10.1).

Table 10.1: Harnessing the abstract as a planning tool for a learning and teaching publication

Moves	Purpose	Questions	Sentence starters
Locate	Describe the broader context within which your study contributes.	What is the broader topic of your study?	[xxx] is an issue of growing concern in universities.
Focus	State the issues, questions, or opportunities that your study explores.	How does your study explore this broad topic more specifically?	This study reports on research into . . . [conducted where and with whom] to explore . . . [linked to above topic].
Anchor	Articulate an overview of your theoretical framework and research design.	What literature, models, or theories did you draw on? How did you gather data?	Our study was informed by . . . [model/theory/work]. The views of [specific study participants] were captured through . . .
Report	Present the key findings arising from your research.	What did you find overall from the analysis of your study?	The results of our study were . . .
Argue	Make an argument with implications.	What are you arguing as a result of your research? What are the broader implications arising from your study?	We argue that . . . Our findings imply that . . . .

Source: Based on Healey, Matthews, and Cook-Sather (2019), modified from work of Pat Thomson and Barbara Kamler (2013)

Reflection 10.1

Using the abstract as a structuring device

I attended a "writing for publication" workshop at the ISSOTL conference in Bergen, Norway, in 2018 organised by Mick, Kelly, and Alison. I have done a lot of inquiry into my own teaching and students' learning experiences but have struggled to put it down on paper. I found the idea of the abstract structure so helpful because it took what I had written and forced me to think about how I had organized it and how I could organise it. Applying the abstract structure provided the flow that I was certainly lacking in the little bit of writing I had started and has motivated me to continue writing my paper. I found that I did not need to modify the "moves" at all.

Joanne Bouma is an associate professor (nursing) at Mount Royal University, Calgary, Canada.

We have reproduced the abstract from our *Teaching & Learning Inquiry* article below to illustrate how Pat Thomson and Barbara Kamler's framework may be applied (Healey, Matthews, and Cook-Sather 2019, 43-44). We have inserted the names of the "moves" in the abstract for purposes of clarity, though they would not normally be included. In this case the anchor move was not relevant, as we did not have a research design.

[LOCATE] There are many general books and articles on publishing in peer-reviewed journals, but few specifically address issues around writing for journals focused on the scholarship of teaching and learning (SoTL). One of the challenges of beginning to write about teaching and learning is that most scholars have become interested in exploring these issues in higher education alongside their disciplinary interests and have to grapple with a new literature and sometimes unfamiliar methods and genres, as well. Hence, for many, as they write up their projects, they are simultaneously forging their identities as scholars of teaching and learning. [FOCUS] We discuss the process of producing four types of SoTL-focused writing for peer-reviewed journals: empirical research articles, conceptual articles, reflective essays, and opinion pieces. Our goal is to support both new and experienced scholars of teaching and teaching—faculty/academics, professional staff, and students—as they nurture and further develop their voices and their identities as scholars of teaching and learning and strive to contribute to the enhancement of learning and teaching in higher education. [REPORT] We pose three related sets of overarching questions for consideration when writing articles about teaching and learning for peer-reviewed journals and offer heuristic frameworks for publishing in the four specific writing genres listed above. We also discuss how to get started with writing, preparing to submit, and responding to reviewers, focusing on the importance of contributing to and creating scholarly conversations about teaching and learning. [ARGUE] Finally, using the metaphor of being in conversation, we argue that writing is a values-based process that contributes to the identity formation of scholars of teaching and learning and their sense of belonging within the SoTL discourse community.

This is, of course, only one way to structure your abstract, and some may find it too prescriptive and constraining, but a clear informative structure that presents the rationale, argument, and contribution of the paper is essential.

Over to You

The abstract, along with the title, is the most important part of your paper, but too many authors complete it in a rush prior to submitting their article. It is key for findability, particularly within proprietary databases that often default to only searching the title, author, abstract, and keywords, not the full text of the article. The abstract should probably go through more drafts than any other section of your paper, and it can play a useful role in planning the structure of your article. We recommend that you think about the following questions:

- What are the key points from your writing that need to be included in your abstract?
- How are you going to structure your abstract?
- Will you start your writing by drafting the abstract or will you leave it until you have finished?
- When you go over your abstract from a searcher's perspective, can you identify what search terms your target audience might be using?

PART 4

WRITING IN DIFFERENT GENRES
Introduction to Part 4

We suspect that many readers will jump to this part of the book because it is practical and provides detailed sets of questions to guide writing. Indeed, the genesis of this entire book can be traced to the set of questions Shelley Kinash and Kayleen Wood, Australian colleagues of Mick's, used to engage workshop participants in planning how to write an empirical research article (Kinash and Wood 2012). We draw on those questions in chapter 12, "Analyzing and Reporting Data: Empirical Research Articles," and we use the approach of posing questions in all the other chapters in this part of the book.

We offer frameworks for eleven forms (what we call "genres") of writing about learning and teaching (empirical research articles, theoretical and conceptual articles, literature reviews, case studies, books and edited collections, conference and workshop presentations, reflective essays, opinion pieces, stories, social media, and applications for teaching fellowships, awards, and promotions). While we present these in a particular order, our goal is not to imply a hierarchy or to value any one over the others. Rather, we start with the genres that might be most familiar and in which many scholars are (or feel) required to publish, and we map the similarities, differences, overlaps, and contrasts among those and the growing number of genres that are—or, to our minds, should be—recognized as legitimate and important. For each genre, we connect the practical approach (suggested by questions that provide a framework) with the human experience of writing (drawing on and developing identity and engaging in ongoing learning).

Each of the eleven chapters in this part of the book explores how scholars define or draw boundaries around a particular genre, and we offer insight into the value of that genre to illuminate the possibilities of writing. Moreover, we present a set of questions as a framework to guide writing in the genre, and, when possible, we pair these questions with real examples from published works.

We open part 4 with chapter 11, "Extending the Conventional Writing Genres: Naming and Clarifying," which digs deeper into the genres of writing to understand the overlaps and distinctions as we see them and the ways in which they might accommodate a wider range of experiences of and perspectives on learning and teaching.

Consider addressing the following questions before you read part 4, and then keep them in mind while you are reading:

- What are your existing conceptions of the eleven genres we discuss in this section of the book? How might considering them within the book's framework—writing as creating and contributing to scholarly conversations about learning and teaching, writing as fostering identities and clarifying values, and writing as a medium for engaging in ongoing learning— inform your understanding?

- What is your sense of the current conventions and affordances of each of these genres of writing, and how can any or all of them be expanded to invite and affirm a greater diversity of scholars of learning and teaching?

CHAPTER 11

EXTENDING THE CONVENTIONAL WRITING GENRES

Naming and Clarifying

Rules are merely tendencies, not truths, and genre borders only as real as our imaginations small. (Vuong 2019, 245)

We need to imagine new genres for sharing insights that are much broader than our current models for publishing. We need to develop much more interplay between product and process. (Bernstein and Bass 2005, 43)

There are many taken-for-granted assumptions about research, writing, and publications. In this chapter we stretch thinking about what publishable scholarship about learning and teaching is and can be. We invite you, as Ocean Vuong suggests above, to enlarge your imagination, and in particular, as Dan Bernstein and Randy Bass argue, to develop different ways to share insights into learning and teaching. Naming the different genres and arguing for their legitimacy supports you, we hope, in writing in different ways depending on who you are and who you want to become, as well as on what conversations you want to contribute to or create. We define what we mean by "genre," note the possibilities and risks of writing in "unconventional" genres, describe key features and formats of the eleven genres on which we focus, and provide some preliminary guidelines for writing in different genres.

What Do We Mean by "Writing Genre"?

As we noted in chapter 1, by "writing genre" we mean *the kind or form of writing* you select. There are many forms in which to write about learning and teaching. For example, writing a research article that draws on data gathered through a research design is a commonly accepted writing genre in many academic disciplines, including in learning and teaching. But it is only one of several genres for communicating about learning and teaching; other possible genres include theoretical and conceptual articles, literature reviews, case studies, books and edited volumes, conference and workshop presentations, reflective essays, opinion pieces, stories, social media, and teaching fellowship, award, and promotion applications. We acknowledge that our use of the word genre blurs the lines between a *type* of writing (e.g., literature review) and the *forum* for writing (e.g., refereed journal, chapter, or blog post). This is intentional, given that *how we write* intersects with *where we write* and *to whom we write* in ways that are hard to separate.

We are also aware that there are other terms for different writing genres. For instance, in some of the health care professions, there exists a genre called "reflective practice case studies." These are clinical case studies generated through reflective practice intended to support healthcare professionals in re-examining care challenges and opportunities through a form of writing that combines research and reflective practice. This is an excellent example of the kind of genre-blurring practice for which we argue in this book. Another example would be the term "essay." One scholarship of teaching and learning (SoTL) journal defines this genre in contrast to research articles:

> Essays on such topics as how SoTL can directly improve student learning outcomes; how SoTL has transformed an academic community/culture; the connections between SoTL and other forms of scholarship; how best to integrate SoTL into higher education; the problems and benefits of international collaboration in doing SoTL and applying the results to college teaching (classroom, online, or in combination). (*International Journal for*

the Scholarship of Teaching and Learning, "Policies – Areas of Submission")

In our terms these could include a mixture of case studies, opinion pieces, reflective essays, stories, and theoretical and conceptual articles. (For other takes on "essays" see Collected Essays on Learning and Teaching (CELT); Academy of Management Learning & Education Editorial Team 2018.)

These examples throw into relief the challenges of categorizing and naming different genres, as we have done, for purposes of discussion and practice. Rather than see this as problematic, we suggest that it is part of an ongoing process of rethinking and revising our ways of engaging, analyzing, and sharing understandings.

The Possibilities and Risks of Writing in Unconventional Genres

Our goal in identifying eleven writing genres is to think both within and beyond the conventional to capture, understand, and communicate the complexity of learning and teaching in higher education in different ways. Working with—and breaking with—what is generally done and accepted offers us space to reflect on our assumptions about writing and publishing scholarship on learning and teaching and invite more voices to be a part of the conversations about higher education. At the same time, it carries risks.

Making space is, to our minds, about expanding possibilities. Rather than labeling what is conventional or unconventional by way of ranking or imposing an evaluative metric on writing genres, our goal is to make space for multiple and diverse forms of writing. Your beliefs about accepted forms of writing will vary according to your disciplinary backgrounds, cultural contexts, and personal and political commitments, so what is conventional to one person might be alternative to another. Yahlnaaw's reflection captures the complexity of naming conventions and the potential perils we face when we make assumptions about what is conventional in the context of learning and teaching research methodologies (Reflection 11.1).

Reflection 11.1

The experience of different presentation genres

Jah! Xaaydaga 'las! Yahlnaaw han.nuu dii kiiGa ga. HlGaagilda Xaayda Gwaii sda.uu hll iigiing. Hey! Wonderful People! My name is Yahlnaaw. I am from Skidegate, Haida Gwaii, British Columbia. Last year I was invited to be a part of conference workshop on different methods to do teaching and learning research or inquiry. It was an exciting opportunity for me; and I valued being included as a student in the workshop. In our planning process, I was quickly placed in a familiar context when working with scholars experienced in Western ways of knowing and being. For me, storytelling is an accepted form of knowledge creation. My workshop co-facilitators discussed storytelling as "alternative" and "innovative." I explained, from my standpoint, that storytelling is not alternative. Colonial knowledges came to this land after Indigenous knowledges. Thus, if anything is alternative, it's colonial knowledges because they came after. What is considered accepted or alternative is not factual, it is subjective and shaped by your social location in society. Thus, for me, talking about people as data is alternative.

Yahlnaaw is a graduate student at the University of Northern British Columbia, Prince George, Canada.

Reviewers also make assumptions based on what they consider conventional. As an author, if you choose to write in a genre that is outside of the conventional in your context, or in a given journal, you are taking a risk. While recognition of the legitimacy of different genres is growing in some learning and teaching publications, a recent experience of Kelly's highlights a challenge of pushing genre boundaries. She submitted an essay to *International Journal for the Scholarship of Teaching and Learning.* As mentioned above, it publishes research articles and essays, yet her essay was reviewed against criteria for an empirical research article. While one reviewer acknowledged that the review criteria were problematic and recommended that the essay be accepted, the second reviewer recommended rejection with these comments:"There is no clear methodology.The empirical material that was provided is very poor. It is not enough to support any argument. There are no clear conclusions." The editor decided major revisions were required and the essay would be sent back to the reviewers for another round of reviews. In responding to the second reviewer, Kelly wrote:

> Yes, from an empirical research article framework your assessment (to reject) makes sense. However, my deliberate intention was to contribute an essay drawing on my reflections of my experiences and published research (including some of my own work).Thus, I ask that you rethink your comments based on the value of submitting different genres to advance SoTL, which draws on recent arguments from international SoTL scholars including Nancy Chick, Gary Poole, Peter Felten, Kathleen McKinney, Karen Manarin, and Alison Cook-Sather.

The essay was accepted following the second round of reviews (Matthews 2019a), yet the process was frustrating, even though Kelly had the experience, peer support networks, and agency to persist (see chapters 26 and 28). As Ronald Barnett (personal communication, July 28, 2019) suggests:"It is incumbent upon authors, especially those who submit papers that are on the fringes of a journal's editorial range, to make it crystal clear at the outset of a paper what it is and what it is not. Sometimes, as Marx said, we have to educate our masters."

Yahlnaaw's reflection and Kelly's story illustrate the importance of openness to multiple writing genres and valuing each in its own right. To this end, we think that naming genres explicitly and clarifying the distinctions and overlaps among them can encourage writers, editors, and reviewers to embrace a diversity of submissions.We are arguing against the creation of a hierarchy that privileges one genre over another.Yet, it will take a collective of brave writers and reviewers to challenge conventional (Western) wisdom and resist the convenience of writing only in dominant genres. It will also involve each of us questioning our own assumptions about writing genres and what counts as publishable work to move this agenda forward.

In making this case, we are by no means diminishing established genres, such as empirical research articles or case studies of practices in Western contexts or storytelling in First Nations contexts. These genres enrich knowledge of learning and teaching in their own ways. Instead, we are arguing for additional ways of contributing knowledge to the growing scholarship of teaching and learning in higher education. We recognize that this values-based stance might come into conflict with the pressure many universities put on writers to embrace particular genres and publish in outlets that "count more" in metrics of rankings and ratings (see chapter 8). We also recognize that each of you will have your own views on the genres and how they intersect with cultural and institutional priorities. Depending on where you are in your career and in what context you are writing, you will need to make decisions that take these metrics and other variables into account. We hope, however, that external criteria will be only one determinant of your choice of genre and outlet and that your own values and scholarly commitments will be an equal driver (see also chapters 4 and 6).

It is also not our intention to draw hard and fast lines between genres and suggest that they constitute discrete, pure categories. Many learning and teaching scholars use a combination of genres. Mick makes that point when he notes that many of his publications are a mixture of conceptual material and literature reviews, often with the inclusion of some mini-case studies (Our Perspectives 13.1). Readers may well find that they also write in genres that do not neatly map to one of the eleven genres we have selected to discuss. For instance, you may write a short piece for a publication such as *HERDSA Connect, Educational Developments,* or *The Conversation,* or you may publish a study guide for students (e.g., Healey and Hill 2019) or a research report required from a funding body or a policy document for your university senate, as Kelly recently did (Matthews, Garratt, and Macdonald 2018). Such publications may include aspects of theoretical and conceptual articles, case studies, opinion pieces, reflective essays, stories, and other genres, and you may find some of the questions we include in our frameworks for these genres helpful in preparing your pieces.

The selected genres we outline in the book overlap in both helpful and confusing ways. In naming these genres we are attempting to clarify the ways in which they differ, each serving a unique purpose and together constituting a rich body of scholarship.

Key Features and Formats of the Genres

The genres we name overlap and do not include every form of academic writing. For example, we chose not to examine dissertations and theses because a large literature already exists on this genre (Aitchison, Kamler, and Lee 2010; Kamler and Thomson 2014; Thomson and Kamler 2016). We also excluded book reviews, classroom notes or curriculum materials, pragmatic how-to-guides, grant proposals, and other genres of writing about learning and teaching, largely because of space constraints. Below we present the key features of the eleven writing genres we discuss—features that apply to academic writing generally and that you will therefore want to consider when writing about learning and teaching. As we have already noted, all are often, or could be, integrated with other genres. For example, case studies often have elements of empirical research articles, empirical research articles can assert an opinion, and so on. A summary table, "The Functions, Appearances, and Publishing Locations of the Eleven Genres," is available in the online resources.

Empirical Research Articles

What the genre typically does: Gathers and uses observable data (e.g., from interviews, surveys, document analyses, reflections, and narratives) to offer evidence to support a particular aim or question. **What the genre typically looks like and where it is published:** Research articles in the natural and social sciences include an introduction, a literature review, sections on methods, findings, discussion, and implications, plus a conclusion. The humanities have different format variations. Research articles are typically published in journals, book chapters, and books.

Theoretical and Conceptual Articles

What the genre typically does: Draws on literature and theories (without presenting new data) to provoke, deepen, or expand thinking about a particular concept or practice.

What the genre typically looks like and where it is published: Theoretical and conceptual articles typically describe the method or approach guiding the writer's process but otherwise do not follow a prescribed set of headings typical of data-driven research articles. They are usually published in journals, as book chapters, or as books.

Literature Reviews

What the genre typically does: Synthesizes what is known and reveals what else we can learn about a topic by reviewing existing research.

What the genre typically looks like and where it is published: Freestanding literature reviews tend to be organized around a guiding question with an introduction and methods, findings, and discussion sections. They are commonly published as journal articles, book chapters, or research reports.

Case Studies

What the genre typically does: Delves deeply into, and provides rich descriptions of, specific examples of successful learning and teaching practices, often within a single course, program, or institution, with the goal of influencing others to enhance their practices.

What the genre typically looks like and where it is published: Case studies are usually organized around a "rich description" of a learning and teaching practice or context and include an introduction, discussion of the case study, and implications for other scholars. Some journals publish case studies, blogs are a common platform for case studies, and case studies might also be included in award or fellowship applications.

Books and Edited Collections

What the genre typically does: Provides an opportunity to go into more depth and breadth about a topic or theme. Edited collections bring together people working in the same field—or different fields—to explore the topic from various perspectives.

What the genre typically looks like and where it is published: Books may involve a mixture of review, conceptual thinking, empirical data, and reflection. Learning and teaching books are published by a limited number of commercial and university presses. Several new publishers are entering the open access market. Special issues of journals share several characteristics with edited collections.

Presentations

What the genre typically does: Communicates your research and stimulates conversations with colleagues in real time.

What the genre typically looks like and where it is published: Presentation formats vary widely and include conference papers, workshops, panel discussions, and posters. Posting slides online following a presentation is a common practice.

Reflective Essays

What the genre typically does: Shares lived experiences of the messy, unfinished, personal, and relational work of learning and teaching and offers analyses of the resulting insights.

What the genre typically looks like and where it is published: Reflective essays are written in the first person and present insights rather than empirical findings or arguments while describing the learning and teaching practice. They are typically published in journals that explicitly name this genre or via blogs.

Opinion Pieces

What the genre typically does: Asserts a value judgement about learning and teaching that draws directly on the writer's experience and informed perspective.

What the genre typically looks like and where it is published: Opinion pieces tend to be short (usually less than 1,000 words), written in the first person, and focused on a single point with no conventions for headings or sub-headings. Blogs are a common forum for opinion pieces, and some journals also publish this genre.

Stories

What the genre typically does: Presents a lived experience in context with the goal of sharing its relevance and importance.

What the genre typically looks like and where it is published: Stories include information about the context, what happened, who was involved, where it happened, and what happened in a narrative flow and are unlikely to have headings at all. Award and fellowship applications typically include a story, and book chapters and blogs are also common venues for publishing stories.

Social Media

What the genre typically does: Enables fast self-publication and quickly raises awareness of your work. Social media can accommodate any writing genre, although stories, case studies, reflective essays, and opinion pieces tend to be more common than publishing a research article, for example.

What the genre typically looks like and where it is published: Social media by definition means to publish online, enabling rapid self-publishing that bypasses peer review. It is emerging as an important genre for scholars that allows online interaction through platforms like Twitter, LinkedIn, Facebook, and many more. And publishing on social media can look vastly different from written text because you can design the layout and use images creatively.

Teaching Award, Fellowship, and Promotion Applications

What the genre typically does: Makes the case and provides evidence that you meet the award, fellowship, or promotion criteria, based, at least in part, on the excellence of your teaching (i.e., evidence of your impact of enhancing student outcomes), support of learning (i.e., evidence of supporting colleagues and influencing support for student learning) and leadership (i.e., evidence of effective leadership of learning and teaching).

What the genre typically looks like and where it is published: In contrast to the other genres, these applications are usually private. Some involve completing highly structured forms, while others emphasize critical reflection and discussion of the impact of activities and experiences structured under a few broad headings. These applications typically go to a committee or panel for assessment.

As we note above, the distinctions between the eleven genres are not hard and fast. We offer these general descriptions to help you decide which genre might be most conducive to any given learning and teaching experience, perspective, or finding you want to share and the identity you want to develop as a learning and teaching scholar. Moreover, as we noted in chapter 1, we extend the term "writing" to include making oral presentations, such as at a conference or in a workshop, because these typically involve working with text and are often a precursor to a publication, summarize existing publications, or present material from a recent publication. We also recognize that not all the genres we discuss are "published," such as most applications for teaching awards, fellowships, and promotions. Yet these genres constitute common and important ways in which scholars engage in conversations about learning and teaching in higher education.

In presenting the genres above we do not wish to reify stereotypes or conventional norms. Because so many of our critical friends and reviewers for our *Teaching & Learning Inquiry* article (Healey, Matthews, and Cook-Sather 2019) wanted clearer descriptions of the boundaries among genres, we have attempted to capture these in the list above. However, we encourage a blurring of boundaries within and between genres. As Lucy Mercer-Mapstone and Sophia Abbot (2020, 233) state in their edited book on student-staff partnerships, "Alternative genres are appropriate and sometimes necessary for sharing the realities of partnership work." In the chapters that follow we point out overlaps between, for example, case studies and empirical research articles, and between reflective essays, opinion pieces, and stories. Another example of blurring boundaries is that we see reflection as a valid form of knowledge generation (Cook-Sather, Abbot, and Felten 2019); so empirical research articles could, to our mind, draw on first-person reflections and never use the word "data." Under the umbrella of "first person" we include autobiographical and self-referential work as well as auto-ethnography, all of which include personal examples.

Yet, as Kelly's story above illustrates, we have some way to go in blurring genre boundaries and thinking beyond Western conventions of research and knowledge creation in learning and teaching, a reality also clarified in the reflections by Yahlnaaw (Reflection 11.1) and Peter Looker (Reflection 3.1).

Guidelines for Writing in Different Genres

In the chapters that follow we present flexible guidelines in the form of open questions to help you frame your writing, and in part 5 we link steps in writing to the different genres. The guidelines are not intended to be perfect or prescriptive but rather to offer steps for getting started by presenting questions for consideration. Our expectation is that you will employ these guidelines creatively, in ways that make sense for you. Not every question has to be answered, or in the order displayed, and, depending on the piece you want to write, we suspect you will think of other questions that should be answered in your publication. All three of us have found these guidelines to be helpful to workshop participants to gain perspectives on their experiences, plan what they want to include, establish the flow of the publication, and find a focus. Figure 11.1 offers a *potential* process for writing for publication—from selecting your genre to submitting your finished piece—using our guidelines. However, we encourage you to reorder, add, remove, or repeat parts of the process as is appropriate for your context, your identity as a writer, and the conversations you want to join and create. Indeed, you may consider producing your own framework of questions for your task, in which case, please share them with us by sending us an email.

Over to You

We argue here for embracing a wide variety of writing genres that enable you to join in and create conversations about learning and teaching in higher education. While we acknowledge that there are overlaps among the genres, we contend that each should be valued in its own right. Questions to ask about working within and extending the conventional writing genres include:

Figure 11.1: Using the guiding questions to write for publication

PLAN

1. Decide on a genre

2. Identify 1-3 potential journals

3. Select relevant guiding questions
   a. write brief answers
   b. arrange your answers into a logical narrative
   c. assign word count to each question

4. Draft a timeline for you and your co-authors

WRITE

5. Draft an abstract that articulates your argument

6. Draft main text

7. Re-order sections, refine, revise, and copy edit

8. Select specific journal and format to their guidelines

GET FEEDBACK

9. Invite feedback from critical friends

10. Revise again

SUBMIT

Source: Based on Healey, Matthews, and Cook-Sather (2019, 35)

- What are your preferred writing genres and why?
- How might other writing genres enable you to communicate about your learning and teaching in important ways?
- Which of the processes in Figure 11.1 work for you and in what order?

CHAPTER 12

ANALYZING AND REPORTING DATA
Empirical Research Articles

The data in a scientific article aims to illustrate the story. . . . We verify, analyse, and display data to share, build and legitimize new knowledge. (Cargill and O'Connor 2013, 25)

To fully understand the ways in which race and racism shape educational institutions and maintain various forms of discrimination, we must look to the lived experiences of students of color . . . as valid, appropriate, and necessary forms of data. (Yosso et al. 2004, 15)

Empirical research articles are perhaps the most common genre of writing about learning and teaching and are considered by many to be the most prestigious genre as they are historically assumed to be the basis for advancing knowledge and understanding, as well as confirming or challenging previous research. As the first quote above captures, Margaret Cargill and Patrick O'Connor recommend analyzing and reporting data through constructing a story. In the second quote, Tara Yosso and colleagues offer an essential reminder that whose and which stories get told depends on what counts as data.

It is difficult to generalize about writing empirical research articles, as what is appropriate depends on your theoretical and methodological approach, the audience you are addressing, and your purpose. Some aspects of these topics may be covered in the guide for authors produced by the journal, book publisher, or other outlet to which you are submitting, but others are for you to clarify and decide.

Analysis of what editors and reviewers say they are looking for, and the weaknesses they identify in papers that they reject or return for substantial revision, can help writers self-evaluate their articles before submission (see chapters 8 and 28). In this chapter, we present a flexible framework to guide the organization and composition of empirical research articles. We also include a discussion of the benefits and complexities of writing such articles, but with the caveat that there is no single right way.

Preparing Empirical Research Articles for Publication

There are many excellent books written about undertaking scholarship of teaching and learning (SoTL) and researching learning and teaching in higher education (e.g., Cleaver, Lintern, and McLinden 2018; Cousin 2009; Daniel and Harland 2017; McKinney 2007; Norton 2009). These texts discuss the wide variety of methodological and theoretical foundations needed to engage in this research. Which of these approaches you adopt can have a significant impact on how you write your article, as is well illustrated in the discussion of increasing the likelihood of publishing qualitative (Rocco and Plakhotnik 2011), quantitative (Newman and Newman 2011) and mixed-methods (Newman, Newman, and Newman 2011) manuscripts in *The Handbook of Scholarly Writing and Publishing* (Rocco and Hatcher 2011). A key theme that emerges from these chapters is the effect of the theoretical and methodological approach adopted on the appropriate structure of the article (Miller-Young and Yeo 2015). For example, the aims and scope section of the journal *Critical Studies in Education* states that it:

> rejects the positivist view that social reality is "out there" waiting to be "found" and that researchers are able to maintain an objective distance from research subjects. Instead, the journal takes the view that researchers generate data rather than find them and that the representation of data is a form of analysis. For these reasons, we do not publish articles that separate "findings" from "discussion,"

whether they have discrete sections named in this way or not. (*Critical Studies in Education*, "Aims and Scope")

Hence, if you are considering submitting an article to *Critical Studies in Education*, you will need to write your article differently from the approach you might take for many other educational journals. Similarly, other journals have expectations—often outlined in their contributor guidelines—that should guide your writing.

What to Look Out for in Writing an Empirical Research Article about Learning and Teaching

An empirical research article, whether published in a journal or as a book chapter, should provide a clear rationale for the study and its contribution to the existing literature, justification for the research methodology used, an analysis of findings, and a discussion of those findings and their implications for the field of study. For learning and teaching journals, the focus of the discussion section is often the implications for enhancing the quality of student learning. Simply describing the educational practice and reporting data are insufficient for this genre, which requires interpretation of data placed within a theoretical or conceptual framework with broader implications linked to the learning and teaching literature. In other words, empirical research articles have to acknowledge the current conversation and extend it through the presentation of primary research, or start a new conversation drawing on compelling new data. As Katarina Mårtensson makes clear in Reflection 12.1, writing an empirical article can be a messy process of drafting, reading, interpreting, translating, and, for some, walking. She signals the time, thought, joy, and frustration that go into writing, which is clearly a more complex process than simply "writing up the research."

Reflection 12.1

The experience of writing empirical articles

Getting started is frustrating. Every time I write an empirical article, I have to think a lot about its content, structure, and main arguments before I actually get to open a new Word doc on my laptop. As if I need to prepare mentally for a long time. It is stimulating and stressful. I start with the structure, titles of sections, and bullet points under headings. This is joyful, as I sense something actually growing in front of me. One source of frustration is the literature review needed to frame my article. I browse other relevant publications. Usually I find a lot. I discover things I hadn't previously read. It is a joy to read it but then, suddenly, I reach a point where I think everything is already written. In a more sophisticated language than what I can produce (I am not a native English-speaking person, and yet I usually publish in English). I have to force myself to believe that I can contribute. At best, I set aside full days of writing, going back and forth between sections of my article. I go back into my empirical data. I enjoy this iterative process. I take long walks, and meanwhile process my writing so that I can revise and improve when I come back. Another joy of my writing is that I usually co-write. So, I send a draft to my colleague/s, and we bounce it back and forth until we are satisfied.

Katarina Mårtensson is a senior lecturer at the Division for Higher Education Development, Lund University, Sweden.

When you write an empirical research article, your argument will unfold across your introduction, literature review, methods, findings, discussion, implications, and conclusion. Your introduction presents your argument in a clear and simple form. Your literature review provides context and traces the strands of conversations in progress that inform your argument. The methods section explains and justifies how you went about gathering data to substantiate your argument, and your findings section presents what your methods yielded. The discussion is the most interpretive section of a research article. It is in this section that you marshal your evidence, make sense of your findings, and present them in a way that endeavors to offer new understandings and convince readers of their importance. The implications section builds on your argument to point to future explorations or practices that follow, according to your argument, from what you have found. One author's experience of developing an argument in an empirical article is presented in Reflection 12.2.

Reflection 12.2

The experience of developing an argument in an empirical article

To me the argument of a paper functions as the soul of the manuscript. It serves as the foundation on which the entire paper is built in terms of literature review, methodology, discussion, and conclusion. In my case, the issues I would want to argue about in a paper are actually identified at the moment I conceptualise a study or inquiry. However, articulating that argument while writing a paper is the most arduous task for me. I have experienced that more than half of my effort in writing a manuscript is spent on building an argument. Most often, in empirical articles, I present my argument in the first part of the manuscript and in subsequent sections I use empirical evidence and my data to substantiate those arguments. While building an argument, I would normally go about discussing what is known and what needs to be known and why it should be known. I try to write the "why it needs to be known" section in a slightly persuasive tone to establish the rationale of the study. I also find it important to weave my argument throughout the manuscript to keep the issue alive and establish a clearer alignment with the other sections of the manuscript.

Amrita Kaur is a senior lecturer at the School of Education and Modern Language, Universiti Utara Malaysia, Kedah, Malaysia.

"Guiding Questions for Planning, Revising, and Refining an Empirical Research Article" presents a series of questions to support the writing of empirical research articles about learning and teaching in higher education. A copy of this resource with only the questions included is available in the online resources. You may find it helpful in planning your empirical research article.

Guiding Questions for Planning, Revising, and Refining an Empirical Research Article*

1. **Why is this topic important in learning and teaching research, to whom is it important, and why at this time?**
Give a clear rationale for your paper and situate it within a broader conversation. For example:

> A gap often exists, however, between the high value teaching centers place on the scholarship of teaching and learning (SoTL) and the support those centers provide for such work. . . . Several models have emerged of teaching and learning centers supporting SoTL on diverse campuses. . . . Such excellent programs model effective ways for teaching and learning centers to ease faculty entry into SoTL. However, these approaches focus so intently on the inquiry process that they may not sufficiently support faculty in the final essential step of scholarship, what Lee Shulman (2004) calls "going public" to make work available for peer review. . . . Faculty active in SoTL often do not see their projects through to publication. This finding is troubling. (Felten, Moore, and Strickland 2009, 40–41)

2. **What previous research has been undertaken on this topic? What is your contribution to the literature and the learning and teaching conversation?**
Identify how your paper fits within the existing literature and what you are adding to existing knowledge and understanding. For instance, the first sentence of the abstract of this article clearly sets the paper in the context of the literature:

> Although academic identity has received attention in the literature, there have been few attempts to understand the influence on identity from engagement with the Scholarship of Teaching and Learning (SoTL). (Simmons et al. 2013, 9)

3. **What is your argument or stance? What questions are you addressing?**

    Being explicit about your argument and the issues you are addressing (and, equally important, what you are not covering) is critical to convincing reviewers that your paper is worth publishing and colleagues that it is worth reading (see chapter 25). Sometimes a single question can summarize the focus of your paper:

    > To what extent do developers consider their prior disciplinary training influences or aligns with their current work? (Little, Green, and Hoption 2018, 325)

4. **What is your underlying conceptual or theoretical framework? If appropriate, what are your hypotheses?**

    Make your conceptual or theoretical framework explicit and, if you are following a positivist framework, clearly state your hypotheses. The authors of one paper state:

    > [We] draw on Meyer and Land's (2005) notion of liminality to apply to SoTL identity development. We describe how navigating among conflicting identities can lead us into a troublesome but deeply reflective liminal space, prompting profound realizations and the reconstruction of our academic identities. (Simmons et al. 2013, 10)

5. **What are your research methods, and what is the rationale for your approach?**
    a. **What data have you collected, and how?**
    b. **Who are your participants?**
    c. **What is the context (e.g., discipline, institution, nation)?**

    It is difficult to generalize outcomes of research in learning and teaching because contexts vary so much (Healey and Healey 2018). Give the reader sufficient contextual information to help them interpret your findings. For example:

    > The data presented in this paper derive from an international online survey entitled "Educational developers' academic backgrounds." It was distributed via the

member networks of the International Consortium for Educational Development.... In total, 1156 developers accessed the survey.... For this paper, we focus on the 878 respondents with highest degrees in four discipline clusters: Education, Humanities, Social Sciences, and STEM fields. (Little, Green, and Hoption 2018, 326)

6. **How have you analyzed the data?**

Detail the analysis you undertook. If you have adopted a quantitative approach, tell the reader which statistical techniques you used. If you adopted a qualitative approach, be explicit about how, for example, you identified themes and what checks you made for consistency of interpretation. For example, one Dutch study reported that:

> Pearson's correlation coefficients were applied to determine relationships between all scales, including the Intention to Show Research-Related Behaviour scale. Considering the multiple analyses, we applied $p < .01$ to compensate for the family-wise error rate (Tabachnick and Fidell 2007). For interpretation, we used the following criteria: $r < .30$ = weak correlation, $.30 < r < .50$ = moderate correlation, and $r > .50$ = strong correlation. (Griffioen 2019, 167)

7. **What are your findings and how do they contribute to the ongoing learning and teaching conversation or create an important new conversation?**

Ensure that you not only present your findings but also discuss how they contribute to, extend, or move beyond the broader conversation you identified in response to questions 1 and 2. One study of using a structured writing group found that:

> Participants especially valued the discipline of weekly sessions and peer feedback. They reported increased skills and confidence in their writing, greater knowledge of the publication process, and intention to continue writing.

Although five papers were published, a 12-month follow-up revealed that original writing intentions were not sustained.... In summary, our key recommendations for an effective SoTL writing program are:

(1) The relevant senior management must support both the program and ongoing time allocations for research and writing.

(2) Ensure participants are ready, motivated, and have the time to devote to the program (easier said than done).

(3) Agreed regular progress is essential, so everyone is at the same stage to get the most from the peer-feedback opportunities.

(4) Recognition of the outcomes by management will reinforce motivation for both program graduates and future participants.

(Weaver, Robbie, and Radloff 2014, 212, 223)

8. **How do your findings compare with previous research?**
   Compare your findings with those reported by others in similar and different contexts. Which confirm and which challenge previous research? Which are new? For instance, in an analysis of self-directed learning (SDL) among geography students undertaking problem-based learning (PBL), the authors state:

   The findings of this study support Srikuman Chakravarthi and Priya Vijayan's (2010) recommendation that support and guidance must be provided to students early in a PBL environment and then facilitate increasing independence in the later years of the students' study. ... It is important to reflect on possible reasons for the geography students' drastic drop in average SDL scores at the beginning of the second-year PBL experience. This is in contrast to other studies where the decrease in students' SDL scores occurred at the end of the first

PBL experience (Litzinger, Wise, Lee, & Bjorklund 2003;
Reio and Davis 2005). (Golightly 2018, 473)

9. **How do you handle and present unexpected findings?**
Research is often moved forward by unexpected findings. Hence
it is important to discuss how they are unexpected and the implications for future research. For example, an early Australian study
of the effects of participation in new learning environments highlighted an unexpected finding:

> It was the approach to the design of and induction into
> the learning environment, rather than the approach
> to content-focused teaching per se, that was centrally
> important to learning opportunities and the resulting
> outcomes in terms of challenges to, and the development
> of, these students' epistemic beliefs. (Taylor, Pillay, and
> Clarke 2004, x)

10. **How does the context influence your findings? What
are the implications for others in different contexts?**
Discuss the impact of your context on your findings and the
relevance of your findings to others in different contexts (Healey
and Healey 2018). For example, a study of how students engaged
with threshold concepts in three seminars in three liberal arts
institutions in the United States concluded:

> The perspectives of students in three seminars likely will
> not (and should not) reframe the literature on threshold
> concepts. Still, scholars and teachers should take seri-
> ously the experiences and insights of students as learners
> (Cook-Sather et al., 2014; Healey et al., 2014). (Felten
> · 2016, 7)

11. **What are the limitations of your research? What
unanswered questions remain? What other questions
follow for future learning and teaching research?**
Add any caveats you have about the limitations of your findings and identify unanswered and new questions that need to be

addressed. For example, Deandra Little, David Green, and Colette Hoption (2018, 334-6) warn that:

> As with any study at the level of discipline clusters, caution is advised. Disciplines are not monolithic, but dynamic. . . . In this study, contrasts emerge not just within discipline clusters, but *within specific fields* in those clusters. . . . Our data specifically look at *research approaches,* and do not speak to how developers' training might influence other aspects of their educational development practice. We do not recommend extrapolating from these data to other domains of their work. . . . Our study explores socialization and imprinting among developers . . . raising several questions for future projects: Which features of prior fields endure most in other aspects of developers' work? Does imprinting differ if our migration into educational development is voluntary or forced? To what extent do developers' assertions of disciplinary distinctiveness denote genuine differences versus an exaggeration of disciplinary identity in an unfamiliar, transdisciplinary field?

As with other sets of guiding questions in this book, select those questions that are relevant to your context, add others as appropriate, and decide the order in which you will address them to communicate effectively with your audience. The questions are based on those in Healey, Matthews, and Cook-Sather (2019, 36-37).

Structuring Your Article: The Importance of Headings and Sub-headings

As Thomson and Kamler write, "Headings are an important tool in the journal article toolkit" (2013, 111). Some indication of possible headings and sub-headings that you might use may have occurred to you in reading our Guiding Questions. A common structure is: Introduction, Methods, Report, and Discuss (IMRaD), but these generic headings give the reader no indication of the subject matter or argument of the article. A good test is this: if you read the title, abstract, and the headings and subheadings of an article, do you obtain a clear idea of what it is about? If not, this may be because the author is only using generic headings, and many readers may give up at this stage, as they are not persuaded that there is something interesting for them to pursue. Here are the headings used in "Demystifying the Publication Process–A Structured Writing Program to Facilitate Dissemination of Teaching and Learning Scholarship" (Weaver, Robbie, and Radloff 2014):

Background
Writing program
    Writing program principles
    Local context
    Selection of participants
Program evaluation
    Aim
    Instruments
Findings
    Personal insights–the self as writer
    Understanding writing and feedback
    Strategies in producing an academic paper
    Submission outcomes
    Feedback on writing program
    Future writing plans
    Lessons for academic development
Conclusions

You will see that although some of the headings are generic, in most cases they make the content explicit with the phrasing of the sub-headings. Similarly, in the article "Conflicts and Configurations in a Liminal Space: SoTL Scholars' Identity Development" (Simmons et al. 2013) the authors use colons to distinguish generic and specific headings:

SoTL scholars' identity: Introduction
Academic identity: Disciplined SoTL scholar versus disciplinary scholar

Troublesome knowledge and liminality
Exploring our SoTL identities: Method
Liminal identities
    Doubt and insecurity: Intrapersonal conflicts
    Developing SoTL identity: Intrapersonal configurations
    The role of SoTL community in building an alternative identity: Interpersonal configurations
Swimming in the liminal sea
Further thoughts
Liminal scholars

The appropriate structure also varies according to the theoretical and methodological approach, as discussed earlier. Thus, for example, the authors' instructions for *Critical Studies in Education* states:

> Apart from "Introduction" and "Conclusion," the Journal rejects generic headings for article sections (e.g., literature review, methodology, findings, discussion). Instead we look for articles with section headings that reflect the substantive contribution of the section to the specific issue at hand (i.e. headings that reflect the article's unfolding argument or its steps in logic). We also prefer to see methodological issues discussed within an article's introduction rather than as a discrete section, although we recognize that sometimes it is more appropriate to deal with methodology separately. (*Critical Studies in Education*, "Instructions for Authors")

Over to You

Empirical research, whether published as journal articles or as book chapters, is key to providing the evidence that underpins informed conversations about learning and teaching in higher education. Developing the skills to write such pieces will maximize the likelihood that editors will accept your work for publication and that potentially interested readers will be drawn to read and cite that work. Questions to ask about writing empirical research articles include:

- Are you sitting on some empirical research about learning and teaching in higher education that you have not found time to write about?
- Which of our Guiding Questions do you think you need to answer to write your article? What other questions are important for you to tackle?
- Which outlets would you consider writing your research article for (see chapter 8)?

CHAPTER 13

ADVANCING NEW PERSPECTIVES
Theoretical and Conceptual Articles

Under the umbrella of conceptual and theory manuscripts, we find a broad array of article types (e.g., taxonomy development, exploratory conceptual modeling, critique of theory). . . . In general, conceptual and theoretical manuscripts do not have methodology sections. There is no argument being made that the broad scope of a body of literature has been explored and new findings are emerging from an analysis. Instead, authors are selectively choosing key pieces of literature that support a particular perspective that they are putting forth for consideration. (Callahan 2010, 302)

While we recognize that some scholars make a distinction between theoretical and conceptual frameworks (Adom, Hussein, and Agyem 2018; Kivunja 2018), the terms are often used interchangeably in the literature. Our main concern in this chapter is to tease out the similarities and differences between writing standalone theoretical and conceptual articles and writing in the other genres we discuss.

Instead of requiring you to present primary data, as we discussed in the chapter on empirical research articles, theoretical and conceptual articles allow you to play with concepts through deeper scholarly consideration with the goal of illuminating new possibilities, including theory building, as emphasized in the above quote from Jamie Callahan. Theoretical and conceptual articles also differ from empirical articles in how they look. The latter, as we noted in chapter

12, typically include an introduction, a literature review, sections on methods, findings, discussion, and implications, plus a conclusion. Theoretical and conceptual articles typically describe the method or approach guiding the writer's process, but otherwise do not follow a prescribed set of headings. They focus on exploring existing literature and established theories.

The argument of a theoretical or conceptual article is speculative, not empirical, hence you build your argument through noting connections, contradictions, gaps, complexities, or other patterns, putting ideas into dialogue with one another, highlighting previously un-noted phenomena. It is important to construct a logic that readers can follow: to move through a series of comprehensible steps that lead the reader to understand your conclusion, even if they might not agree with it. The argument you build in a theoretical or conceptual piece aims to provoke, deepen, or expand thinking in the abstract or hypothetical arena, not the concrete. Developing a logical argument takes practice. Ronald Barnett, acting as a critical friend for this book, agreed to share his framework, "The Distinction between Thesis, Argument, and Argumentation," as an online resource. We found this framework helpful and you might, too.

The distinction between theoretical and conceptual articles and literature reviews is not always clear (Callahan 2010). Freestanding literature reviews, as we argue in the next chapter, *present a systematic synthesis* of research. Theoretical and conceptual articles, on the other hand, *draw selectively* on literature that is relevant to the argument of the piece, and they deepen, expand, or provoke thinking about a particular concept or practice. In this chapter, we offer a flexible guide to the organization and composition of theoretical and conceptual articles, illustrated by a range of examples.

In Reflection 13.1, Kerri-Lee Krause ponders the experience of writing theoretical and conceptual articles.

Reflection 13.1

The experience of writing theoretical and conceptual articles

Writing about higher education policy and strategic issues is a passion of mine. It is a process that enables me to reflect more deeply on issues that I encounter on a daily basis in my academic leadership role. Much of my writing has involved empirically based higher education research outputs, for example quantitative studies of the Australian first year student experience. However, as I developed further experience and expertise as a writer and a higher education leader, I found the recursive research, reflection, and writing process involved in composing theoretical and conceptual articles particularly liberating.

This genre of writing allows me to work through thorny theoretical and conceptual problems, to challenge myself to think about familiar concepts in new ways, and to invite readers to do likewise. The "wicked problem of quality" paper (Krause 2012) was prompted by my concern that the notion of "quality" in higher education is typically under-theorised and rarely problematised; yet, it is foundational to all that we do as educators, leaders, and policy makers. One of the important lessons I have learned is the fundamental importance of developing and communicating a robust theoretical framework to underpin one's work. This practice goes some way towards negating the stereotypical view that educational research is somehow inferior to discipline-based research. I contend that writing about learning and teaching in higher education can and should be deemed as equally rigorous processes to those of conducting discipline-based research.

Kerri-Lee Krause is the deputy vice-chancellor (student life), at the University of Melbourne, Australia.

Writing a Theoretical or Conceptual Paper for Publication

Drawing together existing theoretical and conceptual approaches before proposing new concepts and insights is vital to furthering learning and teaching conversations, whether you are writing in a refereed journal or a book chapter. It is not uncommon to explore particular theoretical and conceptual approaches in depth without utilizing data or testing hypotheses, though the development of ideas that will inform future empirical work is a common outcome. Perhaps most like literary analyses in the humanities, "[theoretical and] conceptual articles offer the exciting opportunity to productively disrupt the ongoing conversation or to change it completely through the creative analysis of existing works that shape something new" (Healey, Matthews, and Cook-Sather 2019, 37).

Theoretical and conceptual articles are described in various ways in different journals. For example:

> *International Journal of Sustainability in Higher Education:* "These papers will not be based on research but will develop hypotheses. The papers are likely to be discursive and will cover philosophical discussions and comparative studies of others' work and thinking." (*International Journal of Sustainability in Higher Education,* "Author Guidelines")

> *Journal of Counseling & Development:* "Articles that provide new theoretical perspectives or integrate existing theoretical views, address innovative—new or adapted—procedures or techniques, discuss current professional issues or professional development (position papers), or offer well-reasoned reactions or responses to previously published articles." (Watts 2011, 308)

Regardless of the outlet you choose, writing a theoretical or conceptual article requires a deep understanding of the relevant literature and hence can involve a long gestation period. It is easy, when exploring literature, to get lost in the detail, go off on tangents, and diminish the strength of your argument. Therefore, theoretical and conceptual articles can be a challenging genre and one that authors, particularly those new to writing about learning and teaching, may find difficult to engage with. As Richard Watts (2011, 311), a writer in the field of counseling, suggests, "Authors often find it more difficult to develop conceptual articles than empirically based articles, which tend to have a more standard format." Similarly, Paul Salomone (1993, 73), another writer in the field of counseling, argued earlier that "the conceptual article . . . is the most difficult to write because a creative leap beyond the mere association of similar ideas is required." Despite—and sometimes because of—these challenges, writing theoretical and conceptual articles can be immensely satisfying (Our Perspectives 13.1).

Our Perspectives 13.1

What attracts you to writing theoretical and conceptual articles?

Kelly: The writing space to think and play instead of trying to prove something about learning and teaching is what draws me to theoretical and conceptual articles. Taking a deep dive into a topic to see how I understand it by drawing on the work of others is a fun intellectual process. The challenge is having time for preparing to write these pieces, and I find I rarely get it. This explains why I have limited experience with publishing in this genre, due to the depth of insight into the literature that is required (also dependent on time). When I see space in my schedule, I now hold that time for theoretical and conceptual articles because I get to read more on a topic, think deeply about it, and then share what I have learned. I enjoy this genre far more than empirical research articles at this stage in my writing life.

Alison: I appreciate the opportunity that theoretical and conceptual articles provide to bring ideas from different arenas of scholarship into dialogue. Like metaphors, which juxtapose two seemingly unrelated things, the conceptual pieces I have written draw on disciplinary concepts outside of my primary field of scholarship and practice (education). I have used these theoretical and conceptual explorations to deepen my understanding of learning and teaching and to argue for particular ways of engaging in both. For instance, the concept of liminality from anthropology helped me and a student co-author to argue for learning and teaching as unfolding in suspended spaces that allow for role revision (Cook-Sather and Alter 2011), and the concept of translation from translation and literary studies let me and a student co-author argue for learning and teaching as literal and metaphorical processes of transformation (Cook-Sather and Abbot 2016).

Mick: I would not describe much of my writing as primarily theoretical or conceptual, and yet I am probably best known for two diagrams representing conceptual arguments that have been reproduced and cited more often than anything else I have written. Both diagrams attempted to summarize the main approaches identified in the literature. In one case, the diagram showed the different ways that students engage with research (Healey 2005; Healey and Jenkins 2009), and in the other, it portrayed the range of ways students may be involved in partnership with staff and other students in learning and teaching (Healey, Flint, and Harrington 2014, 2016). Readers' responses to these pieces taught me that if you can summarize your ideas visually, they have more impact than text alone.

Your perspective: What attracts or might attract you to writing theoretical and conceptual articles or chapters?

"Guiding Questions for Planning, Revising, and Refining a Theoretical or Conceptual Article" outlines questions and offers examples to guide you in writing focused yet rich theoretical and conceptual articles that provoke new thought and debate within the learning and teaching discourse community. A version with just the questions, which you can use for planning your theoretical or conceptual article, is available as an online resource.

Guiding Questions for Planning, Revising, and Refining a Theoretical or Conceptual Article*

1. **What is your overall aim and rationale for this article?**
   Clarify your aim and rationale. These help the reader understand what you are trying to achieve and provide justification for the study, as Kerri-Lee Krause clearly states in her exploration of quality in higher education:

   > This article explores the wicked problem of quality in higher education, arguing for a more robust theorising of the subject at national, institutional and local department level. The focus of the discussion rests on principles for theorising in more rigorous ways about the multidimensional issue of quality. (Krause 2012, 285)

2. **What does your work contribute to the wider field of the scholarship of teaching and learning (SoTL) or higher education research?**
   It is critical to state clearly what you consider your contribution to be. This will help reviewers decide whether to recommend publication and readers to decide whether to continue reading.

   > The growing literature on undergraduate teaching and learning currently lacks an organising framework. This article sets out to provide one, distinguishing between hard pure, soft pure, hard applied and soft applied fields of study, and hence making it possible to highlight generally unremarked similarities and differences between the various research findings. (Neumann, Parry, and Becher 2002, 405)

3. **What theories or concepts are you exploring in your article, and how do you define them for the purposes of your analysis?**
   Answering this question clarifies the subject matter of your conceptual or theoretical article.

The article outlines an "academic literacies" framework which can take account of the conflicting and contested nature of writing practices, and may therefore be more valuable for understanding student writing in today's higher education than traditional models and approaches. (Lea and Street 1998, 157)

4. How was the analysis conducted?

Tell readers how you went about your analysis, as this will help them understand your argument.

Attempts to define SoTL flounder when faced with its diversity. In considering the confusion that can ensue, we see the problem to be one of focus, namely a focus on definition rather than on diversity. . . . In looking for the constitution of SoTL, we focused initially on the internal horizon of *disseminated* SoTL knowledge (i.e. published work). . . . Only when that analysis was felt to be complete did we consider the external horizon of contextual factors that have influence over the internal horizon. This is the theoretical framework for our analysis and result. (Booth and Woollacott 2018, 538-9)

5. Why, and to whom, do these theories or concepts matter in learning and teaching?

The answer to this question clarifies why your article may be important and to whom. As one of the leading philosophers of higher education states:

What is it to learn for an unknown future? It might be said that the future has always been unknown but our opening question surely takes on a new pedagogical challenge if not urgency in the contemporary age. Indeed, it could be said that our opening question has *never* been generally acknowledged to be a significant motivating curricular and pedagogical question in higher education. Be all this as it may, the question (What is it to learn for an unknown future?) surely deserves more attention than it has so far received. After all, if the future is unknown, what kind of learning is appropriate *for* it? (Barnett 2004, 247)

6. **How do scholars discuss and critique these theories or concepts?**

Bring readers into previous conversations about the theories or concepts you address.

> This article firstly reviews and critiques the four dominant research perspectives on student engagement: the behavioural perspective, which foregrounds student behaviour and institutional practice; the psychological perspective, which clearly defines engagement as an individual psycho-social process; the socio-cultural perspective, which highlights the critical role of the socio-political context; and, finally, the holistic perspective, which takes a broader view of engagement. (Kahu 2013, 758)

7. **What new insights or frameworks are you bringing to these theories or concepts?**

Elaborating on the new insights that you bring to the conversation helps readers understand both your thinking and its contribution to, extension of, or branching out from the conversation.

> In this article, we focus on questions that come into view when we look at educational development through the lenses of signature pedagogies and the Scholarship of Teaching and Learning (SoTL). We offer this as a thought experiment in which we consider if SoTL is a signature pedagogy of educational development, simultaneously enacting and revealing the practices, values, and assumptions that underpin the diverse work efforts of our field. (Felten and Chick 2018)

8. **What are the implications of your analysis for researchers or practitioners?**
Address the "So what?" question, as Randy Bass does in this classic SoTL article about "What's the problem?"

> Changing the status of the *problem* in teaching from terminal remediation to ongoing investigation is precisely what the movement for a scholarship of teaching is all about. How might we make the problematization of teaching a matter of regular communal discourse? How might we think of teaching practice, and the evidence of student learning, as problems to be investigated, analyzed, represented, and debated? (Bass 1999, 1)

9. **What further research or actions are prompted by your analysis?**
Identify where you think your argument goes next or how others might build on it.

> Academic developers may advocate student–faculty partnership if they aspire to disrupt some of the neoliberal logics and practices in contemporary higher education, while being aware that it can still be re-appropriated by neoliberalism. (Wijaya Mulya 2018, 89)

*As with other sets of guiding questions in this book, select those questions that are relevant to your context, add others as appropriate, and decide the order in which you will address them to communicate effectively with your audience. The questions are based on those in Healey, Matthews, and Cook-Sather (2019, 37).

Over to You

Writing theoretical and conceptual articles is a challenging, but potentially hugely rewarding, way of influencing conversations about learning and teaching in higher education. This genre allows you to explore and to learn and, in turn, to share nascent or deepened understandings. Questions to ask about writing theoretical and conceptual articles include:

- What learning and teaching topics fascinate you and need, to your mind, deepening or reconceptualizing?
- Which topics intrigue, excite, disturb, concern, or worry you and therefore warrant addressing?
- Which of our Guiding Questions do you think you need to address to write your theoretical or conceptual article? What other questions are important for you to tackle?
- What outlets might be interested in publishing your theoretical or conceptual article?

CHAPTER 14

SYNTHESIZING WHAT WE ALREADY KNOW

Literature Reviews

Many reviews, in fact, are only thinly disguised annotated bibliographies. (Hart 2018, 2)

A quality literature review should not just reflect or replicate previous research and writing on the topic under review, but should lead to new productive work (Lather, 1999) and represent knowledge construction on the part of the writer. (Imel 2011, 146-47)

In response to the rapid growth of the body of literature in higher education, Malcolm Tight (2018b, 607) suggested that "it may be time to spend more effort on synthesising and disseminating what we have already learnt, rather than, or before, undertaking fresh research." Rather than choosing to only generate new research or only synthesize what we have already learned, we suggest, as we do throughout this book, taking a both/and approach. Bringing literature together in a review is a particularly useful endeavor in writing about learning and teaching, where the literature is dispersed across SoTL, educational research, and discipline-based educational research publications. Drawing on scholarship, literature reviews offer an exciting opportunity to synthesize what is known about a topic and reveal what else we can learn.

Our main focus in this chapter is on *freestanding* literature reviews, as opposed to reviews embedded in research articles, theses, and other genres (e.g., Ridley 2012), though much of what we say applies to those as well. As the first quote at the beginning of this chapter indicates, a common error in writing literature reviews is to produce what is effectively an annotated bibliography, sometimes along the lines of A said, B said, etc. In contrast, a quality review, as the second quote above suggests, adds to the literature by producing new insights from existing literature, often contributing "new frameworks and perspectives on the topic" (Torraco 2005, 356). In other words, a good literature review is more than the sum of its parts.

Whereas empirical research articles (chapter 12) are expected to present original data and theoretical and conceptual articles (chapter 13) afford opportunities for speculation and argument, literature reviews integrate previous studies within a new frame. Each of these genres importantly informs the others. As Chris Hart (2018, 11) points out: "It is the progressive narrowing of the topic, through the literature review, that makes most research a practical consideration," and David Boote and Penny Beille (2005, 3) suggest that "a thorough, sophisticated literature review is the foundation and inspiration for substantial, useful research." A few journals, such as the *Review of Educational Research* and *Educational Research Review,* specialize in publishing freestanding, critical, integrative reviews of research literature on education, but most higher education journals publish reviews relevant to their focus.

A variety of terms may be used to describe literature reviews, including research reviews, integrative reviews, and research syntheses (Imel 2011). In this discussion we do not include meta-analyses, which use a statistical procedure for combining empirical data from multiple studies to measure effect sizes, such as John Hattie's (2008) systematic review of over 800 meta-analyses of the influences on achievement in school-aged students. We also exclude discussion of *how* to undertake the literature search and literature analysis, just as we omitted consideration of data collection and analysis, and research methods, in the chapter on empirical research articles. Our focus is rather on demystifying the *writing* of the literature review. To that end we present a flexible guide to the organization and composition of a literature review.

The Nature and Purpose of Literature Reviews

Harris Cooper (1988, 2003) developed an influential taxonomy of literature reviews in education and psychology. His "taxonomy categorizes reviews according to: (a) focus; (b) goal; (c) perspective; (d) coverage; (e) organization; and (f) audience" (1988, 104). We summarize these six characteristics:

- *Focus* – Most authors of literature reviews in education focus on research findings, research methods, theories, or practices and applications.
- *Goal* – The primary goal of a literature review is synthesis or integration. Other goals are a critique of the existing literature, a discussion of strengths and limitations, and the identification of central issues and gaps in the literature.
- *Perspective* – There is a difference between the reviewer advocating a position or remaining neutral. Check whether the journal you are submitting to has a preference for one or the other of these.
- *Coverage* – This concerns the extent to which the author attempts to find and include relevant literature. The coverage can be exhaustive, exhaustive with selective criteria, representative of core material, or dictated by the reviewer's goals.
- *Organization* – Reviews may be organized historically, conceptually, or methodologically.
- *Audience* – Reviews can be written for groups of specialized researchers, general researchers, practitioners, policymakers, or the general public.

See also Grant and Booth (2009) for another classification of literature reviews.

Reviews of relevant literature have a range of purposes. Chris Hart (2018, 31) identifies twelve:

1. Distinguishing what has been done from what needs to be done
2. Discovering important variables relevant to the topic
3. Synthesising and gaining a new perspective
4. Identifying relationships between ideas and practice

5. Establishing the context of the topic or problem
6. Rationalising the theoretical or practical significance of the problem
7. Enhancing and gaining the subject vocabulary
8. Understanding the origins and structure of the subject
9. Relating ideas and theory to problems and questions
10. Identifying the main methodologies and data collection tools that have been used
11. Placing the research into an historical context to show familiarity with state-of-the-art developments
12. Having a body of knowledge to which you can relate your own research findings.

Although Hart claims these purposes are equally important, which ones are relevant vary between different studies and different types of review. For example, Joseph Maxwell (2006) argues that the purpose of a freestanding review is to present a review *of* research, while the objective of an embedded review is to present a review *for* research. This distinction has an important bearing on how the quality of the review is judged. Maxwell (2006, 28) argues that, whereas *thoroughness* is a key indicator of quality of a freestanding review, *relevance* is "the most essential characteristic" of the embedded literature review. Literature reviews can also expose both dominant and silenced voices and perspectives (Walker 2015). It is also important to remember that there are ethical issues involved in undertaking and writing literature reviews (Kara 2019).

Further nuances apply to specific purposes. For example, authors often identify filling gaps in the literature as both purpose and outcome of a freestanding review or as an argument justifying their study in an embedded review. Pat Thomson (2019a) is critical of the gap-filling justification because "the gap filler, no matter how much they struggle to be appreciative, starts from a deficit position. Here is what the field doesn't do. Then the gap filler is going to sort this out. They will fix this important omission." She goes on to argue that a gap in the literature is not an adequate justification for a study

(Thomson 2019b): "It isn't necessarily significant that nobody has written about a particular topic in this specific way before. Nope. The topic may just not be interesting or important enough for anyone to have bothered." A better justification for a study, she suggests, is its *significance*: identify the nature of the topic or problem you are studying and how your review contributes to understanding it better or answering a problem that you or others have recognized. Along these lines, Thomson (2019a) suggests either a "next step" or a "what if" approach to justifying the study:

> The next stepper positions themselves as part of the field and about to make a positive contribution to what has gone before. The what iffer is also positioned as part of the field but as someone who would like to do a little creative work to see what experimentation might have to offer.

We see the logic of Thomson's arguments, although, as Ronald Barnett (personal communication, July 28, 2019) notes, "gap-fillers can be collegial and what-iffers can be isolated on their desert islands." So, when considering the purpose of your literature review, take into account what approach might be at once collegial *and* contribute to or create inclusive and generative conversations.

Prior to undertaking a literature review it may help to undertake a scoping review. These are "a form of knowledge synthesis that addresses an exploratory research question aimed at mapping key concepts, types of evidence, and gaps in research related to a defined area or field by systematically searching, selecting, and synthesizing existing knowledge" (Colquhoun et al. 2014, 1292, 1294).

Writing a Literature Review for Publication

A good indication of the standards and criteria involved in writing a literature review, whether it is published in a journal or as a book chapter, is given in the statement of the aims and scope of the *Review of Educational Research*:

The *Review of Educational Research* (*RER*) publishes critical, integrative reviews of research literature bearing on education. Such reviews should include conceptualizations, interpretations, and syntheses of literature and scholarly work in a field broadly relevant to education and educational research.

The standards and criteria for reviews in *RER* are the following:

1. Quality of the literature. Standards used to determine quality of literature in education vary greatly. Any review needs to take into account the quality of the literature and its impact on findings. Authors should attempt to review all relevant literature on a topic (e.g., international literature, cross-disciplinary work, etc.).

2. Quality of analysis. The review should go beyond description to include analysis and critiques of theories, methods, and conclusions represented in the literature. This analysis should also examine the issue of access—which perspectives are included or excluded in a body of work? Finally, the analysis should be reflexive—how does the scholar's framework constrain what can be known in this review?

3. Significance of the topic. The review should seek to inform and/or illuminate questions important to the field of education. While these questions may be broad-based, they should have implications for the educational problems and issues affecting our national and global societies.

4. Impact of the article. The review should be seen as an important contribution and tool for the many different educators dealing with the educational problems and issues confronting society.

5. Advancement of the field. The review should validate or inform the knowledge of researchers and

guide and improve the quality of their research and scholarship.

6. Style. The review must be well written and conform to style of the *Publication Manual of the American Psychological Association* (6th edition). Authors should avoid the use of unexplained jargon and parochialism.

7. Balance and fairness. The review should be careful not to misrepresent the positions taken by others, or be disrespectful of contrary positions.

8. Purpose. Any review should be accessible to the broad readership of *RER*. The purpose of any article should be to connect the particular problem addressed by the researcher(s) to a larger context of education. (*Review of Educational Research*, "Aims and Scope")

As this list of standards and criteria indicates, high-quality literature reviews in higher education should provide provocative new insights into key issues. But writing such a review is a highly skilled task involving several stages:

> Authors of review articles are expected to identify an appropriate topic or issue for review, justify why a literature review is the appropriate means of addressing the topic or problem, search and retrieve the appropriate literature(s), analyze and critique the literature, and create new understandings of the topic through one or more forms of synthesis. (Torraco 2005, 356-7)

Unlike a theoretical or conceptual article, which draws on literature to provoke the forward-looking generation of new concepts, a literature review looks back at what has already been written and presents it in a new way. So, while it looks back, it also influences thinking—and, potentially, practice—going forward.

In "Guiding Questions for Planning, Revising, and Refining a Literature Review," we identify a series of questions that break this task down into more manageable steps, illustrated with examples from higher education freestanding reviews. A version with only the questions included is available in the online resources. You may find it helpful in planning your literature review.

Guiding Questions for Planning, Revising, and Refining a Literature Review*

1. What is the focus and aim of your review? Who is your audience?

Identify your focus and, if appropriate, clarify your target audience, as the authors of this review of the literature on the concept of excellence in teaching and learning do:

> The literature review set out to address three main questions: How is the term "excellence" used in the context of teaching and the student learning experience? What are the key conceptualisations of excellence? What are the implications of usage and conceptualisations for future policy in relation to promoting or developing excellence? (Little et al. 2007, 1)

2. Why is there a need for your review? Why is it significant?

Tell readers about the importance of the topic or problem and why a literature review is an appropriate way of addressing it.

> Mentorship is a defining feature of UR [undergraduate research]. As more and different types of colleges and universities strive to meet student demand for authentic scholarly experiences, it is imperative to identify what effective UR mentors do in order to ensure student engagement, quality enhancement, retention, and degree-completion. (Shanahan et al. 2015, 359)

3. **What is the context of the topic or issue? What perspective do you take? What framework do you use to synthesize the literature?**

   A good literature review is creative. Describe the context and your perspective and framework, as these authors do in this quote from a literature review on designing educational development practices:

   > Their conceptual review yielded a framework with six foci of practice (skill, method, reflection, disciplinary, institutional, and action research or inquiry) that was drawn from an analysis of the design elements of the educational development practices in the research they reviewed and from an analysis of the conceptual, theoretical, and empirical literature cited by those articles. (Amundsen and Wilson 2012, 90).

4. **How did you locate and select sources for inclusion in the review?**

   Provide details of the sources you selected and your selection criteria so that readers can assess your conclusions. Search engines are not neutral (Noble 2018). Consider tracking and reporting the search terms and resources you used to find the materials in the review, because words matter. For instance, in the past US authors often used the term "freshman" for first-year students; scholars from other areas of the world didn't. Searching different databases can lead to differently skewed results. Consider snowball searching as well: start with base articles, then follow who cites whom and who is cited by whom. This approach reduces the problem of overly restrictive keywords, especially in fields where terminology is changing. For example, a review of teacher identity in universities focused van Lankveld et al.'s (2017) search:

   > On the basis of title and abstract screening, we selected the following studies: empirical and review studies published in the English language in peer-reviewed journals that were concerned with adult university teachers and that focused principally on teacher identity. . . . We

chose to limit our search to 2005–2015. (van Lankveld
et al. 2017, 327)

5. How is your review structured?

Inform the reader how you have structured your review. Try where
possible to use informative headings rather than generic ones. For
example, the authors of this review of the scholarship of teaching
and learning (SoTL) literature structured their report as follows:

> Introduction
> Defining SoTL
> SoTL in the disciplines
> SoTL and educational development
> SoTL recognition and excellence
> National and international SoTL initiatives
> Student engagement with SoTL
> Main findings and recommendations
> (Fanghanel et al. 2015, 2-3)

6. What are the main findings in the literature on this topic?

By providing both an overview of findings already documented in
the literature and a framework for your synthesis of those findings,
you help readers make sense of what is already known. For instance,
a review of the literature on students as partners found that:

> Trends across results provide insights into four themes:
> the importance of reciprocity in partnership; the need to
> make space in the literature for sharing the (equal) real-
> ities of partnership; a focus on partnership activities that
> are small scale, at the undergraduate level, extracurricular,
> and focused on teaching and learning enhancement; and
> the need to move toward inclusive, partnered learning
> communities in higher education. (Mercer–Mapstone
> et al. 2017a, 1)

7. What are the main strengths and limitations of this literature?

By assessing the main strengths and limitations of the literature you provide a critical analysis rather than a descriptive summary. A Norwegian analysis of the research–education nexus argued that:

> Overall, the evidence reveals a highly complex and multidimensional picture on the research–education relationship at different levels such as national, organisational/institutional, curriculum and individual. This complexity and multidimensionality and the lack of unambiguous definitions of the two core terms, research and education, make it challenging to define a clear set of measurable indicators to measure the impact of the research–education relationship on study quality. We thus argue that it is important to distinguish between and combine three types of indicators, i.e., input, process and output indicators, highlighting the importance of student-active learning forms. (Elken and Wollscheid 2016, 8)

8. What conclusions do your draw from the review? What do you argue needs to be done as an outcome of the review?

Identify your main conclusions and the areas where further research could usefully focus. A study of professional identity development concluded that:

> Further research is needed to better understand the tensions between personal and professional values, structural and power influences, discipline versus generic education, and the role of workplace learning on professional identities. (Trede, Macklin, and Bridges 2012, 365)

As with other sets of guiding questions in this book, select those questions that are relevant to your context, add others as appropriate, and decide the order in which you will address them to communicate effectively with your audience.

Over to You

Writing a quality literature review can be a challenging but also an inspiring venture. Most research begins with a review of the relevant literature, but standalone reviews need to be more systematic and add to knowledge and understanding. In other words, a freestanding review needs to be more than simply a summary of the pre-existing literature; to contribute to the scholarly conversation, it should also provide new insights that will guide the future development of the field. As you consider the steps that we and others provide for writing a review, also keep in mind how this work draws on and reveals your own identity, either implicitly or explicitly. Questions to ask about writing literature reviews include:

- What topics will be of interest and significance to others as well as fascinating to you—enough for you to consider writing a standalone literature review?
- Which of our Guiding Questions do you think you need to address to write your literature review? What other questions are important for you to tackle?
- What is the extent, scope, and significance of the existing literature as it deals with your question or problem?
- What outlets might be interested in publishing your literature review?

CHAPTER 15

FOCUSING ON PRACTICAL EXPERIENCES

Case Studies

A case study is an empirical inquiry that investigates a contemporary phenomenon in depth and within its real-life context, especially when the boundaries between phenomenon and context are not clearly evident. (Yin 2018, 18)

Case studies are a genre of scholarship that, as our opening quotation indicates, delves deeply into specific examples of learning and teaching practices, usually within a single course, program, or institution. Case studies allow authors to move from anecdotal approaches to more systematic ones. As Lee Shulman (2004, 29) argues: "There is a powerful strategic value in writing and analyzing cases that have been written by members of a case forum, and in systematically exploring the tough question 'what is this a case of.'" Some learning and teaching journals have specific sections for case studies (e.g., *The Journal of Learning and Teaching in Higher Education*, *Journal of Scholarship of Teaching and Learning*), though they may be called "instructional articles" (*International Journal of Teaching and Learning in Higher Education*), "practice reports" (*Student Success*), or "classroom notes" (*International Journal of Mathematical Education in Science and Technology*). Several universities and scholarly outlets publish examples of interesting practices in edited volumes or web-based collections. Some case studies are semi-fictionalized to maintain anonymity.

There is a growing interest in *impact case studies* as research-funding bodies demand evidence of impact (Green 2019). In the UK Research

Excellence Framework, 25% of the assessment weighting is given to the reach and significance of impact case studies. "Impacts on students, teaching or other activities both within and beyond the submitting HEI [higher education institution] are **included**" (REF2021 2019, 90); though this was not the case in the 2014 REF when impacts needed to be wider in reach than the submitting higher education institution (Kneale, Cotton, and Miller 2016).

Writing a case study about your practice can be an excellent way to enter the world of publishing about learning and teaching. It can help you build your confidence and begin to develop your identity and voice as a writer. But case studies are as valuable a genre for experienced learning and teaching scholars as they are for inexperienced scholars. They are often more accessible than research articles, and the additional information about context and process usually provided in a case study can be powerful in persuading colleagues to change their practices. In this chapter, we offer a flexible framework to guide the organization and composition of both peer-reviewed and non-refereed case studies, along with discussion of the benefits and complexities of writing in this genre to ensure criticality and the illumination of broader implications. We focus on standalone case studies as opposed to case studies included to illustrate particular practices within other genres, though many of the points we make apply to both.

Case Studies of Practice: Critical Analysis to Advance Learning and Teaching Scholarship

Case studies might sound a bit confusing as a genre because we often think about case studies as a pedagogical approach or a method. Case-based learning is common in business, law, medicine, health-related disciplines, and engineering, where case studies are analyzed to identify problems and propose solutions. This pedagogical approach has also been used in learning and teaching in higher education (Schwartz and Webb 1993). The term "case study" is, moreover, used to describe a research design through which scholars collect and present data (Tight 2017;Yin 2018). Many publications using this last method would be classified in our empirical research article genre.

In this chapter we are using the term case study to highlight a practice rather than to constitute a method; we use the term to signal a genre of scholarship that delves deeply into the specifics of practice. These pieces of writing tend to be brief, scholarly explorations of specific practices, examples, or initiatives that could either be continuing or one-off projects. Case studies are not always about successful implementations; those about instances where things didn't go according to plan can be at least as useful. Key for both is solid reflection and analysis. Importantly, case studies offer a great deal of context with a strong rationale for the practice being presented. In this sense, you could think of case studies as a way to tell a story about learning and teaching: a story rich in context and focused on the experiences of learners and teachers (see also chapter 20).

As we noted in chapter 11, the boundaries between case studies and some empirical research articles and reflective essays are blurred, and case studies may also appear in blogs. The characteristics of each genre are best seen not as mutually exclusive but rather as overlapping and falling along a continuum. Many scholarship of teaching and learning (SoTL) research articles, for instance, are constructed around an in-depth analysis of classroom practices. Here we discuss case studies that are generally shorter pieces, based on an analysis of practice and provisional discussion of evidence of impact. The latter might include evaluations based on students' and academics' views, reflections of participants, data on outcomes (e.g., assignments), and adoption of the practice by others.

Some case studies will have the potential to be developed into full research articles with the addition of a robust theoretical or conceptual framework and more refined method. Similarly, the analysis contained in some research articles pertaining to practice in a specific department or institution could be elaborated on in a case study through detailing the context in which it occurred, discussing how it was implemented, and considering what might need to be changed to suit different contexts. Sometimes, the whole of a research article may be based on one case study (e.g., Marquis et al. 2016), or more than one case study may be compared within a research article (e.g., Hill, Walkington, and King 2018).

Since a case study offers a deep and detailed dive into a specific example of learning and teaching practice, your argument in this genre is built in reference to the particulars of the course, program, or institution combined with evidence of its impact. While your argument might be built through your introduction, literature review, methods, findings, discussion, implications, and conclusion, as in an empirical research article, a case study is likely to be more focused, and the argument will be concentrated on how the findings might or might not be replicated or applicable in other contexts.

In Reflection 15.1, Jessica Riddell discusses the experience of writing a case study on the co-creation of a podcasting course at a Canadian university (Liatsis, Pohl, and Riddell 2018).

Reflection 15.1

The experience of writing a case study

After reading an article about publishing as the final frontier of students as partners (SaP) (Healey, Healey, and Cliffe 2018), I was inspired to co-publish with students for the first time this past year. After a transformative experience co-creating a course with two student collaborators, we chose to share our experiences in the form of a case study because we felt that the genre was less intimidating and would allow us to include multiple voices and perspectives in our journey of co-creation. Other forms of SoTL—research articles, for example—tend to homogenize voices and unify a journey that felt rather disingenuous. Instead, we wanted to invite into the conversation the challenges and delights that animated our journey. In our paper we set out to engage in critical self-reflection grounded in the relevant SaP literature in an authentic manner that did not efface the contested conceptual terrains we navigated together. The writing and publishing experience was eye-opening: the students demonstrated a level of persistence and commitment in countless rounds of revisions that exceeded my expectations. As a seasoned writer, but a novice SaP co-author, my initial impulse was to reframe and rewrite the case study, but the genre itself created spaces for me to reflect as a partner rather than as a professor or editor. This opportunity has re-shaped my conception of scholar, learner, and mentor, and I have a newfound appreciation for the case study as an essential component of SoTL.

Jessica Riddell is the Stephen A. Jarislowsky Chair of Undergraduate Teaching Excellence at Bishop's University in Canada and the executive director of the Maple League of Universities.

This example shows the potential overlap with another category: autoethnography. Although we do not focus on it here, this genre can be understood as spanning case study and reflective essay genres (Deitering, Schroeder, and Stoddart 2017).

Writing a Case Study for Publication in a Refereed Journal or as a Book Chapter

The publication criteria for case studies in *International Journal for Students as Partners* (*IJSaP*) state:

> These publications are brief, scholarly explorations of specific practices, examples or initiatives, including continuing and one-off projects. They discuss the context and rationale for the work, place the case study in the context of the relevant literature, analyze the implementation of the initiative, identify strengths and weaknesses, and offer critical analysis of impacts on students, staff, practice, and policy as appropriate. Case studies do not need to include a theoretical framework or make a significant original contribution to the field, however, purely descriptive case studies are not acceptable (a maximum of 3,000 words). Case studies should include an abstract (150 words).

Criteria for Review

- Presents an analysis of the implementation of an initiative
- Contextualizes the initiative through the citation of relevant literature
- Identifies the strengths and weaknesses of the initiative
- Critically analyses impacts on students, staff, practice, and policy as appropriate

(*International Journal for Students as Partners,* "Submissions")

In writing a case study, whether for a journal article or book chapter, you should provide a rich description of the context, position the practice within the relevant literature, analyze the implementation of the initiative, identify strengths and weaknesses, offer critical analysis of impacts on students and faculty/academics, and call for changes to practice and policy, as appropriate. Case studies advance the learning and teaching conversation through documenting examples of practice, provoking reflection on them, and offering the opportunity for others within the learning and teaching community to adopt them. However, case studies that are descriptive, without analysis or critical reflection, are unlikely to be published in a scholarly journal or book chapter. Our "Guiding Questions for Planning, Revising, and Refining a Case Study" can help you frame case studies and ensure that your writing in this genre is critical and illuminates broader implications. A copy of the questions is available in the online resources. You may find it helpful in planning your case study.

Guiding Questions for Planning, Revising, and Refining a Case Study*

1. What is this a case study of?

Tell the reader what learning and teaching research and practice areas your case study illustrates. Why should the reader be interested in reading what you have written? For example, the author quoted below positions her case study in the context of the literature on the research-teaching nexus.

> The curriculum design of the new degree course in English launched in 2006-07 was underpinned by modules that aimed to encourage students to engage with scholarship and experience research at first hand. The integration of a research ethos within the English provision mirrored the top right-hand quadrant of the "curriculum design and research-teaching nexus" model . . . proposed by Healey (2005, 70; Healey and Jenkins 2009, 7). (Orsini-Jones 2013, 1)

2. **Why should your case study matter to other scholars?**
   Give the rationale for your case study and explain why it matters. What problem does it address? One book chapter presents a case study of redistributing grades (marks) for a group project between team members with the following justification:

> Group projects are often criticised by both staff and students because frequently when they are assessed team members are credited with identical marks. . . . The use of peer and self assessment techniques help to develop skills of responsibility, autonomy, judgement and self-awareness. Knowing that the group marks will be reallocated to reflect the contribution of individuals helps to discourage the "freeloader." (Healey and Addis 2004, 116)

3. **What is the context of your case study (e.g., discipline, institution, nation)?**
   Give the reader sufficient contextual information to help them interpret your findings. In a case study of preparing obituaries of key geographers in a philosophical module on the development of the discipline, the author stated:

> Society, Space and Social Science is a compulsory human geography module at the University of Gloucestershire.

The module aims to place human geography in the wider social sciences as well as provide students with an understanding of the changing nature of geography. Some members of the module teaching team have research interests in the historical development of geography. To this end staff are eager to illustrate to students how research can and does inform teaching and that some research and literature searches can be fascinating and illuminating. (Harrison 2004, 14)

4. **From whose perspective is the case study written? Who was involved in the practice?**
   Provide details of the faculty/academic staff, student, and other participants. Whose voices are represented in the case study? For example, a podcasting course from a liberal arts university in Canada

   > was designed by two student leaders (station managers at the university radio station) in collaboration with a faculty collaborator . . . [and] had an enrolment of 15 undergraduate students from a diverse range of programs. (Liatsis, Pohl, and Riddell 2018, 115-116)

   > (See also Reflection 15.1.)

5. **What did your practice look like?**
   Describe the main features of the educational practice. The Canadian podcast case study discussed

   > an experiential learning course comprising a 12-episode podcast series dedicated to transformative learning in higher education. . . . Three teams of five students each identified four professors who were particularly effective in facilitating conditions of transformative learning by soliciting feedback via a student survey, interviewing their peers, and examining professors' engagement as educational leaders. (Liatsis, Pohl, and Riddell 2018, 115-116)

6. **How did you collect evidence about impacts of your practice?**

Discuss the sources of evidence of the impacts of your initiative. For instance, the authors of a study that involved the selection and training of two experienced students to be leaders of a Closed Facebook "students-only" community that provided advice and directed queries to appropriate channels stated:

> A participatory action research methodology was deployed for the reflective evaluation stage. . . . The two student leaders, facilitators of the Closed Facebook, and four academic project staff members answered the following questions. (Kek et al. 2017, 120)

7. **What were the outcomes arising from the practice described in your case study?**

Identify the change that resulted from the practice. For example, in a study of integrating student peer review into a large, first-year science course, the authors reported that:

> The student peer review exercise provided students with the opportunity to reflect on and improve their work prior to submission. Survey results showed 78% of students agreed that peer review developed their ability to give constructive feedback. Training and resources provision for the teaching staff was crucial to the integration of peer review activities. Supported teaching staff were able to engage with and support the students, and the students valued this engagement and guidance. (Dowse, Melvold, and McGrath 2018, 79)

8. **How do you handle and present unexpected findings?**

Unexpected findings can move the conversation about a particular topic in new directions. It is therefore important to explain in what way they are unexpected and what the implications may be for future research. For example, an early study of students and faculty working on a SoTL project together found:

Engaging students in our SoTL project was unexpectedly valuable for the faculty members as researchers. Because we were accountable to our student researchers, we collaborated more diligently than we might have otherwise. . . . We additionally found that our study increased student interest in research mentoring. . . . Students who heard about their peers' involvement in the study expressed interest in becoming future research partners. This was an unanticipated and highly welcome indication that students may have their own compelling motivations for joining us in this kind of work. (Wymer et al. 2012, 6)

9. **What lessons have you learned, and what will you do differently as a result?**
Reflect on what you have learned and what you would do differently if you were to implement the initiative again.

It was very difficult for students who are barely able to read journal articles in English to enter an equal partnership with lecturers in an Academic Writing course who have published in those journals. In retrospect, it is clear that empowering (disadvantaged) students to be able to articulate their voice in such a partnership required much more time and effort than we realised. (Wijaya Mulya and Aditomo 2020, 60)

10. **What are the implications for others in different contexts?**
Discuss the impact of your context on your findings and the relevance of your findings to others in different contexts. The Canadian podcast study concluded that:

Four key factors were necessary to turn this from an idea into an academically rigorous credit course:

1) Purpose: We believed that this was an important intervention to ensure the sustainability and relevance of the student-run radio station.

2) Passion: We were committed enough to devote countless hours to this project and students were inspired to engage in this project in meaningful ways.

3) Mentorship: A faculty sponsor, mentor, and champion were essential in the process to design and implement an academically rigorous course.

4) Empowerment: It is essential that a liberal education institution encourage and empower students to go above and beyond in their learning in order to cultivate change in their environments. (Liatsis, Pohl, and Riddell 2018, 120-121)

As with other sets of guiding questions in this book, select those questions that are relevant to your context, add others as appropriate, and decide the order in which you will address them to communicate effectively with your audience.

Case studies may also appear as chapters of edited collections by institutions or scholarly bodies (e.g., Guest and Lloyd 2013; Healey and Roberts 2004). Since for many authors a case study may be their first publication about learning and teaching, using a set of questions, such as those above, as a guideline can support the development of a writing voice and identity.

Writing a Case Study for Publication on a Website or in a Blog

Most case studies are published not in refereed journals but on institutional websites or in blogs. The Advance HE Knowledge Hub includes many case studies; a recent collection they published featured case studies on action research (Arnold and Norton 2018). Helen May (2013) provides a short guide to writing case studies for Advance HE. University College London publishes some lively case study stories demonstrating inspiring teaching practices and projects. Mick's website features several hundred examples of "mini-case studies," most of which are brief summaries of interesting practices organized into themes (e.g., engaging students in research and inquiry; students as partners and change agents) with references or contact details, where further information may be found. Some are summarized from published articles or information on websites, and others are written specifically for the collections. Some case studies may be presented as stories (chapter 20) or appear in blogs (chapter 21).

Over to You

Case studies are an important genre for communicating about your learning and teaching practices and influencing others to enhance their practices. The aim in writing your case study, whether it is less than a single page or several pages long, is to communicate the key details of your practice to colleagues in other departments, institutions, and countries. Therefore, it is important to ensure that you: give readers sufficient information to help them decide whether to adapt your practice or idea to their context; minimize use of discipline-specific terminology; and avoid institutional or discipline-specific acronyms. Because the genre requires both critical reflection on practice and focused analysis in writing, developing the capacity to write case studies can contribute to you becoming a well-rounded and effective learning and teaching scholar. Questions to ask about writing case studies:

- Which of your learning and teaching practices are effective and sufficiently innovative to be of interest to others as a case study? Could these practices be applied in a different disciplinary, institutional, or national context or to a different group of students—age, background, previous experience—than is covered in the literature?
- Which of our Guiding Questions do you think you need to address to write your case study? What other questions are important for you to tackle?
- For what outlets would you consider writing your case study?

CHAPTER 16

TELLING A BIGGER STORY

Books and Edited Collections

The real point about writing books is that, like mountains, they are there. Some of us cannot resist the challenge; but it's hardly rational behaviour. (Albert 2000, 14)

As the title of this chapter suggests, a book or an edited collection can tell a bigger story than any of the other genres we explore. That is not only because books and edited volumes are longer. It is also because the conceptualization and review processes are different, and a book project can create a new conversation often containing a greater number and diversity of voices, which is more challenging to accomplish in the other genres. Whether a book deepens and extends an established conversation or creates a new one, it requires substantial time and sustained energy, as is emphasized in our opening quote and as is confirmed by Paul Weller (2007, 389), who notes that it "can be a daunting, exhausting, but ultimately exhilarating experience." This chapter covers both books and edited collections. Both are important forms of writing, but they call on different skills and make different demands on authors and editors.

There is plenty of advice on writing academic books (e.g., Black et al. 1998; Germano 2016; Haynes 2010; Luey 2011; Porter 2010). Here we begin by discussing what distinguishes writing books about learning and teaching from writing in other genres. We then examine the changing publication landscape and how this change affects choosing a publisher for a book on learning and teaching. Next, we elaborate on how and when to prepare and submit the book proposal. Finally, we include a section discussing some of the issues involved in editing a collection of articles or chapters on learning and teaching.

Books as a Writing Genre

We note above that writing a book is a major way of creating and contributing to conversations, as is writing in the other genres we discuss in this volume. Books about learning and teaching, however, differ from the other genres in three main ways.

First, they are much longer and typically take more time—both to write and to be published—than the other forms of writing. In terms of length, 80,000–100,000 words is common for mainstream publishers, though educational professional associations, such as SEDA (Staff and Educational Development Association) and Advance HE (previously HE Academy) in the UK and HERDSA (Higher Education Research and Development Society for Australasia), publish shorter guides and publications, typically 10,000–35,000 words. This means that the topic needs to be large enough to sustain, or offer multiple angles on, an argument and keep the interest of the reader, but not so large that the book loses coherence. It also means that a book project will commonly stretch over 2–3 years, perhaps less when you have co-authors—although, as we have discussed, co-authoring can also sometimes prolong writing projects (see chapter 7). The necessity of this sustained engagement is worth considering alongside all your other commitments.

Secondly, criteria and processes for evaluating books differ from those of other genres. In comparison to empirical research and theoretical or conceptual articles in journals in particular, where the key criteria for acceptance is a particular notion of the quality of the scholarship and the contribution to the academic literature, with books, much more emphasis is placed on the audience and what will be of interest to potential readers. Furthermore, for journal publications, the key gatekeepers are the editors and the reviewers, who are normally educational scholars. With books, although reviewers are still asked their opinion, the commissioning editor (who advises the publishing house on what books to publish) and the publisher's editorial board or a senior manager (who decide on whether to offer a contract) have a key role in deciding on the commercial viability of the project. They are rarely educational scholars. Hence, as Gary Smailes (2010) notes, "It's your job to convince publishers that your book has what it takes to make it in the marketplace that that publisher specialises in." Where books are part of a series, you will also have to convince the academic editor that your book will make a scholarly contribution to the literature.

Thirdly, where you are in your career trajectory is a consideration, given that books about learning and teaching carry different degrees of respectability across disciplines. Most academics who consider writing a book about learning and teaching will only undertake it after they have gained experience writing in many other genres, although there are exceptions (such as Chanelle Wilson, a scholar early in her career with whom Alison co-edited the book *Building Courage, Confidence, and Capacity in Learning and Teaching through Student-Faculty Partnership*). Some may also have written and edited books in another discipline before they become interested in writing about learning and teaching, as is the case with Mick. If you are considering writing a book about learning and teaching, it is important to find out, first, whether your discipline values such a focus and, second, whether it values books less or more than, or as much as, other forms of publication.

One of the consequences of the first two of these differences is that there are relatively few discipline-based books about learning and teaching in higher education, as is revealed by a perusal of the list of references in *Teaching and Learning in Higher Education: Disciplinary Approaches to Educational Enquiry* (Cleaver, Lintern, and McLinden 2018). One exception is in the field of medical education where the size of the market supports several texts (e.g., Swanwick, Forrest, and O'Brien 2018). Most writing about learning and teaching in specific disciplines appears in discipline-based journals or as chapters of edited volumes, or as discipline-specific examples illustrating broader arguments in general learning and teaching journals. Therefore, your book will need to appeal to a multi-disciplinary readership.

Some books about learning and teaching are texts aimed mainly at faculty, staff, and graduates new to teaching and supporting learning, some of whom may be undertaking a certificate course in learning and teaching (e.g., Hunt and Chalmers 2013; Race 2014). The majority, however, are aimed at new and experienced faculty and staff, and sometimes campus leaders and students as well, interested in topics within higher education (e.g., Hay 2011; Hutchings, Huber, and Ciccone 2011). A few are monographs aimed primarily at other higher education researchers (e.g., Fanghanel 2011). Some books are only available in hardback and e-book formats and are reliant on library sales (e.g., many of the higher education books published by Springer). A small but growing number of publishers are focusing on the e-book market, and some, including the publisher of this text, are making PDF versions of some or all their books available on open access platforms (e.g., Fung 2017). Other publishers may make your book open access on the payment of a fee (e.g., Gleason 2018). A small number of authors are experimenting with self-publication (e.g., Roberts 2018). Examples of authored and edited books from a range of publishers are shown in the online resource, "Selected Books about Learning and Teaching in Higher Education."

The Changing Publication Landscape and Choosing a Publisher

Change characterizes the publishing industry. Although in recent years there have been several takeovers and mergers among some of the large commercial publishers, in the same period many new smaller publishers have emerged, who are, as Anthony Haynes (2010, 27) describes, taking advantage of "the development of faster, smarter, less expensive technology" and providing "a burgeoning of opportunity for academic authors." He goes on to suggest that "we already live in a golden age for academic authorship—and it is possible that there is a platinum age to come."

From time to time publishers also move into and out of particular markets. For example, a few years ago Routledge took over Kogan Page's higher education list and the Society for Research into Higher Education (SRHE) moved its series from the Open University Press to Routledge. Hence, it is quite possible that you may obtain a contract with one publisher, but your book will end up being published by a different one. Even more common is that staff move on and your editor changes during the publication process.

There are relatively few publishers of learning and teaching in higher education books, most of whom are commercial publishers or university presses, so it should not take too long to produce a short list of potential publishers who have an active list of related books, though you may need to search harder for some of the new publishers. Scanning the reference list of recently published learning and teaching articles and books should give you a start. Some of the larger publishers have series, sometimes associated with professional associations, which may mean that some or all the royalties go to the association. Once you have a short list of potential publishers and have examined the details of recent books that they have published, you might try talking to recently published authors about their experiences. Alternatively, or in addition, you could seek the advice of colleagues who have experience writing books. This should help finalize your short list and decide the order in which you will approach the publishers, or help you choose several to approach at the same time.

In the case of our book, in September 2018 we examined the web pages of the principal publishers of learning and teaching books in higher education to decide if they would be a good fit for the book we had in mind. As a result, we had expression-of-interest conversations with the Routledge SEDA Series editor, who was enthusiastic about the idea, and Advance HE (previously the HE Academy), with whom Mick has published several open access texts previously. However, Advance HE had only just recently been formed from a merger of three organizations and had not yet decided on their publication strategy. Hence, at that stage, our plan was to work on a proposal to send to Routledge. We also sought the advice of two colleagues, one in the UK, Sally Brown, and one in the US, Peter Felten, who had each published several books on learning and teaching and had been critical friends for our *Teaching & Learning Inquiry* (*TLI*) article. Peter mentioned that Elon University was launching an open access books initiative through the Center for Engaged Learning.

After reading their prospectus and participating in a Skype conversation with him and Jessie Moore, the series editors, we decided that we would prepare a proposal to submit to them. There were two key factors in our decision. First, the book would be available as an open access publication at no charge to readers (or to us). This was attractive as it meant the book would reach a much wider audience than with publishers selling the book, and this benefit far outweighed the fact that we would receive no royalties and a significant part of the marketing of the book would be down to us. Secondly, there was the enthusiasm for the book idea from the series editors, both highly respected authors in learning and teaching, whom we knew well and had worked with previously. Unlike at large publishers, the senior managers, commissioning editors, and series editors at Elon are the same people, and we felt we could talk to them as experts in the field. If they had not also been our publishers, they would have been two of the people we would have approached as critical friends to request they comment on our draft text.

Writing a Successful Book Proposal

Most publishers have their own proposal form that you should use. Based on a perusal of several of these, we list below the kind of questions that need to be addressed:

- *Title*—How can you best capture and communicate the subject matter of your book in a few words? Consider including a subtitle to clarify the focus and give more words for search engines to discover your book.
- *Overview*—What question will your book answer? What are the distinctive features of your book? What is the main argument you are making? How does the book move existing scholarship

forward? State all of this succinctly, in a few highly accessible words.

- *Purpose, scope, and motivation*—What is the aim and scope of the book? Why do you want to write it? How did the idea originate?
- *Fit*—How does the book fit with the publisher's existing list and, where relevant, a particular series?
- *Markets*—Who are the potential audiences? Why would they want to read the book? What needs does it meet? What benefits will it provide to readers? What is the core and ancillary readership? What interest will there be internationally?
- *Need*—Why does a book need to be written on this topic? What comparable and competing texts are there (you should list the author, date, title, publisher, length, and price of each)? Can the market support another book? How does your book differ (i.e., does it fill a gap in the literature)?
- *Length*—What is the expected length of the book in words? How many figures and illustrations will it contain?
- *Contents*—What is the structure of your book? Present a contents page including preliminary and end material, and section and chapter titles. For each chapter, add a brief summary and approximate number of words.
- *Authors' names and qualifications*—Why are you the right person or people to write this book? Give a brief biography or CV, including affiliations, qualifications, main publications, awards, and other relevant achievements.
- *Delivery date*—When do you expect to submit the manuscript, given either as an actual date or a number of months after signature of contract?
- *Reviewers*—Who would you recommend as potential reviewers of your proposal?

In her *Chronicle of Higher Education* column, Rachel Toor provides some useful advice that we reproduce in Reflection 16.1.

Reflection 16.1

Preparing an academic book proposal

"When writers start telling me what they're working on and I feel my eyes start to glaze over, I ask how they got interested in the topic. That shifts the conversation from an information dump (on me) to the story of whatever fired them up in the first place. . . .

"Remember, the book proposal is an act of seduction. The overview is your chance to get personal with the editor and make her want you. This is where you connect the prose with the passion, and yes, even for academic books, or maybe, especially for academic books, there *has* to be passion."

"A good book proposal will take you—and the reader—back to that initial flush of enthusiasm, even if it means recalling the pain of when that big old beast bit off a chunk of your leg. If you can remember what originally incited your interest, and narrate that story, you can draw someone in. . . ." (Toor 2013)

Rachel Toor is an associate professor of creative writing at Eastern Washington University's writing program in Spokane, US. She writes a monthly column for The Chronicle of Higher Education.

The advice on when to submit a proposal varies. Some suggest doing it before you start writing the manuscript, as you may obtain some useful guidance on content, structure, and style of writing (Salter 2018). Others suggest leaving it until you have a draft of all or most of the book, as the nature of your book may change during the writing process and you will normally only have one attempt to pitch your idea to a publisher (Knox 2018). This could prove to be a high-risk strategy as extensive rewriting may be needed. Even if you send in the proposal early, it is unlikely, unless you are a well-known author, that you will be offered a contract until you can provide at least some sample chapters, and in some cases the entire manuscript.

It is acceptable to submit your proposal to more than one publisher at the same time as long as you tell them that you are doing that, you ensure each proposal is sent to an appropriate editor, and you tailor your argument directly to the interests of each publisher. However, by taking this approach there is a danger that, if there is a major flaw in the proposal, you miss the opportunity to address it before sending the proposal to another publisher. Anecdotal evidence suggests that the rejection rate for book proposals in higher education is quite high, so you need to ensure that you produce a polished, well-argued, detailed, and well-written case. As with other genres, ask one or two critical friends to look over your proposal before submission.

In our case, we prepared a proposal in December 2018 after our initial conversation with the publisher, but we decided not to submit it until March 2019, by which time we had an initial draft of around a third of the text and had rethought some of the contents and structure of the book. We signed a contract in April; completed the first draft in June; sent it out to our critical friends for review; spent August and September revising and responding to reviewers' comments; and finally submitted the completed manuscript at the end of October, just over a year from our first discussions of the project. If we take into account the time writing our *TLI* article (where we formulated many of our arguments as well as our approach to writing about writing), it was closer to twenty-one months. From submission of the draft manuscript to publication took a further eight months.

Preparing a book proposal should help you to clarify the focus of your manuscript, but you may start to write your manuscript before you submit a proposal to a publisher. The Guiding Questions below might help you in the planning process, and they are also available in an easy-to-download format as an online resource. The emphasis in these questions is on the process of planning the manuscript rather than what questions should be answered in the text. Hence examples from published books are not given.

Guiding Questions for Planning an Academic Book*

1. What is the "bigger story" that you want to tell with this book? How can you capture it in a way that engages editors and reviewers?
2. How will you select a publisher to approach? What criteria might you identify to help you choose?
3. How much of the book will you draft before approaching a publisher?
4. How will you decide on the contents so that you achieve a balance between depth and breadth that will be of interest to your intended readership, thereby providing appropriate coverage of your topic within the publisher's word limit?
5. How will you ensure that you build a convincing argument through the text and are not diverted down interesting but distracting side-tracks?
6. If you are co-authoring the book, what process will you use to draft, revise, and edit the manuscript?
7. What kind of schedule or set of deadlines will you generate for drafting and revising, bearing in mind your other commitments over the several months or years the project can extend?
8. Which critical friends will you approach, and at what stages of drafting and revising, to obtain feedback on both content and style prior to submission of the manuscript?

As with other sets of guiding questions in this book, select those questions that are relevant to your context, add others as appropriate, and decide the order in which you will address them to communicate effectively with your audience.

If the book is successful, you may be invited to write a second edition. In theory this should be considerably easier to do than writing the first edition, and for some it may involve primarily updating and covering some additional topics. However, for others it may mean a complete rewrite, as Mark Corrigan (2019a) found when writing the second edition of *Social Media for Academics* (Corrigan 2019b).

Editing a Learning and Teaching Collection

Some of what we have said about writing a book about learning and teaching also applies to editing one. But there are also significant differences, as William Germano (2016, 117) reminds us: "Writing a book may be hard and lonely, but editing a collection is very public labor." In assessing proposals for edited volumes, publishers are looking for answers to the 4Cs—coherence, contribution, coverage, and contributors (Brennan 2016). Nevertheless, despite the demand for coherence and cross-referencing, the potential to sell individual chapters is attractive to some publishers. In comparison to special issues of journals, edited volumes are usually "much more integrated, cross-referenced, and *intentional*" (Chapnick and Kukucha 2016a). This is well illustrated in *Enhancing Learning and Teaching in Higher Education* (Lea 2015), where each chapter interweaves insightful commentary with case studies, practical examples, and opinion pieces, as well as debate pieces and "Dear Lecturer" comments from students. A good book editor will "carefully move, delete, rewrite and generally improve the text to ensure a consistency of approach and emphasis throughout" (Weller 2007, 397).

Editing a book can help develop your connections, enable you to contribute to the field, and enhance your profile (Thomson 2013b), though some discourage pre-tenured faculty from undertaking the task (Chapnick and Kukucha 2016b) because of the time and energy involved and because edited volumes tend to be valued less in reviews for promotion. In the UK an edited book may be submitted to the national Research Excellence Framework, but not an edited special issue of a journal. However, for contributors to an edited volume, an article in a special issue of a journal counts more than a chapter in an edited book.

Before deciding whether to propose an edited volume to a publisher for the first time, Emma Brennan (2016), editorial director and senior commissioning editor at Manchester University Press, suggests:

The first question a prospective volume editor should ask themselves is whether they can do (and want to do) what commissioning editors do all the time:

- persuade busy people to spend time writing for your volume
- keep them to a strict timescale
- impose specific house style guidelines
- critique, edit and even cut the work of friends, colleagues and senior figures in your field.

When commenting on this chapter, Ronald Barnett (personal correspondence, August 28, 2019) noted:

> Excellent advice—but the phrase "herding cats" comes to mind. One has to be very specific and keep on repeating oneself and even then, many contributors just won't follow the script. I would stress the timescale. Work out all the stages involved and then double it. And even then, there will be one or two who just keep one hanging on … and one has to decide whether to say "thank you but we have had to move on …." It can be immensely frustrating.

It isn't always difficult and frustrating, though. Alison and her colleague, Chanelle Wilson, found the contributors to their edited collection responsive and responsible, and the full manuscript went to the publisher within the month that it was due.

There is plenty of other advice on editing books and special issues of journals available in the sources cited in this chapter (e.g., Muller 2012; Palgrave Macmillan n.d.; Thomson 2013c), not least of which is keeping in close contact with your book publisher or journal editor about significant changes as the collection develops from what was proposed, particularly in contents and length—advice that also applies to book authors.

The Guiding Questions below may help you in planning an edited collection of learning and teaching articles (and are also available in the online resources). The emphasis of the questions is on the planning process.

Guiding Questions for Planning an Edited Collection of Chapters or Articles*

1. What is the "bigger story" that you want to tell with this edited collection? How can you capture it in a way that engages editors and reviewers?
2. Would an edited collection benefit your career at this time given the context in which you work?
3. Is the collection best published as an edited book or a special issue of a journal? Will you invite contributors or put out a call for proposals?
4. How will you select a publisher or journal to approach? What criteria might you identify to help you choose?
5. Will you invite contributors to draft their chapters/articles before or after you approach a publisher or journal editor with a proposal?
6. What kind of schedule or set of deadlines will you generate for drafting and revising. Keep in mind your own commitments over the several months or years the project can extend, and keep in mind that not all contributors will make all the deadlines you specify.
7. What process will you set up for authors to have the opportunity to respond to and review one another's chapters/articles?
8. How will you balance offering constructive and supportive feedback to contributors with striving to create a coherent collection?

*As with other sets of guiding questions in this book, select those questions that are relevant to your context, add others as appropriate, and decide the order in which you will address them to communicate effectively with your audience.

A few experienced authors progress from editing single books to editing a book series. Pat Thomson (2019c) argues that a good series has "an identity. It stands for, and has, a particular point of view on a field. So in its own distinctive way, editing a book series is another way to contribute to the wider scholarly conversation."

Over to You

Writing a book or editing a collection is a significant enterprise and not one to be undertaken lightly. However, the bigger canvas and the different review process provided by this genre make it conducive to creating and contributing to scholarly conversations in more ambitious ways. Questions to ask about writing books and edited collections include:

- What big ideas are you passionate about for writing a book or editing a collection on learning and teaching in higher education?
- Which of our Guiding Questions will help you begin your book manuscript or prepare your book proposal?
- If you are considering putting together an edited book collection, how do you address the 4Cs—coherence, contribution, coverage, and contributors?

CHAPTER 17

TALKING ABOUT LEARNING AND TEACHING

Conference and Workshop Presentations

A talk is always better if you don't just think about what you want to say, but also how your audience will respond. (Thomson 2019d)

I go, of course, for two main reasons: to share what I know and to learn what others have to say. Academic conferences are places of teaching and learning. They are also, like all social sites of learning, places to practice identities, relations to knowledge, and positions to others present or absent. I can read a published article, sure, but I also value being close to the people who have expertise, to follow close up the moves their minds make, to see what I can about who they are. I want to hear their voices, where they speak with certainty and when they pause. I go to fill up on ideas. (Robinson 2018, 144)

Presenting about learning and teaching at conferences and other scheduled meetings, such as workshops, seminars, and symposia, is a major professional activity for scholars, and it provides many opportunities and challenges that differ from other genres of scholarship. Presentations afford you opportunities to explore research ideas and findings before submitting them for formal publication, discuss published work and its application to practice, co-create new ideas, investigate research agendas, and exchange practices. Moreover, there is evidence that teaching approaches travel in large part from person to person, through personal connections, rather than through published arguments (Huber 2009). Conferences and workshops provide important social opportunities for ideas and learning and teaching practices to travel. Although most presentations are made orally, they are usually text based, even if only in terms of speaking notes.

As emphasized in the two quotes at the beginning of this chapter, in preparing a talk you should think as much about *how* you are going to communicate effectively with your audience and how they are going to respond as about *what* you are going to say. This chapter explores ways in which you can make the most of the opportunities provided by conferences and similar meetings to share and learn about interesting learning and teaching research and practices. It will cover writing proposals and making presentations in the form of papers, workshops, and posters. The chapter concludes with a call to contribute to the redesign of these events to enhance the learning of both presenters and participants.

The Nature of Conferences

How you prepare to present at conferences and similar events depends on the presentation format (see Conference Presentations below) and the type and purpose of the event. Learning and teaching conferences range from international to institutional and from general to discipline-specific meetings. Some are small, with 30-100 delegates, and others have 500+ participants. They also vary in their purposes. Some, such as the annual conference of the Society for Research into Higher Education (SRHE), are primarily for researchers to present and discuss their work. Others, including many institutional and disciplinary annual conferences, aim to bring researchers and practitioners together to discuss the application of the latest research and to exchange practices. For many SoTL conferences, the distinction between researchers and practitioners is blurred and most presenters and participants have both identities.

Each of these conferences has its own culture. Hence the first step to take when deciding whether to apply to present at a particular conference—or, if you are fortunate and you receive an invitation to give a keynote (Peseta 2018; Wilson 2018), facilitate a workshop, or contribute to a symposium—is to learn what you can about the likely participants, their backgrounds, and their expectations. What is the mixture of teaching staff and faculty, educational researchers, learning support staff, administrators, and students? Do they share the same context (e.g., from the same institution, country, discipline) or are they mixed? What prior level of knowledge and understanding do delegates have of the topic you are presenting? Talking to someone who has been to the conference before, or to the meeting organizers, is important to avoid making inappropriate assumptions about participants' identities, knowledge, and contexts.

Surprisingly little research has been undertaken into the nature, impact, and experience of academic conferences (Conference Inference Blog; Henderson, Cao, and Mansuy 2018; Popovic 2018; Rowe 2018). Nicholas Rowe (2018) reports that while delegates at scientific, academic, and professional conferences largely feel their needs are being met, they "are divided as to the long-term worth and benefit of conferences, particularly when they consider how their activities and contributions were viewed and appreciated by others" (714). The latter point reflects that while a considerable quantity of work is presented at conferences, only a relatively small proportion is available outside the event itself, and therefore its wider impact and recognition are limited (Rowe 2017).

Given that "conferences are recognised in research on academic careers as important sites which have a *plethora of indirect benefits*," there is also interest in the impact of caring responsibilities on academics' conference participation (Henderson 2019). Conferences are not neutral spaces with equal access. Institutions should consider providing extra financial support to their staff, faculty, and students with caring responsibilities and those who need care themselves, so that they may participate in conferences. Similarly, organizers need to consider how to make their conferences care-friendly by, for example, planning for how caregivers of participants may be involved in conference activities and by providing access to childcare facilities.

One of the indirect benefits of participating in conferences is the development of a network of critical friends (see chapter 26), but as Christine Cheng wisely recommends, value people—don't network. In her view, "networking is too instrumental—and it doesn't work in the context of academia. . . . What's more helpful is building a long-term relationship" (quoted in Pell 2019; see also Cheng 2019). This may be easier to achieve at smaller events.

In the remainder of this chapter we draw on the limited literature available on how to prepare conference proposals, create conference presentations, and design conferences better for learning. Participating in and helping to shape conferences are forms of creating and contributing to conversations about learning and teaching and can play a significant role in shaping your identity as a scholar (see also the series of blog posts on "Giving a Conference Paper?" that Pat Thomson curated on Wakelet).

Conference Proposals

The principles for choosing an appropriate outlet for your work are discussed in chapter 8. Regional, national, and international conferences normally require you to submit a formal proposal for peer review as much as six to nine months prior to the conference (Cassidy 2018a). Typically, regardless of the proposed format, written abstracts from 300–1,000 words are required, and they are assessed using similar criteria. For example, all submissions for the SRHE 2019 conference were judged by the following criteria:

- Originality of questions addressed
- Effective use and clear explanation of research methodology
- Clarity of the research aims and objectives and outcomes
- The extent to which the work is rooted in the relevant literature
- Significance of the research and the contribution added to what is known about the area researched

- The quality of the data (where applicable) and the reliability and significance of the conclusions
- The quality of evidence presented, whether derived from empirical work or scholarly analysis (SRHE 2019)

These criteria are not dissimilar to those used by internationally refereed journals. Most of the advice on selecting a title (see chapter 9) and writing an abstract (see chapter 10) also apply to writing conference proposals. One key difference is that many learning and teaching conferences will look at proposals not just for your content but also for how you are going to engage the audience during the presentation. As you work your way through these or other criteria, consider not only *what* you want to present but also *how* (what format). Think about how both these choices will situate you in this particular conversation about learning and teaching and contribute to the development of your identity as a scholar within that conversation. As with predatory publications, though, beware of predatory conference invitations (see chapter 8).

Conference Presentations

Most learning and teaching conferences offer a range of presentation formats, including papers, posters, workshops, symposia, and panel discussions. Some (e.g., SRHE) also offer video presentations to be inclusive of those who cannot attend in person for financial, geographical, or other reasons. Here we focus on the first three formats, as these are the most common. All may be presented individually or with co-authors.

Papers

The term "paper" is unfortunate as it suggests a written document that some presenters may be tempted to read out. The term "talk" might be more appropriate, particularly for a conference on learning and teaching. As Ronald Barnett (personal communication, July 28, 2019) suggests, audiences want you "to talk to them, as if in their living rooms or in a café." He goes on to note that there are many challenges of public speaking:

> Eye contact with all members of an audience, speaking to the person in the back row, visibly clear PowerPoint slides, but not reading the slides, speaking to the audience, having a conversation with the audience, being a little self-referential, having some humour, keeping to time, dealing respectfully with questions, being inspiring, provoking, stimulating, energising the audience, making the audience think . . . If the furniture allows, too, clear the podium out of the way, and engage directly with the audience (with a lapel mike).

Presenters commonly have 15–20 minutes to present their papers or give their talks in sessions, which are typically 1–1.5 hours in length. They are usually allowed 5–10 minutes to respond to questions, either immediately or, where presentations are linked, as in a symposium, questions may be grouped together at the end of a session. Increasingly in learning and teaching conferences (e.g., ISSOTL, SEDA), participants are encouraged to engage with the audience. The guidance for ISSOTL presenters provides a model of good practice (Chick et al. 2017). This can be challenging when the time you have been allotted is limited, but it can be achieved using short activities, such as a "quiz," or asking participants to discuss a question in pairs and then inviting selected pairs to share their answers, either in plenary or with another pair.

If you accept Pat Thomson and Barbara Kamler's (2013, 170) advice to "never write a conference paper. Always write a draft of the article that will be submitted," then many of the suggestions made in earlier chapters about writing journal articles and book chapters apply to "writing" your conference paper, including the frameworks in chapters 12-16. However, presenting a paper orally is, or should be, very different from reading out your draft. While some people read papers aloud, particularly in the humanities, we recommend against it at learning and teaching conferences. You may want to make an outline, perhaps an annotated one with key phrases or points you want to be sure to say, but you should not prepare a text that is more appropriate for someone to read silently.

Preparation is key to a successful presentation. It is especially important to check timings and be prepared to be flexible so that you can cut portions, if on the day you unexpectedly have to complete your presentation in a shorter period than you had expected or if participants become particularly engaged in one portion of your session. If you are using a PowerPoint presentation to support your talk, try to avoid text-heavy slides; consider using images to stimulate thought, but be sure to explain them. Avoid reading directly from the slides—your audience can read as long as the font is large enough (James and Mendlesohn 2005; Mendlesohn and James 2015; Nottingham 2014; Roberts 2018).

A paper affords you an opportunity to develop and practice your scholarly voice in its spoken form, ideally in dialogue with those in your session. How people perceive what you say will shape how they see you fitting into one or more conversations about learning and teaching.

Workshops

At higher education conferences, workshops often run for 45–90 mins in parallel with other sessions, such as paper presentations and discussion sessions, although three-hour workshops are not uncommon. Pre-conference workshops are sometimes built into the program of national and international conferences and are usually scheduled for a half or whole day. Sometimes keynote speakers also offer a workshop, where the ideas outlined in their talks can be explored and applied in greater depth with a smaller group. Workshops vary in size, with 10–50 delegates being common, though we have presented workshops with over a hundred participants. Facilitator styles vary widely, but the key characteristic of workshops is that they involve participants in active learning (Barrineau, Engström, and Schnaas 2019; Barr and Tagg 1995; Healey and Roberts 2004). A presenter giving a lecture and at the end simply inviting some questions does not in our view count as a workshop (nor is it good practice for paper presentations). For us, the quality of a workshop depends on the appropriateness and design of the activities and how they are linked to meet the objectives of the session.

Sometimes the whole of the workshop may be designed around an activity, such as a role-play exercise, or a series of activities, such as generating and sorting ideas, sharing practices in small groups, or discussing the application of materials provided by the workshop leader. In other cases, these activities may be interspersed with mini presentations by the facilitator. In these kinds of workshops, a clear structure with realistic timings is critical for the success of the session. Most will end with some action planning where delegates can reflect on the relevance and application of the ideas discussed to their own contexts. Some workshops are more fluid and begin with a negotiation with the participants on what aspects of the topic they want to discuss, perhaps with different groups focused on different aspects. Giving participants a choice in what they do helps avoid the usual practice that everyone does the same thing. Alice Cassidy (2018b) discusses different ways of involving participants, but many may be adapted from those recommended for use with students in class (Cassidy n.d.; Haynes et al. 2012; Strawson et al. 2012). You can also use workshops to invite feedback from participants to inform your scholarly thinking and writing.

Workshops afford you an opportunity to develop the pedagogical as well as scholarly aspect of your identity. One of the most exciting aspects of studying learning and teaching is that you can consider the relationship between content and process, and thinking intentionally about facilitation of a workshop, as a professional development opportunity for all involved, is part of that consideration (Torosyan and Cook-Sather 2018).

We provide below our Guiding Questions for presenting papers and workshops at learning and teaching conferences. A version you can add your answers to is available in the online resources.

Guiding Questions for Planning a Presentation at a Learning and Teaching Conference*

1. Who is your audience? How much prior knowledge will they have of your topic? How do you allow for members of the audience who come from different countries and cultures?

2. What equipment will you need? Communicate in advance with the conference organizers about computers, internet access, projectors, flipcharts, lapel or roving microphones, etc.

3. Do you need a set of PowerPoint slides? If they are needed, limit the number of words per slide and use images to stimulate thought. Avoid reading from the slides during your session.

4. How long do you have for your session? How will you split this between talking and activities? To ensure that the session is interactive, aim to have an activity at least every 15–20 minutes.

5. How will you structure your presentation? How will you grab the attention of the audience at the beginning? How will you maintain their interest during the presentation? What key message will you leave them with at the end? Consider telling stories to illustrate your talk, and think about your talk as a conversation you are having in a café. Ensure that your contribution and argument are clear to participants.

6. What activities will you include to engage participants with your topic? These can be individual as well as group activities.

7. Would it help your audience to have a copy of your slides or a handout in advance, or should you lay them out on chairs or hand them out at the door?

8. What is the physical layout of the room? Do you want, if possible, to move the chairs to encourage group discussions? Do you need to ask the participants to sit

next to some others, perhaps near the front, to encourage discussion?

9. How will you deal with the unexpected? It is best to practice the presentation out loud so that you can get the timings right and plan what you would cut, or add, if the unexpected occurs.

As with other sets of guiding questions in this book, select those questions that are relevant to your context, add others as appropriate, and decide the order in which you will address them to communicate effectively with your audience.

Poster Presentations

At scientific conferences, posters are numerically the most prevalent way of disseminating research findings, and it is not uncommon to have several hundred posters on display in the same session (Rowe and Ilic 2015). Although posters are not used to the same extent at learning and teaching conferences, they are an important way to communicate research findings and practices. Presenting a poster can be an effective way of planning to write a paper (Thomson 2019e). Presentation software allows you to create a poster as a single slide and export it into a format that can also easily be added to a website. You can print your poster on paper or cloth, depending on whether you wish to reuse it or are worried about the ease of transporting it (Cassidy 2018b). There are numerous websites that provide guidance on designing academic posters (e.g., Pennsylvania State University 2005). Karen Manarin (2016) provides an interesting discussion of undergraduates presenting their research using posters in an English literature class that can serve as a model for learning and teaching conferences. Nicholas Rowe (2017, 143) has a useful checklist:

1. Check the author instructions for size and format before you start. Use the biggest format they allow.
2. Title: Keep titles short, meaningful, and designed to attract attention.
3. Fonts: If you are unsure of your font sizes, print samples and view from different distances. Aim for a continuity of font style and application.

4. List authors as per author guidelines. Include titles, degrees etc. only if required.

5. List affiliations briefly. Consider an institutional logo, or even a QR code that links to an appropriate web page.

6. Follow the desired formatting of the event. Use your own sub-headings to signpost the work from beginning to end.

7. Start: State your problem or issue clearly. Outline the context, then state what the work sets out to do.

8. Keep all methodologies brief and to the point.

9. Use bullets, diagrams, and spacing to break up text. Give important points their own space. You can always provide further detail in your explanations, or in supplementary material or a short paper for delegates to take away.

10. Present only a summary of your main findings, or those that are most noteworthy. Present them clearly and use illustrations/diagrams where it helps clarify the point.

11. Show clearly what your findings mean and how they offer a solution (or not) to the problem you set out to solve.

12. Identify the next steps that need to be taken, or what your findings mean for current practice. Highlight what you have achieved through your research.

13. Offer supporting references only briefly—you can include more detail separately as supporting information.

14. Give your contact details on the poster. Include a QR code that links to your institutional or professional web page. Consider business cards of your poster or make sure you have a web address that is easily photographable near your title and author information.

The traditional poster design, at least in the sciences, has recently spawned a debate, stimulated by a video made by Mike Morrison (2019) in which he critiques most posters as being overly technical and not communicating their findings effectively (Greenfieldboyce 2019). Morrison proposes instead a template in which the main research finding is placed in plain English in large letters in the center of the poster, with a brief summary elsewhere. Others have suggested variations on this design (e.g., Faulkes 2019; Vande Pol 2019). The debate highlights the importance of communicating your take-home message effectively—a theme that runs throughout this book, whether it is in the title (chapter 9), the abstract (chapter 10), the text (chapter 24), or the conclusion (chapter 30).

There is also increasing use of digital poster presentations on interactive screens. Attendees can zoom in or out and swipe to view more of your slides—important for accessibility and useful to everyone. Participants may also be able to contact you, via the e-presentation system used, to engage in a conversation regarding your poster (Masters, Gibbs, and Sandars 2015).

Poster sessions vary in their formality. If you are presenting a poster at a small- or medium-sized conference, you will often just chat with anyone who is passing who appears interested in your poster. At a large conference, you may be faced with talking to several people at the same time, in which case having a prepared set of talking points may be useful.

A poster is like an intersection of an elevator speech and a visual representation. It also affords you an opportunity both to develop your presentational voice and to be in dialogue, since conference delegates often ask questions when they stop to look at posters.

Toward Learning Conferences

Most conferences appear to be designed more for the benefit of the presenter than of the delegates (Skelton 1997). This is, perhaps, not surprising given that having an accepted presentation is often a requirement for obtaining the financial support to attend. However, it is somewhat ironic that most of our time at learning and teaching

conferences is spent listening to presentations even though we—
as educational developers—know the many benefits of active
involvement of participants for learning and use these active strategies
with our students (Cassidy n.d.; Gibbs 1988). The argument for active
learning is, if anything, stronger for adult learners (Knowles 1970).
This tension between what educators preach and what they practice
has not gone unnoticed (Elton 1983; Haley, Wiessner, and Robinson
2009; Kordts-Freudinger, Al-Kabbani, and Schaper 2017), and several
authors have discussed the characteristics of "learning conferences"
(Louw and Zuber-Skerritt 2011; Ravn 2007; Ravn and Elsborg 2007)
and how to promote learning at learning and teaching conferences
(Popovic and Cassidy 2018; Campbell and Popovic 2018).

Some learning and teaching conferences have moved in the direction of being more interactive and include audience engagement in
their selection criteria (not applicable for posters, but essential for
workshops). For example, ISSOTL specifies these requirements for
conference proposals:

- Planned opportunities for active audience engage-
  ment in the session are described
- Opportunities for audience participation in the
  discussion are included
- Effective pedagogical practices are demonstrated.
  (ISSOTL 2020)

These examples are elaborated in the full ISSOTL conference
pedagogy statement (Chick et al. 2017), and Jennifer Meta Robinson
(2018) offers an illuminating reflection on the experience of organizing and participating at SoTL conferences.

Presenting is an opportunity to facilitate a conversation in real
time and allows scholars to learn with others. At the end of your
presentation, rather than asking if anyone has any questions, come up
with some questions to ask the audience—this can create a focused
discussion that informs their thinking. Or better yet, generate discussion throughout your presentation by pausing to ask participants to

answer questions. This is common practice in workshops and could easily be integrated into paper presentations and keynotes.

Over to You

Whether you appreciate conferences or would rather steer clear of them, there is no avoiding that they are an important facet of academic life (Thomson 2017b). If you are a discipline-based scholar interested in learning and teaching, you may have to choose between participating in a disciplinary conference or a learning and teaching one, though many larger disciplinary conferences have learning and teaching strands within them. If your disciplinary conference does not, you might consider offering to convene such a strand yourself. As a scholar of learning and teaching, you may want to consider not only how you can best benefit from the experience of participating in a conference but also how you can best help make it a learning experience for others. Questions to address about conference and workshop presentations include:

- Do you have a scholarly contribution that you would like to present at a conference or in a workshop to share findings, obtain input, or both?
- Which conferences attract the kind of participants who would be interested in your topic and with whom you want to be in conversation?
- How can you best show that you meet the proposal criteria for the conference and presentation format in which you are interested, and how does that format contribute to the development of your voice and identity as a scholar of learning and teaching?
- How can you make your conference or workshop presentation lively and interesting and, where possible, engage participants actively such that you further everyone's learning?
- If you are organizing a learning and teaching conference, how might you structure it to making it primarily a learning event?

CHAPTER 18

REVEALING THE PROCESS

Reflective Essays

Reflection, like language itself, is social as well as individual. Through reflection, we tell our stories of learning. (Yancey, 1998, 53)

We believe that the time has come both to legitimate critical reflection as a form of scholarly writing about teaching and learning, and also to make all SoTL writing more explicitly reflective—making space for the conditional and the human aspects of our inquiries and our partnerships. (Cook-Sather, Abbot, and Felten 2019, 23)

Have you had an experience of learning or teaching that you want to examine for how it has informed your own thinking or practice? Do you want to write for readers in an informal and personal way without necessarily having to situate your experience and what you learned from it in published research? Might you want to use your writing not only to capture what you already understand about the experience but also to learn further? If you answered "yes" to any or all of these questions, you may want to consider writing a reflective essay for publication. If you want to tell a story of your learning, as Kathleen Blake Yancey suggests reflection allows, you can join the growing number of people helping to legitimate this genre of writing, as Alison and her colleagues, Sophia Abbot and Peter Felten, suggest it is time to do. We use the term "reflective essay" to refer to a particular genre—a personal, contemplative, critical analysis based on lived experience but not necessarily grounded in your own data or others' research. We are not referring to expository essays or "disciplined provocations" (Academy of Management Learning & Education Editorial Team 2018, 397) but rather to a form of essay writing that allows both authors and readers to explore more freely.

Such explorations can both reveal and further learning. As Jenny Moon (2013, 80) puts it: "We reflect in order to learn something, or we learn as a result of reflecting." Her emphasis on the educative power of reflection echoes that of John Dewey (1933, 6), who framed reflection in learning as an intellectual undertaking characterized by "active, persistent, and careful consideration of any belief or supposed form of knowledge in the light of the grounds that support it and the further conclusions to which it tends." David Boud, Rosemary Keogh, and David Walker (1985) introduced emotion into this intellectual process, suggesting that reflection entails not only returning to an experience for the purposes of evaluation but also attending to or connecting with feelings associated with that experience. Tacking between experience and interpretation, or what Donald Schön (1987) called "reflection-in-action," is demanding intellectual and emotional work. It includes analyzing "prior understandings which have been implicit" (Schön 1987, 68) and making them explicit such that they can more intentionally inform future action. These iterative processes are messy and unpredictable, and the results are not provable in any scientific sense. While learning theory tells us that such processes are the heart of learning (Illeris 2018), writing about them rarely finds a place in traditional forms of scholarship. That's where reflective essays come in as a particular form of meaning making.

A growing number of scholars are arguing that "much academic discourse limits practitioners' and readers' opportunities to engage in the very critical reflection and knowledge construction that are, ostensibly, the desired outcomes of a rigorous approach" (Cook-Sather, Abbot, and Felten 2019, 16; see also Sword 2009). Such arguments contend that traditional forms and conventions of scholarship are neither broad nor inclusive enough to represent the complexity and nuance of the scholarship of teaching and learning (SoTL) (Bernstein and Bass 2005; McKinney 2007) and prevent us from seeing learning and teaching from a wide range of perspectives (Manarin 2017). We see very different sides of learning and teaching if we bring emotion and identity more centrally into our writing (Sword 2017a) and make space for analyses of "who we are and how we got to be this way" (Gravett and Bernhagen 2018, 2). In her work to "re-theorize Donald Schön's theory of reflection for use in the writing class-room," Kathleen Blake Yancey (1998, vi) argues for thinking about how we might "use reflection as a mode of helping students develop as writers." Building on this re-theorizing, we argue that reflective essays invite all authors, not only students in writing classrooms, to share the messy, unfinished, personal work of living and to critically analyze learning and teaching as those authors experience that work.

In this chapter we discuss what the reflective genre can accomplish, spell out what to strive for and what to avoid in writing a reflective essay, offer recommendations and a framework of guiding questions for planning, revising, and refining a reflective essay for publication, and note where to find examples of reflective essays.

What Can the Reflective Genre Accomplish?

While traditional scholarly writing requires that authors focus on crafting original, logical arguments substantiated or proven by bodies of data and situated within the literature, reflective writing makes space for idiosyncratic, still emerging, or intellectually and emotionally vulnerable presentations not generally welcome in traditional scholarly writing (Sword 2009). As one faculty scholar wrote:

> The informal nature of the reflective genre of writing lowers the bar for participation in sharing ideas, with the result of increasing the number of participants whose experiences are shared. As a scientist by training, I had no time, education, or inclination to prepare a rigorous academic treatise on my experiences in the classroom; but the reflective genre allowed me to share the experiences and ideas . . . with a wide academic audience

who may benefit from these insights. (Quoted in Cook-Sather, Abbot, and Felten 2019, 20).

Equally important, reflective writing can contribute to efforts to combat systems and practices of domination (hooks 2003) because, according to one student author, it gives "marginalized students more of a voice" and "helps us realize that our voices matter, our stories matter, we matter" (student author quoted in Cook-Sather, Abbot, and Felten 2019, 23).

Reflective writing can also be more accessible to readers. As a student scholar argued, "[It] has the unique power to draw readers in, regardless of their positionality or experiences, because it allows the reader to imagine herself or himself in the shoes of the writer" (quoted in Cook-Sather, Abbot, and Felten 2019, 22). Such accessibility is particularly important for student readers if we want to "take students seriously as an audience" for SoTL (McKinney 2012b, 4) or any published writing about learning and teaching.

What Should You Strive for and What Should You Avoid?

Reflective essays are written as informal, first-person accounts; they show, as opposed to tell, through offering vivid, detailed examples instead of simply stating that something happened. They offer analysis of lived experience that illuminates the day-to-day practicalities of the work and insights gained into the potential of such work in higher education. Such analyses might include offering explanations and interpretations (not assuming examples speak for themselves); making assumptions explicit; clearly articulating insights and conclusions; and making connections across points. Finally, because they focus on lived experience, reflective essays include a small number of citations of existing literature, rather than the extensive number expected in some other genres.

Reflective essays present analyses of lessons derived from experience and explain how those lessons have affected you. They include personal statements that reveal uncertainty, complexity, and challenge as well as new understanding and excitement. Candid acknowledgments of the messiness of the work upon which authors reflect can model brave, engaged, responsive practice in learning and teaching in higher education; they can assure academics, staff, and students alike that their "experiences, sometimes doubt or difficulties, are communal and not just individual hurdles" (student author quoted in Cook-Sather, Abbot, and Felten 2019, 21).

Given reflective writing's emphasis on personal experience and emotional as well as intellectual insight, you should **avoid**:

- Writing in a distanced (third-person, "objective") voice about your own or others' work
- Focusing too much on subject matter or research outcomes and not enough on *experiences*, both positive and negative
- Describing what happened rather than conveying what those experiences felt like
- Including extensive references to theoretical frameworks and other scholarship rather than digging into your own partially formed, messy, contradictory perspectives
- Presenting content-based outcomes and implications rather than the details of exploring, experimenting, and struggling through the process necessary to achieve them.

How Might You Go about Writing a Reflective Essay?

Writing a reflective essay requires a mindset and style that differ from much other scholarly writing. It is premised on your being willing to take a hard look at your own assumptions and experiences. Taking such a hard look means wrestling with the ways of thinking and being you might take for granted and that are challenged when you begin to analyze them. It also means acknowledging conflicts and even contradictions when you consciously and intentionally identify and examine your thoughts and experiences. Reflective writing can, therefore, "be a means of becoming clearer about something" (Moon 2006, 2).

One of the greatest challenges of reflective writing is finding language to name all of these things that are not typically addressed in forms of writing privileged in Western academic contexts. Reflective essays afford authors a space to share publicly what they have experienced and discovered. They need not be confessional or overly vulnerable making, but they do require a certain amount of bravery since, depending on one's discipline, revealing any uncertainty can be dangerous. For this reason, some scholars choose to publish their essays anonymously (Anonymous 2014). This point links to our discussion in chapter 4 about developing an identity or identities as a writer.

In contrast to empirical research articles, reflective essays neither marshal evidence to prove something nor strive to convince anyone of anything in particular. Instead, they aim to offer readers glimpses of the messy, unfinished, personal work of learning and teaching—the lived experience and the sense people make of it—so the argument is more an assertion of what is worthy of attention. Reflective essays may or may not draw on data, although they certainly draw on lived experiences, and they aim to make an argument in the sense of enacting a process of interpretation of that experience and reasoning regarding its importance. The reasoning is of an affective as well as analytical kind—a coherent explanation and declaration more than a contention or defence.

Because the reflective essay genre is unfamiliar to many authors, it can be helpful to draw on guidelines for how to approach it. In "A Short Guide to Reflective Writing" the University of Birmingham (2015) defines what reflective writing is and why it is important, offers a model of reflection, and provides short examples of reflective writing. Similarly, Monash University (n.d.) offers a resource called "Reflective Writing in Education" in which they discuss the purpose and structure of reflective writing in education and offer several illustrative examples. Using guides such as these and the framework we offer below can support you in moving your writing through multiple revisions in order to find words to name those qualities of experience and insights that are typically not given voice in publications—experiences of struggle, uncertainty, and risk-taking, and insights that are idiosyncratic, still emerging, or intellectually and emotionally vulnerable.

Below we offer a set of guiding questions for planning, revising, and refining a reflective essay for publication annotated with further explanation and examples. A copy of the framework with just the questions is available in the online resources.

Guiding Questions for Planning, Revising, and Refining a Reflective Essay*

1. **What situation, scenario, or event are you reflecting upon?**

   Give readers a sense of the focus of your essay. What set of circumstances, precipitating event or ongoing process, or catalyst for exploration and analysis prompted you to write the essay? Consider opening with some sort of vivid image or intriguing statement, such as:

   > "I don't know anything about chemistry," I thought, as I read an email informing me that my first placement as a student consultant with the Students as Learners and Teachers (SaLT) program would be in an organic chemistry lab. I was a political science major. What could possibly qualify me to work with a STEM professor? (Daviduke 2018, 151)

2. **Who is doing the reflection and what are their roles in the situation, scenario, or event?**

   Identify authors up front, giving as much detail as is appropriate and necessary for readers to understand the position and perspective from which they are writing. Does the piece have a single author? What role did that person play? Does it have multiple authors? Do they write in one voice or multiple voices? For example, one reflective essay opens with this explanation by two academic and two student authors:

   > The following is our collective attempt—staff- and student-centric, both in terms of outcomes and reporting—to unpack the complexities of our collaborative endeavour in 2017. We juxtapose our respective experiences of navigating the "normative hierarchical

university paradigm" (Mercer-Mapstone et al. 2017a, 18) to present a more collaborative and balanced discussion of our partnership. (MacFarlane et al. 2018, 144)

3. What is the broad teaching and learning context of your reflection?

Give a sense of the kind of institution, geographical location, cultural norms, etc. within which you are writing. For instance:

> At the time of this project, I (Tanya) was working at the Edinburgh University Students' Association, supporting student representation, and I (Hermina) was a first-year student representative from the School of Health in Social Science. It was through a University of Edinburgh Innovative Initiative Grant project related to Tanya's PhD research (focusing on co-creation of the curriculum) that we began to work together closely. (Lubicz-Nawrocka and Simoni 2018, 157)

4. What prompted your reflection on this topic or situation?

It is helpful to readers to know why you were inspired to write the reflective essay. For instance, Liz Dunne, Derfel Owen, Hannah Barr, Will Page, James Smith, and Sabina Szydlo (2014) wanted to reveal the behind-the-scenes process that led to the establishment of an institutional initiative that became an international inspiration and to tell the story through the voices of those who might not otherwise have been heard:

> "Students as Change Agents" at the University of Exeter is an initiative that has become extremely successful, impacts strongly on the way that students are listened to and work in partnership at the University, and is beginning to influence ideas and practices nationally and internationally. Perhaps as with many such initiatives, the story of this success has been dependent on the commitment of individuals who have believed in

its philosophy and values and who have contributed to making it work.

This piece outlines the development and growth of Students as Change Agents from the perspectives of six key players. It highlights some of the "back story," the times before the initiative was successful, the long journey and the voices of some of the people who have supported this development, from the first seeds of an idea to a major institutional initiative. (Dunne et al. 2014, 1)

5. **How did you structure your approach to reflection?**
Sharing the details of your approach can help make visible the context within which and the process through which you developed your reflection. These need not take the form of methodological defences; rather, they model approaches to reflection. For instance:

We decided to draft individual written reflections of our experiences co-facilitating . . . guided by two questions:

1.   In your opinion, what worked in our co-facilitation process and approach? Why did it work?
2.   In your opinion, what did not work in our co-facilitation process and approach? Why did it not work and what should we have done differently?

We shared and read these written reflections and then met to "reflect on our reflections.". . . We discussed how they resonated as a group, and what seemed worth elaborating on. . . . Ultimately, we continued to come back to prominent threads across our reflections that resonated with us all: idealism and conflict, and labels and leadership. (Mercer-Mapstone et al. 2017b, 2)

6. **How can you convey to readers the particulars of your experience rather than assume familiarity with or understanding of how the experience unfolded?**

Be sure to show rather than tell—to create vivid scenarios and analyses that reveal rather than just describe what you learned, such as:

> I was sitting with people who have been involved in this area of practice for a long time, reminding us where things had started. At the same table, a student shared her own understandings of partnership based on her own very recent experiences. The conversations, sometimes characterized by conflict and at other times by consensus, reminded me of the importance of individual experience and the need to collectively develop understandings of what partnership means to a particular group of people, within a particular setting, at a particular time. (Brost et al. 2018, 134)

7. **What did you learn from the reflection that others can benefit from reading about?**

Every reflective essay will have different lessons to share, and it is helpful at some point in the essay to make explicit what you learned and what you are sharing with readers. For instance, a student author writes at the opening of his essay:

> Through my time working with my faculty partner, I learned pedagogical tools, discovered new ways to enhance my own learning, and formed a friendship. In this essay I share a number of the pedagogical issues my faculty partner and I explored and how these explorations transformed my own learning. (Wynkoop 2018, 1)

As with other sets of guiding questions in this book, select those questions that are relevant to your context, add others as appropriate, and decide the order in which you will address them to communicate effectively with your audience. The questions are based on those in Healey, Matthews, and Cook-Sather (2019, 37).

Where to Find Examples of Reflective Essays

The genre of reflective essay is designated as such in two journals—*International Journal for Students as Partners (IJSaP)* and *Teaching and Learning Together in Higher Education (TLTHE)*—and other journals include reflective writing but may not name it as such. For *IJSaP*, authors have written reflective essays that "zoom in" on different moments and lived experiences of partnership (Brost et al. 2018); detail the launching and development of student-faculty pedagogical partnership programs (Goldsmith et al. 2017); and unpack the complexities of a collaborative undertaking (Macfarlane et al. 2018). With some exceptions for guest-edited issues, *TLTHE* is devoted almost entirely to reflective essays. Guest-edited issues often focus on themes, such as "Growing Deep Learning," an issue edited by Ken Bain (2013), and "Crossing Thresholds Together," an issue edited by Peter Felten (2013). They might also present the work of faculty, staff, and students in a particular institution or geographical location, such as Italy (Frison and Melacarne 2017) and Australia (Matthews 2017). The reflective essays in *TLTHE* aim to offer windows onto the development of pedagogical insights that academics and students gain when they collaborate on explorations of classroom practice and systematically reflect on that collaboration. Some of the ideas discussed in this chapter may also help you write applications for fellowships and teaching awards where the criteria emphasize evidence of reflective practice (see chapter 22).

Over to You

Reflective essays combine stories of lived experiences with critical analysis of those experiences to produce accessible representations of learning and teaching. They invite you to share more personal stories of who you are as a learner and teacher, and they allow you to develop a voice for naming the emotions as well as the insights generated through learning and teaching. Questions to ask about writing reflective essays include:

- What experience of learning or teaching might you examine for how it has informed your own thinking or practice?
- What aspects of your experience of learning or teaching might best be conveyed through first-person, informal narrative and analysis?
- How can you engage in, as well as model, learning through writing in this genre?

CHAPTER 19

PROVOKING THOUGHT

Opinion Pieces

I want my scholarship to have a public purpose. . . . Whereas academic writing takes months, years, even decades to publish, editorials and thought pieces can have an immediate impact. (Sara Warner, quoted in Kelley 2016)

Moving from silence into speech is for the oppressed, the colonized, the exploited, and those who stand and struggle side by side a gesture of defiance that heals, that makes new life and new growth possible. (hooks 1989, 9)

To be a scholar is to create and share new knowledge. Indisputably, we value discipline-based, empirical research as knowledge creation in the academy (Boyer 1990), and we typically focus on reporting research results when we publish that work. As we become scholars of learning and teaching, however, what we *think* and *believe* also matters, as does who we are and where our voices are and are not heard, because we are engaged as human beings in the lifelong work of learning. Aside from, and in addition to, any research we might conduct, we have experiences, formulate judgements, and take stands informed by values, perspectives, and experiences that shape and are shaped by our identities and our practices. Usually we limit the sharing of these value judgements to informal corridor conversations with peers. We know from research that these conversations are powerful exchanges that can shape our practices (Biesta, Priestley, and Robinson 2017; Roxå and Mårtensson 2015), yet we rarely translate these informed opinions into formal publications. As Sara Warner notes in the quote at the beginning of this chapter, editorials and thought pieces—sometimes called op eds in news outlets and what we are calling opinion pieces—can have an immediate impact, and using one's voice, as bell hooks suggests, especially for those who have been oppressed and exploited, can be at once defiant and healing—an integral part of education as "the practice of freedom" (hooks 1994).

The genre of opinion pieces allows us to assert a value judgement about learning and teaching based on considered experience and informed perspective. The genre privileges subjectivity, as the intention is to share informed perspectives that make no claim of objectivity. The genre also privileges the author—someone using "I"—who is central to an opinion piece as someone with expertise, experience, or a unique standpoint. Indeed, the voice in which we express our thoughts and beliefs is part of the message, differs from others' voices, and takes courage, creativity, and conviction to develop (Robbins 2016; Sword 2009). In this sense, and compared to traditional research articles, the opinion piece genre recognizes different ways of knowing and expressing knowledge that can more readily enable a diversity of voices, especially those that have been underrepresented, to join the scholarly conversation about learning and teaching.

Our metaphor of writing as *contributing to and creating conversation* is easily applied to this genre. An opinion piece invites you to use your own voice, acknowledge your position and context, draw explicitly on your experience, and write in a conversational tone to share stories of practices linked to value judgments informed by knowledge and subjective experiences. However, writing an opinion piece involves more than stating ideas, claims, or critiques. We communicate *what* we think and believe—our opinion—along with *why* we think it, in order to persuade and provoke readers in ways that require us to be both passionate and analytical.

In this chapter, we discuss what the opinion piece genre can accomplish, and we explore qualities of effective opinion pieces that are published in academic outlets or online media platforms. We also present a framework to guide you in writing an opinion piece with examples drawn from published opinion pieces, and we conclude with reference to some examples.

What Can the Opinion Piece Genre Accomplish?

The work of an opinion piece complements other genres that privilege objectivity and primary research. Expressing an opinion clearly and persuasively can "sway hearts" and "change minds" (Duke University n.d.). Opinion pieces "give people more opportunity to develop their arguments" (Wood 2017) and reach a broader readership, particularly when they are printed in open access journals, news outlets, or blogs. The genre of opinion pieces can accomplish many things, as signaled in Our Perspectives 19.1.

Our Perspectives 19.1

What the genre of opinion pieces has offered us

Alison: I have appreciated the opportunity that opinion pieces afford to blend critical insights based on lived experience with consideration of the wider import of those insights and experiences. An opinion piece (Cook-Sather and Porte 2017) I co-authored with a student from a group underrepresented in higher education, for instance, allowed us to articulate the importance to both of us, from different angles, of clarifying the way particular participants and processes in higher education get named (in this case "hard-to-reach" students). Through writing this piece, we clarified our own perspectives and commitments and contributed to ongoing interrogation of the terms we use and the effects they have, particularly on those marginalized and harmed by the academy.

Mick: I enjoy reading provocative, well-written opinion pieces, though I have limited experience of writing them. Several years ago, I wrote an article for the *Times Higher* in which I expressed the opinion that "disability legislation may prove to be a Trojan horse, and in a decade, the learning experiences of all students may be the subject of greater negotiation" (Healey 2003a, 26). It attracted quite a bit of attention at the time, though the prediction proved to be hopelessly over-optimistic!

Kelly: I had not considered writing an opinion piece until someone invited me to do so (Matthews 2016). After initial concern, I gave myself permission to embrace drawing on my experience and owning my voice. Bringing literature and experience together to take a stance in a short, focused piece of writing was powerful for me. Because of the short length and clear focus, people regularly talk to me about that work. I get the sense that it has had more reach than most of my research articles. It is challenging to write a short piece, and I always think of the expression: I didn't have time to make it short.

Your perspective: What has the genre of opinion pieces offered you, or what might it?

Sara Warner's point, quoted at the opening of this chapter, about the immediate impact of editorials and op eds signals the potential of opinion pieces to reach more people and speaks to a growing movement for scholars within the academy to reach into the public sphere. Penning an opinion piece about learning and teaching, whether in an academic journal, a news outlet (e.g., *The Guardian, New York Times, The Conversation,* the *Times Higher Education* magazine, *The Chronicle, SRHE News Blog,* and other learned society newsletters), or a blog (e.g., *Inside Higher Education* blogs), gives you the potential for a larger readership. In short, opinion pieces can engage the broader public in ways that traditional academic publications rarely do (Leigh 2008).

Opinion pieces invite writers to appreciate that what they think matters, and then share their views publicly, which might feel uncomfortable; publicly sharing a value judgement might seem to require a high level of expertise and standing in the academic community. Yet, the voices of scholars, including undergraduate students, with unique standpoints can enrich the learning and teaching practices that unfold in increasingly diverse classrooms and university communities. Reflection 19.1 describes how Alexander Dwyer, as a then-undergraduate scholar, had to navigate insecurities and identify his unique perspective to write an opinion piece for publication in an academic journal.

Reflection 19.1

The experience of writing an opinion piece

Working on an opinion piece (Dwyer 2018) gave me a degree of intellectual and creative freedom. It enabled me to explore some of the more abstract ideas I was thinking about based on a research project I was involved in that explored how students are engaged in higher education. But it also allowed me to draw on my experiences, observations, and frustrations (emotional reactions). I was motivated to write an opinion piece because I felt like I had something to say. However, I did wonder if I was credible enough to have an opinion and this did impede my initial writing process. But I was able to move beyond this by focusing instead on asking myself what was unique about my perspective. As a student who was working in a different way with academics, I observed some of the social and professional interactions that are like the "backstage" of higher education that most students don't get to see. I identified my unique perspective. In addition, thinking about my work as (in a small way) giving a voice to students who are underrepresented in academic publications helped me see the work as fundamentally valuable. This helped me move beyond my feelings of self-doubt and the belief that I lacked credibility and power to speak about the institution.

Alexander Dwyer was an undergraduate student at The University of Queensland, Australia, at the time he wrote this opinion piece.

What Should You Strive for and What Should You Avoid?

Opinion pieces are short, focused works that put forward an informed judgment related to learning and teaching practices, policies, or research agendas. "Provocative" and "relevant" are common adjectives used to describe opinion pieces, which are often intended to provoke thinking and change or advance the current learning and teaching conversation. Thus, they might illuminate a need, contradiction, opportunity, inequity, or new way to think about learning and teaching. They can also draw attention to existing practices that would benefit from recognition, acknowledgment, and expansion. Sometimes, opinion pieces are a way of suggesting a future research agenda or a theme for a conference session. No matter the topic, opinion pieces help define your identity as a learning and teaching scholar because they require you to embrace your voice, share your standpoint, and assert a value judgment.

Opinion pieces tend to adopt a persuasive writing style that draws on considered analysis of the topic. A strong opinion piece communicates *what* you think—your opinion—and *why* you think it explicitly connected to *who* you are. In communicating all of these, you can own your stance by using "I" and adopting a conversational tone with readers. The platform for publishing your opinion piece will inform the style and tone you adopt. In an academic journal, you might strive to connect your opinion to other academic literature. In contrast, you might avoid referring to academic outputs that are not open access if you publish your piece through the media, instead drawing on conversations in public forums.

Academic Focus

Opinion pieces for academic journals usually range from 1,500–3,000 words depending on the outlet. They might also be called editorials (often written by journal editors or invited by editors, although not all editorials are opinion pieces), points for debate, or opinion essays. However, not all learning and teaching journals will publish opinion pieces, so if you do not see the genre listed as a submission type for a given journal, consider contacting the editor to inquire.

As an example, the journal we co-edit, the *International Journal for Students as Partners (IJSaP)*, publishes opinion pieces that are "short and thought-provoking pieces, stating a position and supported by a persuasive argument." The criteria for review are:

- Addresses a current issue or debate related to partnership in teaching and learning
- Advances interesting, innovative, provocative, and/or critical ideas about partnership
- The argument should be supported where appropriate by academic literature, experience, and/or evidence.

(*International Journal for Students as Partners*, "Submissions")

You will want to consult journal guidelines about their specific requirements because many editors have a sense of the topics they prefer for opinion pieces, or they might not accept this genre. Furthermore, the genre can overlap with case studies and reflective essays (see chapters 15 and 18), so you might also want to communicate with the editor about the ideal genre for your work. For example, if you find you are describing your practice in detail to support your opinion, then a case study might be a better option. In short, the lines between genres are variable, so communicating with editors makes sense before writing or submitting your work.

Public Focus

When writing for media outlets or through blogs, you are likely to have tighter word limits. Like journals, other outlets will have guidelines to follow. Many universities offer guidance on writing for a public audience, including opinions for news outlets. For example, tips from Carleton College (2016), Duke University (n.d.), and Association for American Colleges and Universities (Mintz 2019) offer overlapping advice that is summarized below.

- Make a single point
- Aim for 600–800 words, but always check with the outlet as word lengths vary
- Communicate your single point at the beginning of the piece
- Tell your readers why they should care about the topic
- Give examples and be specific
- Embrace your personal voice
- Use the active voice

- Have a call to action
- Relax and have fun

How Might You Go about Writing an Opinion Piece?

Like composing a reflective essay, writing an opinion piece requires a mindset and approach that differ from what might be required to write in other genres. Rather than reporting results or describing your rigorous research design, opinion pieces ask you to consider your standpoint, draw on your experience, and assert a value judgment. Like reflective essays, they allow you to present your reflections, but an opinion piece is persuasive, as you explain your rationale or the thinking that shaped your stance. For Ronald Barnett (personal communication, July 28, 2019), writing an opinion piece means

> leaping into a different mindset. Adjectives such as pithy, bold, forthright, clear, authoritative, and confident should be the order of the day. Eschew nuance, qualifications (a & b produced c & d & e but then f & g & h). Brevity is key: short phrases, short sentences, short paragraphs. Even terseness. One is trying to be attractive and translucently clear to busy readers who are not academics.

Once in the mindset, a helpful way to understand the elements of an opinion piece is to draw on our Guiding Questions below, which include examples drawn from a selection of opinion pieces. In our online resources, you can access a version with just the questions to easily use yourself. We suggest you answer each relevant question and then order them to give you a structure. With this framework in mind, review some of the examples we present below to identify the different ways writers go about writing an opinion piece.

Guiding Questions for Planning, Revising, and Refining an Opinion Piece*

1. **What is the broad topic you are writing about?**
   Give readers a sense of the focus of your opinion piece. What is the area or topic you will discuss? What was the impetus for

exploration and analysis that led you to write the piece? You can be as straightforward as:

> I'm a researcher who focuses on raising disability awareness in educational settings. (Bialka 2018)

2. **What is your opinion or stance on the topic?**
Before moving into arguments, be explicit about your stance. State it succinctly and ensure it is clear in your title, as the example below demonstrates:

> What Straight-A Students Get Wrong

> If you always succeed in school, you're not setting yourself up for success in life. (Grant 2018)

3. **Why are you writing this opinion piece?**
Be sure to tell readers who you are and how who you are shapes the piece. Arguing for representation and equity, eight students from the University of Toronto's Scarborough campus show how this can be done:

> We come from a diverse range of racialized or gendered identities and abilities. We have all directly been impacted by or witnessed the damaging effects of colonialism and Western hegemony. As such, we hold a heightened sense of urgency to dismantle broader power structures in society, be they related to race, gender, age, sex, experience, or anything else in between. (Bindra et al. 2018, 10)

4. **Who is your intended audience? Who are you writing it for, specifically?**
You might have multiple different kinds of readers within the broader arena of higher education, and naming them is productive. In his piece on straight-A students, Adam Grant explicitly speaks to this group of students:

> If your goal is to graduate without a blemish on your transcript, you end up taking easier classes and staying within your comfort zone. (Grant 2018)

5. **How did you come to form this opinion? What literature or experiences are you drawing on to support your opinions?**

   Related to who you are, give readers a sense of how you came to your current stance, as such:

   > My argument arises from my identity as an undergraduate student studying anthropology, my experience as a student partner over the past two years, and a synthesis of my thinking following research projects exploring conceptions of SaP [students as partners] from students and staff in partnership and institutional leaders responsible for implementing the partnership. (Dwyer 2018, 11)

6. **What examples will you use to illustrate the argument for your opinion?**

   Examples bring experiences to life and can give readers a strong understanding of your argument and stance. You can draw on an example from research, or tell the story of your own or someone else's lived experience. A story of exclusion of one person can be powerful, as presented here:

   > AnnCatherine Heigl, a sophomore at George Mason University, recently attempted to join all eight sororities at her school. All eight turned her down.

   > The reason the sororities denied AnnCatherine is because she has a disability: Down syndrome. (Bialka 2018)

7. **How might your opinion make a difference for others—in practical application or in terms of policy?**

   Identify what actions might arise from your opinion piece; this is your call to action for the scholarly learning and teaching community. Rajani Naidoo does this in her piece on equality in higher education systems:

> What options do we have to remedy this situation? First, we could try to stop policy-makers focusing on world-class universities as if these exist in a vacuum. Second, we could redirect the focus through our own research and policy advocacy to develop strategies on how national and global systems of higher education could potentially interact to reduce inequality.
>
> Third, we need to avoid dichotomising access, quality education and research excellence. It is very important to avoid seeing these as necessary trade-offs, but to find ways to link these in a positive sum manner. (Naidoo 2018)

As with other frameworks in this book, select those questions that are relevant to your context, add others as appropriate, and decide the order in which you will address them to communicate effectively with your audience. The questions are based on those in Healey, Matthews, and Cook-Sather (2019, 39).

Over to You

Opinion pieces occupy an important niche within publishing, and they achieve different goals from other publication genres. Particularly in writing about learning and teaching, which is practice based and always entangled with our subjective realities, opinion pieces offer you a powerful opportunity to deepen, expand, affirm, change, connect, and complicate scholarly conversations in ways that research articles, case studies, and reflective essays often cannot. Questions to ask about writing opinion pieces include:

- What have you formed a value judgement about that can enrich ongoing conversations in the learning and teaching community?
- How will you draw on your lived experiences, evidence, or research to illustrate your stance?
- Where will you share your opinion piece and in what ways will that choice of venue influence how you write it?

CHAPTER 20

SHARING EVERYDAY LIVED EXPERIENCES

Stories

Stories are everywhere. We hear them, we read them, we write them and we tell them. Perhaps on occasions we feel them. We use them to motivate others, to convey information and to share experience. (McDrury and Alterio 2003, 7)

Stories speak. Stories imagine. Stories bring worlds into being, making up the fabric that is stitched together by the symbolic and the material, coloring possibilities with our desires, and inviting us as participants in the work of co-creating futures. (Dutta 2018, 94)

Stories are a way for people to share their experiences and to pass on history from one generation to the next. They are everywhere, as Janice McDrury and Maxine Alterio suggest, and they both capture what already exists and bring worlds into being, as Mohan Dutta argues. In Spanish, the word "history" translates literally to the word "story" in English. Storytelling underpins community in many Indigenous and First Nations cultures as a form of knowledge creation and knowledge sharing that both precedes—as Yahlnaaw points out in Reflection 11.1—and disrupts Western knowledge conventions (Sium and Ritskes 2013). In our daily lives, most of us share stories with our friends, peers, and colleagues as a way of connecting with them. Stories are more than an exchange of facts and events; they convey the complexities of our lives, including emotions and aspirations. Yet, stories in this sense are often thought of as oral. Stories are also written.

For Gerardo Patriotta (2016, 557), written stories "are arguably the most subtle tool of ontological inquiry, insightful meditations on how individuals, faced with questions and enigmas related to human existence, make sense of their 'being in the world' (Heidegger 1962)."

In other words, stories capture how we *become* and *are being* in the world. Stories connect people, and communities grow around shared stories and sharing stories together, whether written or oral. While stories are a common way that we share what is happening in our learning and teaching and communicate our lived experiences and realities, stories are not a common genre for publication in academia; they are typically not considered research in the dominant Western tradition of research, even though many scholars would argue that good research "tells a story." However, a lot of written research is dull and difficult to connect with—the stories do not come to life. So think about the readers of your research and try to capture them, as good stories do, with a compelling narrative flow. Stories create space for imagination and even embellishment.

For these reasons and because we want to draw attention to academia's often exclusive practice, we include stories as a genre for writing about learning and teaching. In doing so, we acknowledge that stories overlap with other writing genres. For example, it is common to weave stories into reflective essays or refer to essays as stories (Cook-Sather 2019), to draw on stories as data for research articles that might use a narrative inquiry method, to include stories in teaching award or fellowship applications, and to evoke stories to support judgments posed in opinion pieces. This integration of stories across genres provides further evidence of the messy overlaps among the writing genres we explore in this book. However, stories are also distinct as a genre and can stand alone as a genre for writing about learning and teaching.

Unlike presenting and analyzing data (chapter 12), exploring theories and concepts (chapter 13), and formulating new insights from literature (chapter 14), storytelling enables us to speak from lived experiences, our own and others', while sharing the details of the context and people involved, so that readers can learn with us and from us. A written story paints a rich picture of practice and experience in a specific place and time and can reveal a process of becoming (Cook-Sather 2019; Dutta 2018; Patriotta 2016).

In this chapter, we offer a flexible guide for organizing and writing stories about learning and teaching. Our focus is on stories that are stand-alone, while we acknowledge that stories can be included in other genres. We begin by discussing what stories, as a genre, offer learning and teaching scholars.

The Work of Storytelling as a Genre for Learning and Teaching

Unlike most of the genres we discuss, the genre of stories needs explanation and a rationale because it is not a commonly published form of writing about learning and teaching. For Elizabeth Quintero (2018, vii), stories have a clear connection to education:

> We do learn from each other's experiences. We learn from children. We learn from colleagues we have yet to meet. [Through stories] the webs of connection among academic research, pedagogy and influence open the possibility for new methodologies, new positionality and new theorizing that are inclusive rather than exclusive.

Understanding the human experience of being a learner and a teacher (or both) is an important part of learning and teaching scholarship. Stories offer a productive genre to capture that human experience. Janice McDrury and Maxine Alterio (2003) situate storytelling as a pedagogical and professional development tool that prompts reflection in a powerful way because stories touch individual lives. Likewise, Hunter McEwan and Kieran Egan (1995, viii) argue:

> A narrative, and that particular form of narrative that we call a story, deals not just in facts or ideas or theories, or even dreams, fears and hopes, but in facts, theories, and dreams from the perspective of someone's life and in the context of someone's emotions.

Increasingly, education scholars are positioning storying as both a method (research tool) and methodology (stance as a researcher shaping your choices in research design), and a genre worthy of recognition and respect. Stories demand that writers engage in learning and teaching conversations in a different way from most other genres. Louise Phillips and Tracey Bunda (2018, 10) argue that: "Across the globe, storytelling enables connection with the other. . . . The relationship with others is at the core of storytelling and storying—there must be tellers and listeners. The fate and creation of the story depends on being with others."

The genre of stories is a particularly accessible way of contributing to and creating conversations because it is embraced by learners and teachers in every context and at every level of discourse (from informal to highly crafted), and it is equally well suited to carrying meaning in Indigenous and First Nations cultures and Western cultures.

What Stories of Learning and Teaching in Higher Education Can Look Like

Elizabeth Mackinlay (2016, 2) tells her story, or what she calls "storys," of her experience of learning and teaching in higher education in a book that begins:

> In one hour I will meet them, the new students who have enrolled in our introductory Women's and Gender Studies course at my university. I have been awake half the night hunched over my laptop trying to get my lecture just right, knowing how important it is to make a good initial impression with first year undergraduate students. I flip through my lecture notes and can't explain why but I am terrified. How will students respond to this course? Have I framed Women's and Gender Studies as a most necessary way of knowing, being and doing in the world? Am I being too theoretical or not intellectual enough, and how sound is my disciplinary knowledge in relation to theory, history and philosophy anyway? Is striving for gender justice important to them and have

I the right kind of pedagogical tools within my reach to convince them it is? Are my definitions of sex and gender too simple? Are they accessible while at the same time giving an understanding of why these two words still matter? Will I stammer over words and phrases as I stumble for clarity and conviction in my place as a feminist educator? I stare down at my coral pink dress and wonder; do I look feminist *enough* to be teaching this course? And what does teaching and learning *like a feminist* mean anyway?

This excerpt demonstrates what a learning and teaching story can look like. Whether you can relate to the particular disciplinary context Elizabeth Mackinlay describes or not, by sharing her experience she is inviting a connection with readers who have questioned themselves as teachers and scholars. The story is left to the reader to interpret. In this way, a story is not imposing a conclusion but rather inviting exploration of a fellow traveler's experience of learning and teaching. "Storytelling reveals meaning without committing the error of defining it" (Arendt 1970, 105). There is no single meaning of a learning and teaching story; the writer conveys experiences and invites readers into a kind of conversation to make their own meaning that intersects with each reader's identity, experiences, context, and way of seeing higher education.

We share the above excerpt of Mackinlay's story to signal the qualitative and technical difference of the story genre compared with other genres we have focused on in this book. By writing stories about learning and teaching, authors are "piercing the curtain," according to Gerardo Patriotta (2016, 568), by exposing "the human-made and human-making world to scrutiny, thereby retrospectively revealing all the effort that goes into the social construction of everyday life." Through stories, writers can teach others to examine and communicate what learning and teaching in their context means to them, offering insights "that lie unexplored, overlooked, neglected, or hidden from sight" (Bauman 2013, 27). Peter Felten (2019, 2) argues for storytelling as a potential for scholars interested in engaging in pedagogical partnership, yet the guidance extends to stories on learning and teaching in general: "By recognizing some of the constraints and limitations of storytelling, we might intentionally seek out stories that explore complex and even contrary experiences and perspectives." He offers four observations on and about the nature of stories:

1. Stories condense and simplify.
2. Stories tend to portray actions and experiences as coherent and purposeful.
3. Stories tend to be told by those with the most power.
4. Stories obscure some perspectives even as they reveal other ones.

(Felten 2019, 1-2)

How we understand and draw on stories as a writing genre will vary and evolve over time, as signalled in Our Perspectives 20.1.

Our Perspectives 20.1

The importance of storytelling as a learning and teaching writing genre

Kelly: Like most people, I love a good story. However, until recently, I assigned stories about learning and teaching to corridor conversations with colleagues or a form of data collection (e.g., narrative inquiry). I did not write my own stories or encourage others to do so because my early career was focused on publishing research that counted at my university. Now, I value sharing written stories about everyday experiences of learning and teaching because they create opportunities to describe the messiness of pedagogical practices, including the failures and unexpected things that can happen that we would rarely include in traditional research formats. Writing a story also enables more people to contribute to the higher education conversation, including students. I now curate a blog at my university that includes everyday stories (University of Queensland Institute for Teaching and Learning Innovation, "News").

Mick: I often try to enliven workshops by telling the back stories to case studies or practices that I present. However, it was not until we wrote our *Teaching & Learning Inquiry* paper (Healey, Matthews, and Cook-Sather 2019) that I started to write some personal stories, a practice we have continued in this book (in each Our Perspectives section). I hope they help to bring the narrative alive and reveal some of the messiness and the challenges of writing as well as some of the highlights.

Alison: While stories of lived experiences have informed all of my research, creating forums within which the stories can be analyzed and engaging in my own analyses of my stories are more recent practices for me. I created the journal *Teaching and Learning Together in Higher Education* (*TLTHE*) in 2010 to provide a space for students, faculty, and staff to draw on their own stories of pedagogical partnership and to reflect on and analyze their experiences. I have also published my own stories of ongoing learning, such as about my experiences of discussing pedagogical partnership across languages and contexts (Cook-Sather 2018c), to share with readers how this work is never finished and how we can all learn from one another's experiences without having to conduct formal research on them. The stories that inform essays in *TLTHE* and the stories I share in published forums aim to capture the human experience, and to express the feeling, of learning and teaching that, as Zygmunt Bauman, Michael Hviid Jacobsen, and Keith Tester (2013) note, can otherwise remain hidden.

Your perspective: What, to your mind, is the importance of storytelling as a learning and teaching writing genre?

Writing a Story to Share

Traditional peer-reviewed outlets, like journals, do not publish standalone stories. However, stories captured as data and then analyzed as part of a research project may be found in learning and teaching journals reported as an empirical study, for example. This makes sense because capturing people's stories offers rich insight into the complexities of what it means to learn and teach in higher education. As a source of data, stories offer endless interpretive possibilities. Stories are generative. In this book, we are advocating storytelling as a genre in itself in which writers author their own stories, recount the stories of others, or invent stories that are left to readers to interpret. Stories can be shared in blogs (for example, see David Pace's blog, *Decoding the Ivory Tower*, or University College London's blog), professional society newsletters, books, and even in the mainstream media (e.g., BBC Stories). We return to a discussion of blogs in chapter 21.

While telling stories about our learning and teaching practices is commonplace to us, many of us will struggle to write them. First, learning to write in many academic disciplines teaches us distance and objectivity as we write up our research, as Kelly highlights in Our Perspectives 20.1 and as David Pace discusses in Reflection 20.1, describing the "extraordinarily liberating" experience of sharing stories. Second, we have to identify a generative story about our learning and teaching that connects to the ongoing conversations of a community. In other words, stories also require us to speak within a designated conversation or community of colleagues—as Phillips and Bunda (2018) indicate—or to find a way to say something new. While we may or may not directly cite other scholars, the story we are writing is being written for an audience and will be shaped by others.

Reflection 20.1

Confessions of a SoTL blogger—Telling stories is liberating

Leaving the world of scholarly writing to begin a blog felt transgressive. Who was I to say that my stories, anecdotes, and observations were worth anyone else's time? What was I doing presenting my own successes and failures, my values and experiences, in such a public arena? We need academic prose to produce a scholarship of teaching and learning that is "public" and "accessible for exchange" as a basis for collective reform of instruction. But it often hides the personal histories, unique encounters, political context, and values that are always a part of our teaching. The experience has been extraordinarily liberating. I wake at 4:00 in the morning, unable to go back to sleep because ideas for new entries have come bubbling up during the night. My pedagogical observations are no longer separated from the experiences that drove me to write about teaching in the first place. I realize now that scholarly writing always required the self-amputation of a part of myself. I will continue writing traditional articles on teaching and learning because I believe in this work, but I am reveling in having another place where I can share both the thoughts and the stories that have emerged from a half-century in academia.

David Pace is professor emeritus, History Department, Indiana University Bloomington, US. He blogs at Decoding the Ivory Tower.

As an example of the challenges and possibilities of storytelling, Kelly (Matthews 2019b) recently shared a story about observing a colleague teaching in a large, 500-person first-year subject on the first day of the semester. Because the story was being shared in an institutional blog, Kelly avoided naming the subject or going into details about the disciplinary content, although she acknowledged her colleague by name (after seeking permission). The story consisted of Kelly describing her experience of watching a colleague's class and then adapting his practice in an effort to create an inclusive learning space. She did not want readers to get distracted by the discipline (mathematics) because the story was about inclusive pedagogies that can cut across disciplinary boundaries. Kelly also did not cite any literature. Stories might cite literature but do not have to. In this example, her audience was the broad teaching community at her university—mostly comprised of academics who are not scholars of learning and teaching, but are higher education teachers. In the Elizabeth Mackinlay (2016) story discussed above, on the other hand, the author did cite other scholars whose work resonated with hers and shaped her thinking and practices.

Finally, writing an impactful learning and teaching story means sharing our vulnerabilities in ways that we would not in our research but might, for instance, share in reflective essays. Sharing our emotional experiences and even our mistakes reflects the lived experience of learning and teaching—the building blocks of powerful stories, which we attempt to display through the "Our Perspectives" and "Reflection" sections included throughout this book. Yet, in doing so, we are making our vulnerabilities public, which goes against the grain of much academic writing. This is evident in Elizabeth Mackinlay's excerpt, where she shares all the questions swimming in her thoughts the night before a new teaching semester begins.

The Guiding Questions below can help you write a story that provokes rich insights into the lived experiences of learning and teaching and that is also ripe for other media (there are a number of good teaching podcasts that are story based, and stories can also work well in video, simple animation, and digital storytelling, too—see chapter 21). A copy of the questions is available in the online resources.

Guiding Questions for Planning, Revising, and Refining a Learning and Teaching Story*

1. **What is your story about?**
   Let your readers know what your learning and teaching story is about. The example below is the opening lines of a story from a blog post about attempting to teach and assess problem-solving:

   > We thought we had these great ideas to engage students in problem-solving. We thought students would like the idea of being enterprising, thinking like entrepreneurs. In a course about innovation and leadership at a university that is all about creating change for a better world, solving complex problems as core assessment tasks seemed like a no-brainer. We were wrong. (Smart and Heynen 2019)

2. When and where does your story take place?

Describe the context of your story for readers. The example above signals the context, and here is another showing how context can be shared and used to draw in readers:

> It was the first lecture in a first-year course. He introduced the course and the teaching team. He did what you would expect in a first lecture. But then he did this simple yet powerful thing. (Matthews 2019b)

3. Who are the people in your story?

Just as you do with context, identify the people in your story. Drawing from the same story example above, the main character is formally introduced:

> I was observing Professor Peter Adams a decade ago—he is now the President of our Academic Board. (Matthews 2019b)

4. What happens first in your story, and then what happens next?

Give readers a sense of the events unfolding so they can visualize what is happening, as Liz Mackinlay does here:

> I have been awake half the night hunched over my laptop trying to get my lecture just right, knowing how important it is to make a good initial impression with first year undergraduate students. I flip through my lecture notes and can't explain why but I am terrified. (Mackinlay 2016, 2)

5. How did the people involved, including yourself, react or respond?

Give readers as sense of the emotional lives of the people in your story. In the below example, a student scholar, Dionna Jenkins, reflects on how she first reacted to and then evolved through her experience:

I came into this partnership more fearful than I would like to admit. . . . I subconsciously held onto this fear for some time, but as the semester progressed I grew more comfortable allowing myself to just take a chance and let my ideas flow. In the end, I began to see that differences between partners are nothing to fear. (Wildhagen and Jenkins 2020)

6. **Why are you sharing this story? What is the message you would like readers to hear?**

Readers will come to their own conclusions based on their read of your story, yet you can signal what the people in your story learned, as demonstrated below:

We learned in the context of teaching entrepreneurship that student ownership of the entrepreneurial idea from its genesis is crucial. In any teaching context, we learned the importance of trusting students by sharing ownership for decisions in the curriculum that academics usually make *for* students instead of *with* students. (Smart and Heynen 2019)

7. **How will you end your story?**

There are so many ways to end a story. Here is one example:

Do everything in Love, in the broadest sense. Guard hearts, intention, and deeds during the course of the partnership. . . . Do not be discouraged, stand firm on truth, care for others the way we long to be cared for. Have faith in one another, stay hopeful when challenges loom, and after all wrap everything we do in Love. (Chen and Ho 2020)

*As with other sets of guiding questions in this book, select those questions that are relevant to your context, add others as appropriate, and decide the order in which you will address them to communicate effectively with your audience.

Stories are perhaps the most inclusive of the genres we discuss in this book. This is in part because every other genre also tells a story of some sort, whether we use that term or not, and also because stories are part of every other genre. As a stand-alone genre, stories make arguments in the sense that reflective essays do: by presenting experiences and processes of reasoning about those in narrative form. The argument you make in a story, then, is one that speaks from lived experience, by sharing details of that experience, in relation to the context and people involved. Like a reflective essay, a story uses first-person pronouns, and the narrative offered often reveals a process of becoming (Cook-Sather 2019; Dutta 2018; Patriotta 2016).

Over to You

Writing our stories of learning and teaching enables us to communicate in different ways than in the traditional forms of written research and other genres described in this book. More people can be included as authors of this genre, and stories can reach beyond learning and teaching scholars because of their accessible nature. Although crafting a generative story is very different from writing an empirical research article, case study, or opinion piece, it still allows and requires us to contribute to the ongoing learning and teaching conversations, or create new conversations, by asking us to always consider how our story connects with readers. Think about stories you can share that might, as McDrury and Alterio (2003) note, motivate others, convey information, or share experience. Questions to address about writing your learning and teaching story include:

- What learning and teaching stories would you like to tell? Why do you want to tell these particular stories? Which will you write about first?
- Which of our Guiding Questions do you think you need to address and in what order to write your story? What other questions might you address?
- Where will you publish your story? How does it connect to, extend, or change conversations in the learning and teaching community?

CHAPTER 21

ENGAGING IN
SCHOLARLY CONVERSATIONS ONLINE
Social Media

[To engage with social media is] to experiment with form rather than content, to find ways to make an academic concept accessible to a broader public. (Perry 2015)

Ten years ago, we would not have dreamed of quoting from a blog. Look at how quickly academic publishing norms have changed. Last year, Alison and Kelly co-authored an editorial with two students that directly cited tweets (Cook-Sather et al. 2018). And here we are now, opening a chapter with quote from David Perry's blog. Indeed, our reference list for this book reveals the many blogs that have shaped our thinking. That is because social media is a part of all our lives and offers opportunities for those of us writing about learning and teaching to reach a wide and varied audience, as Perry suggests above. While using social media in learning and teaching is common practice (Rowell 2019), we do not enter here into the debate about whether it is a genre in and of itself, or simply a platform to publish and share our writing. For the purpose of this book, we name it as a writing genre that has a specific purpose distinct from other genres. The key distinction is the capacity to self-publish in a way that is quick and easy and that bypasses traditional peer review.

In this chapter, we discuss what social media is, with a specific focus on blogs, Twitter, and listservs; which genres lend themselves to being shared via social media; and why social media creates new opportunities for learning and teaching scholars.

What Is Social Media and Why Use It?

Media refers to mass communication. If we are a bit older, we might associate mass media with broadcast news, either on TV or in print—in the analog days. Today, mass media has gone digital, the internet has given us social media, and many print journals have moved online. In Reflection 28.2, Sally Brown recalls when peer review used to happen through the mail.

For Pat Thomson (2016b, 101), a prolific user of digital media, "Social media is an umbrella term used to describe websites and web-based platforms and applications that allow users to make, curate and share content, and to communicate with each other." Now, through social media, we can share our work online directly without having to go through a peer-review process—we can self-publish. While you would not publish a full research article as a blog post on your personal website, you can share pre-published versions via ResearchGate or other academic social networking sites, as more and more scholars are doing (Meishar-Tal and Pieterse 2017) (for more on promoting your work see chapter 29). Yet, self-publishing that bypasses peer-review processes can raise concerns because a level of credibility and trust come from publishing in known and established learning and teaching outlets. Thus, deciding what to self-publish and what to send through peer review is important.

Social media offers a means of contributing to and creating conversations about learning and teaching as public scholarship (Chick 2019), as captured by David Pace in Reflection 20.1. Yet, we all know colleagues who feel that "social media has made scholars impatient, vicious, and dull" (Fraser 2019). Cal Newport (2016) makes a strong case that the constant distraction of social media and email diminishes the capacity for the deep work required of scholars. We do not need to be distracted by social media, however, if we use it purposefully. For Patrick Iber (2016), Twitter enables connection with other academics and people outside of the academy, particularly journalists and editors. Lee Skallerup Bessette (2016) claims that Twitter changed her life for the better but also cautions that it "does very little to protect those who are the most vulnerable, amplifies the most extreme and hateful elements of our society, and keep[s] trying to monetize in ways that take away the core features that brought us all to the platform to begin with." Using social media to contribute to ongoing learning and teaching conversations means being deliberate and thoughtful about what you say and how you want to interact.

David Perry (2015) contends that blogging enables you to reach a broader audience and, in particular, a non-academic audience. Inger Mewburn and Pat Thomson (2013, 1105) found that "academic blogging may constitute a community of practice in which a hybrid public/private academic operates in a 'gift economy'" by contributing to scholarly conversations and peer learning. Tweeting and blogging about your published research *might* affect the impact of your research, as discussed in chapter 29.

Regardless of reach or impact, blogging offers an opportunity to write in a style different from that of traditional academic journal and book writing. Blogging lends itself to sharing learning and teaching stories (see chapter 20). Blogging, according to the Textbook and Academic Authors Association website, can be a means of improving writing:

> Whether it's getting into a writing routine or just refining your writing, blogging can help you. Make sure to allow for comments (even if you moderate them before hand) on your blog so that you can receive feedback that will help improve your writing. If your writing contains too much jargon, your audience will tell you. If you're trying to find your voice, blogging can help you form one. (Textbook and Academic Authors Association 2015)

Pat Thomson (2016c) argues that blogging makes you a better academic writer for seven reasons. She asserts that blogging:

- can help you to establish writing as a routine
- allows you to experiment with your writing "voice"

- helps you to get to the point
- points you to your reader
- requires you to be concise
- allows you to experiment with forms of writing, and
- helps you to become a more confident writer.

Furthermore, blogging enables rapid communication of teaching practices and analyses. The time frame to publish can be minutes (if it is your website or LinkedIn account), compared to publishing a practical case study in a journal, which may take 6–15 months.

Not only can you share and promote your published work through blogs, LinkedIn, Facebook, and Twitter, you can also include imagery, color, and audio in ways that are less common in traditional academic publishing (although this is shifting with video abstracts, for example). You can potentially reach new audiences as well as extend your existing academic communities, and you can engage with your existing scholarly communities in new or different ways, making your work easily accessible. And you can do it yourself, bypassing publishers and slow peer-review processes.

Although there are multiple benefits to engaging in social media, you might not want to, and that is 100% okay. Alison does not use social media and only recently wrote an invited blog post; Kelly uses both for professional purposes; and Mick is starting to use both, but prefers to share and read via academic listservs more than Twitter (see Our Perspectives 21.1). A listserv distributes messages to subscribers on an electronic mailing list. Mick, for example, finds the Staff and Educational Development Association (SEDA) listserv particularly valuable. Farhad Manjoo (2010) calls listservs "one of the most important things on the Internet." There are many other listservs for learning and teaching in higher education (Corrigan 2010). John Lea, a well-published author and a frequent contributor to the SEDA listserv, reflects on his experience in Reflection 21.1.

Reflection 21.1

The experience of contributing to listserv discussions

I'm not a fan of Twitter. I find its word limit restrictive, but I appreciate how useful it is in spreading information. I'm more a fan of the opinion piece, particularly those with a punchy polemic. But it takes time to polish that kind of narrative. For me, the listserv sits nicely between them, acting as a source of information but also as a forum for discussion. The unwritten rule is that an unpolished narrative is enough—perhaps containing some wit, perhaps with a sharp provocative comment. Yes, you can provide information, particularly in answer to a direct question, but this form of social media surely comes into its own when it provokes and compels others to join in a debate. It takes confidence to come in on a debate which is well underway, but, for me, it comes closest to the way that debate takes place in face-to-face situations, except that the audience can be much wider. And you can always come back to reflect on (or correct) what you said before. And I love it when somebody contacts me "off piste" to say that they are listening and lurking, or just to say hello!

John Lea is the research director for the Scholarship Project, UK.

For many people, particularly for writers who have grown up on social media, there is a "fear of missing out" or FOMO. Social media allows us to keep up with discussions of learning and teaching, to self-author, and to include voices of those who might not be as readily included in traditional publishing formats. However, if you are new to social media, the plethora of possibilities can feel overwhelming. We recommend starting with one platform, perhaps one that a trusted colleague suggests and is able to support you in learning.

Our Perspectives 21.1

What is your experience with and attitude toward social media?

Mick: Though I've used LinkedIn for some time to keep up to date with contacts, I'm a relative newcomer to most social media. On Twitter (@MickHealey3) I'm more a lurker than a contributor, as I find the 280 characters too limiting for what I normally like to say. I also read quite a lot of blogs (particularly in preparation for writing this book), but I've only written a handful of posts myself. I'm on several higher education listservs, which help keep me informed about learning and teaching events, new publications, and topical issues. I also join in listserv conversations from time to time and send details of events, publications, and resources that I think may be of interest to the community.

Alison: While I respond to invitations from others on LinkedIn and Facebook, I do not actively use those social media platforms or Twitter because I already spend too much time with technology and I am introverted and easily overwhelmed by input. While some people might experience "fear of missing out" (FOMO), I experience the "joy of missing out" (JOMO). This choice to avoid social media has not appeared to affect my writing profile (although perhaps my social media-savvy friends who post and tweet about my work make up for my absence!). In my relative technological solitude, I am a prolific writer with an extensive record of scholarship and citation, which suggests that you can be an active participant in scholarly conversations without having your own social media presence.

Kelly: I use some social media professionally, which started as a requirement to "disseminate" as part of a funded grant application. I have come to appreciate social media but still actually don't like it much. I am active on Twitter (@kellymatthewsuq) and occasionally share posts through LinkedIn. By sharing what I am reading via Twitter, I am able to support other scholars. By curating an institutional blog and monthly "Teaching Community Update," I can shape conversations around learning and teaching that offer nuance as a counterbalance to an increased focus (at my university) on "marketing-driven" stories that don't always capture the full story of learning and teaching.

Your perspective: In what ways, if any, are you currently using social media to share your learning and teaching work, and how might you further leverage it?

What Genres Lend Themselves to Publishing through Blogs

Through social media, Kelly publishes—as words or videos—examples of practice, reflections, reviews of other published works, stories, conversations between herself and others, and guidance on everyday work practices, such as managing emails (Matthews 2019c) and saying no (Matthews 2019d). These publications speak to the range of genres suited to social media and the ways genres can be blurred through social media. By using a poll feature with real-time results, she is also enabling exchange, which is evident in a blog post on email use where over seventy colleagues from her university shared their approaches (or lack thereof) to managing their inbox (Matthews 2019c). In a literal sense, real-time interaction is possible through curated blogs and Twitter posts. Yet, these creations and contributions require time to curate and monitor in ways that a published piece in a journal or book does not. Particularly in social media with public comments enabled, "trolling" or hurtful comments that attack personally (usually anonymously or via fake accounts) are possible in ways that are not an option in a journal publication, for example. The capacity for back-and-forth online communication is possible with social media, but if you engage in such exchanges you will want to consider the implications and potentially avoid the comments option at the end of a blog post.

There are many examples of excellent blogs, both written and in video format, from learning and teaching scholars or organizations;

to find some, view Feedspot's "Top 100 Higher Education Blogs and Websites to Follow in 2020" and *Geeky Pedagogy*'s list of blogs and podcasts. With the help of Kelly's Twitter network, we have curated a list of blogs, which is available in the online resources: "Curated List of Blogs and Multimedia Resources about Learning and Teaching in Higher Education."

How Do You Go about Publishing a Blog and Sharing via Twitter?

If you are new to Twitter, consider these recommendations from Lee Skallerup Bessette (2017) for scholars wanting to get started on Twitter:

- Tweet links to what you are reading
- Share links to your own work
- Invite questions or comments on a topic you are pondering
- Promote the work of other scholars
- Offer insights from conferences or talks (welcomed by those unable to attend)
- Follow journals, societies, organizations, and scholars to stay up to date
- Use the "Like" function often, retweet, and follow others to grow your followers

There are also many ongoing learning and teaching in higher education conversations on Twitter that you can join. These can be found by searching hashtags, including: #LTHEchat; #EdChatEU; #ecrchat; #AcademicChatter; #studentsaspartners; #studentsuccess and many more. If you are considering starting a regular blog—becoming an academic blogger—Tom Crick and Alan Winfield (2013) have ten suggestions that might be of interest and use to you:

1. Write about yourself and your life.
2. Find your blogging voice.
3. Be clear what your blog is for.
4. Blog as yourself.

5. Think about how controversial you want to be.
6. Remember: A blogpost is a publication.
7. Let your university know about your blog.
8. Think about how often you want to blog.
9. Use social media to promote your posts.
10. Blog because you want to.

We do not want to give the impression that sending a tweet or publishing a blog means writing freely with little attention to detail. For Mick, drafting a single tweet can take up to thirty minutes because he wants to link to the best websites, ensure that he tags the right people, and then communicates concisely with limited words. Kelly can send a tweet in a matter of minutes, but a blog post still takes anywhere from one to ten hours. Since the content of your blog post could be any of the genres we discuss elsewhere in part 4, we suggest you consider the writing genre first and determine your word limit. Then follow the writing process outlined in the chapter on that writing genre, while also considering the blog platform you will use.

Social media encompasses a variety of writing genres, and articulating your argument matters. A strong tweet is an argument communicated concisely and is limited in length by the platform. If you are tweeting to share your published work, go beyond just naming the title with a link; quote the argument in a way that clearly captures your contribution to the scholarly community. Opening a blog post with the argument invites readers to read with purpose and follow your narrative flow. Writing for social media has to move beyond the descriptive to assert a position or argument.

In the Guiding Questions below we share suggestions to get you started on a blog post on learning and teaching. A version with just the questions is available in the online resources.

Guiding Questions for Planning a Learning and Teaching Blog Post*

1. **What do you want to share about learning and teaching via a blog post?**
   - Focus on a single key message or purpose in a blog post. As for any genre, your thesis or argument needs to be clear to you and clearly communicated to readers.
   - Blog posts tend to be short and sharp. If you are publishing through an organizational blog (e.g., *The Conversation*, a university blog), a word limit will typically be set for you. If you are self-publishing, set yourself a word limit.

2. **Why is a blog the ideal platform to share your views about learning and teaching?**
   - Consider where you are in your career and the institutional metrics that count at your university. Perhaps publishing an opinion piece in a journal first is more helpful to your aspirations. Then write a shorter blog post to promote the published piece to bring more people to your work.
   - If you are seeking the quick interaction with readers that social media enables, what forms of interaction do you want (e.g., comments, quick polls)?
   - Are you writing about a time-sensitive topic where quick publication matters?

3. **What writing genre (or combination of genres) is best suited to communicate what you intend?**
   - Are you sharing a reflective essay, an opinion, or a story? Then refer to chapters 18, 19 or 20 respectively to draft the piece.
   - Are you seeking to promote a published work through a blog post? If so, focus on the key outcome and write about why others should read your published work.
   - Have you tried a pedagogical practice that you want to tell others about? Consider framing it as a case study (chapter 15) or a story (chapter 20).

4. **What blog platform will you use?**
   - There are many blog platforms. Will you use an institutional or professional learning and teaching society platform, or will you self-publish using your own blog site? Self-publishing means regularly posting and doing all the formatting yourself, but there are many easy options, as Patrick Dunleavy (2016) outlines.
   - Do the features of differing blog platforms matter for how you want to communicate? For example, if you want to embed a short video animation or imagery, then you will want a platform that easily enables that (a quick web search on blogging platforms will reveal options).
   - Are you able to code, or do you need a platform that allows easy formatting?

5. **Who will read the contribution and offer feedback to you?**
   Whether you are self-publishing or publishing through an organization, someone needs to read your draft and offer critical friend feedback (see chapter 26).

6. **When will you share it and how will you promote it?**
   - There is research on the best time of day (not midnight) and days of the week (Monday to Thursday) to make your blog public (Terras 2012).
   - Will you use Twitter or Facebook to promote your blog post?
   - If you are blogging through an organization, how will they promote your post? (See chapter 29.)

As with other sets of guidance questions in this book, select those questions that are relevant to your context, add others as appropriate, and decide the order in which you will address them to communicate effectively with your audience.

Over to You

Social media enables self-publication immediately to the web via blogs, Twitter, Facebook, and the like. You can curate what you want to share, when, and how. In doing so, you can write in one genre or embrace a mix of writing genres in a way that traditional publications might restrict or exclude. Publishing via social media still requires the hard work of writing and editing, but it frees you from the constraints of academic peer review and enables connection that many scholars (though not all) revel in. In what ways might social media allow you to experiment with form rather than just content, as Perry (2015) suggests in our opening quote, and make an academic concept accessible to a broader public? Further questions to address about engaging in scholarly conversations on social media include:

- What social media platforms are you signed up for or would you be interested in joining?
- How active would you like to be on social media?
- How can you leverage social media to expand your learning and teaching scholarship?

CHAPTER 22

APPLYING, REFLECTING, AND EVIDENCING

Teaching Awards, Fellowships, and Promotions

The NTF [National Teaching Fellowship] changed my life—enabling me to gain a Professorship . . . and focus on educational development. (Peter Hartley quoted in Association of National Teaching Fellows, 2018).

As a scholar interested in writing about your teaching, you are likely to be faced at various stages of your career with applying for a teaching award, a teaching fellowship, or a promotion based, at least in part, on the excellence of your teaching (i.e., evidence of your impact of enhancing student outcomes), support of learning (i.e., evidence of supporting colleagues and influencing support for student learning) and leadership (i.e., evidence of effective leadership of learning and teaching). Success in these applications can have a significant impact on your career, as the quote at the beginning of this chapter indicates. Core to these applications is evidencing the impact of your teaching on student learning and supporting colleagues. For senior awards, fellowships, and promotions, evidence of leadership of learning and teaching beyond your department and institution is often critical. Similar issues arise if you, like many colleagues around the world, apply for an HEA Fellowship under the UK Professional Standards Framework (UKPSF). Your publications about learning and teaching are a key source of evidence of experience and impact in these applications.

In this chapter, we unpack the nature of these forms of writing, present a flexible guide to the organization and composition of these applications, and discuss what to look out for to enhance your chances of success. As in previous chapters, we conceptualize these genres as engaging in conversations, in this case with assessors. These conversations are, however, different from those in the other chapters in this part of the book as these applications are private between you and the assessors, whereas the other chapters discuss engaging in public conversations. Nevertheless, in all the genres examined you are in a process of exchange regarding learning and teaching. We begin the chapter by putting the discussion of applying for teaching awards, fellowships, and promotions in the context of the debate over the status of teaching and the standing of research on learning and teaching within higher education.

What Is the Status of Teaching and Research into Learning and Teaching?

In the last twenty-five years there has been much discussion of the lower status of teaching, and research into learning and teaching, compared with discipline-based research, in Australasia, North America, and the UK (Bennett, Roberts, and Ananthram 2017; Cashmore, Cane, and Cane 2013; Chalmers 2011; Hutchings, Huber, and Ciccone 2011; Macfarlane 2011; Vardi and Quin 2011)—unless you happen to be in the field of education. As Locke (2014, 24) notes, "It is clear that to progress to the most senior positions, a research record is usually needed, and that pedagogical research is not valued as highly as other disciplinary research." While significant progress has been made in correcting the imbalance, more success has, at least until recently, been achieved in the area of recognition (e.g., fellowships) than in the area of reward (e.g., promotion and tenure). However, funds to support national teaching award and fellowship schemes as well as research into learning and teaching have fallen in the last decade, and some programs have closed (e.g., Carnegie Academy for the Scholarship of Teaching and Learning (CASTL) in the US; initiatives funded by the Higher Education Funding Council for England; and the Australian Learning and Teaching Fellows scheme) or been cut back in terms of the reward given to recipients (e.g., UK National Teaching Fellowship Scheme). In contrast, at the institutional level, we have seen growth in the number of scholars being promoted, at least in part, on the basis of their excellence in teaching and in their support of and leadership in learning.

With the growth in many countries of positions focused on educational support, career pathways have been developed, often up to full professorship. Evidence of excellence in teaching may be a necessary, but not sufficient, criterion for promotion and tenure, particularly at higher levels. If you are making a case for teaching excellence, some universities expect evidence of engagement with research into learning and teaching (Locke 2014). For example, a criterion for promotion of teaching-focused staff at level C and above at The University of Queensland since 2007 is "the dissemination of their work on the scholarship of teaching and learning including publication in high quality peer-reviewed outlets and other mechanisms appropriate for the discipline and target audience" (University of Queensland 2019). To promote the rewarding of educators and education leaders in research-intensive universities, Dilly Fung and Claire Gordon (2016, 6) argue for a "strength-based promotions strategy" in which "the criteria and the format of applications should enable an individual's claim for promotion to be considered holistically, on the basis of the strength of the overall contribution made in their context, rather than through a standardised 'tick box' approach." In a few disciplines, such as chemistry and medicine, specific posts as lecturers and professors in higher education are reasonably common, but they are rare in most subject areas.

As with the status of teaching versus research, there is concern that scholarship of teaching and learning (SoTL) and pedagogic research do not have the same standing as discipline-based research in national research assessment exercises (Cotton, Miller, and Kneale 2017; Fanghanel et al. 2016; see also chapter 2). For several years in Hong Kong this concern was addressed by allowing participants to submit work to their research assessment exercise under any of Ernest Boyer's (1990) scholarships—discovery, integration, application, and teaching—thus extending what counted beyond just discovery research. They used the same criteria, as developed by Charles Glassick, Mary Huber, and Gene Maeroff (1997), to evaluate the submissions for all four scholarships with the addition of threshold, advanced, and exemplary levels (Carnegie Foundation for the Advancement of Teaching 2006):

1. Goals of the project
2. Preparation for scholar's work
3. Methods used to conduct work
4. Evidence gathered to demonstrate impact of work
5. Reflection on work
6. Communication of results to others

Dilly Fung and Claire Gordon (2016, 7) argue that where education-focused scholarship "is undertaken and where it makes a genuine impact on student education and on the practices of other educators, it should be recognised in promotion criteria alongside other markers of effectiveness and impact." Kathleen McKinney (2007, 97-99) provides some useful advice on documenting SoTL work for the reward system.

What Are Teaching Awards and Fellowships?

Though the nomenclature varies, teaching awards are usually made for past achievements, while many fellowships, though recognizing previous experience, also have expectations as to future activities by those appointed. Awards occur at institutional, national, and international levels. Thus, for example, at the University of New South Wales, Australia, you can apply to become a Scientia Education Fellow; at the University of Nebraska Omaha, US, you can be nominated for an outstanding teaching award; while at the University of Liverpool, UK, you can apply for a learning and teaching fellowship. Several countries have national teaching awards and fellowships, such as 3M Fellows in Canada, Ako Aotearoa national tertiary teaching awards in New Zealand, and the National Teaching Fellowships (NTFs) in the UK. There are also a few international-level programs, including HEA Fellowships, which, though based in the UK, have been adopted by an increasing number of higher education institutions globally; and the ISSOTL Fellows Program, which is open to the international membership of the society.

Most teaching awards and fellowships are interdisciplinary, but some are discipline-specific, for example, the Taylor & Francis Award for sustained contributions to teaching and learning of geography in higher education, Chemistry Educator of the Year in Australia, and the Law Teacher of the Year in the UK. The POD Network, in the US, has several awards, including the POD Innovation Award, which recognizes creative ideas for educational development, and the Robert J. Menges Award for Outstanding Research in Educational Development.

How to Write Your Application for a Teaching Award, Fellowship, or Promotion

Given the wide range of different types of teaching awards, fellowships, and promotions, it is difficult to generalize about writing your application. Perhaps the most important advice is to ensure that you address all the application questions and criteria as fully as you are able within the constraints of the structure and the word limit requirements of the application.

Some applications, particularly those for promotions, are largely based around the kind of material that appears in a curriculum vitae (CV) and involve completing a tightly structured application form. Others explicitly say not to include lists, instead emphasizing critical reflection and discussion of the evidence of impact of a *selection* of activities and experiences structured under a few broad headings, sometimes in the form of a portfolio. There are several useful guides to developing teaching portfolios (e.g., MacPherson Institute 2019; University of Hong Kong 2019; Weston and Timmermans 2007). Engaging in writing a reflective teaching portfolio can contribute to the development of a scholarly teaching community (Pelger and Larsson 2018).

Examination of numerous examples of applications points to a set of topic areas and questions that appear frequently; we list these below in "Guiding Questions for Planning, Revising, and Refining an Application for a Teaching Award, Fellowship, or Promotion," also available for download in the online resources. The weighting given to different aspects depends, of course, on the context of the specific application, with some applications placing the emphasis on evidence of excellence in teaching practice and others emphasizing evidencing the positive impact of your educational leadership. Some of the topic areas in the Guiding Questions may not be explicitly asked for in the application form, but if an interview or a dialogue is part of the application process, then that may be the place to cover them.

Guiding Questions for Writing an Application for a Teaching Award, Fellowship, or Promotion*

A. Your philosophy and context

1. What is your teaching and learning philosophy and your philosophy of educational leadership? What principles and values underlie your teaching, support of learning, and leadership practice?

2. If you are applying outside your institution, how has the context of your institutional role and your discipline affected the opportunities you have had to develop your excellence? What is the status of and level of recognition for learning and teaching, and research into it, in your discipline and at your institution—and how has this affected you?

B. Your story

3. How did you become passionate about teaching, supporting, and leading learning and, where appropriate, engaging in research into learning and teaching?

4. What is your story and how might it best be illustrated with a selection of examples? What critical incidents in your development as an excellent teacher, supporter, and leader of learning have you faced in your career? How did you respond, and what impact did those responses have on the quality of student learning or the teaching profession?

C. Your impact on students

5. What are your reflections on the key innovations you have developed as a teacher, supporter, and leader of learning? What rationale or theoretical frameworks underpinned them? What evidence do you have that they have had a beneficial impact on student learning and the teaching profession?

6. How have you incorporated research, scholarship, and evaluation into your professional practice? What impact has your research into learning and teaching had on influencing and enhancing student learning?

D. Your impact on colleagues

7. How have you supported and influenced your immediate colleagues to enhance their practice as teachers, supporters and leaders of learning, and their engagement in pedagogic research? What evidence do you have that your efforts, through supporting colleagues, have enhanced student learning or the teaching profession?

8. What impact have you had on colleagues beyond your department at institutional, regional, national, and international levels?

E. Your continuing professional development (CPD), its impact, and your future plans

9. How do you ensure that you continually develop as an excellent teacher, supporter, and leader of learning and as a pedagogic research practitioner? What difference has your CPD made to you, your students, and your colleagues?

10. What is next? What are your plans for future projects and initiatives? How would this award/fellowship/promotion help your development and affect your students and colleagues?

As with other sets of guidance questions in this book, select those questions that are relevant to your context, add others as appropriate, and decide the order in which you will address them to communicate effectively with your audience.

Preparing an application for a teaching award, fellowship, or promotion is a highly personal process that makes our identities as learning and teaching scholars explicit. Writing about our teaching, particularly in a critically reflective manner, does not come naturally to

many and can be quite an emotional experience. Not being successful with such an application can be more upsetting than having
our submissions in other writing genres rejected (see chapter 28).
Though it is not common, we have all known colleagues who have
been psychologically damaged by the experience. In Reflection 22.1
a colleague reflects on the experience of applying for an NTF, but
not being successful until the second attempt. For other reflections
on people's experiences of being NTFs, see Association of National
Teaching Fellows (2018) and Advance HE "National Teaching Fellowship Scheme 20th Anniversary."

Reflection 22.1

The experience of writing a National Teaching Fellow-
ship application

Writing a claim for a National Teaching Fellowship was the hardest
piece of writing I have ever done. Using clear evidence, I had to
claim that I was an excellent lecturer and that I had helped others
to be excellent. There's one word for someone who proclaims
their own excellence and that is "arrogant." I despised having to
write in this way, but I had a clear goal. My teaching incorporated
sustainability into the English curriculum at a time (2008) when
it was very rare to consider the continuing ability of the Earth
to support life within the walls of an English classroom. I wanted
to share with others that it is possible to do so, and that it can be
done successfully, both in terms of developing students' awareness
of issues of great importance to their future and in terms of developing their subject-specific academic ability. The NTF claim was an
intensely personal account of teaching philosophy and experience,
and writing it helped me to reflect on what I was doing, why I
was doing it, and how I could do it better. But I was unsuccessful
in my application the first time and it hit me hard—it was such
a personal account that my claim to excellence being rejected
felt like I had been rejected as a professional and a person. But I

understood what I had to do to improve, and I was successful the second time round.

Arran Stibbe is a professor of ecological linguistics at the University of Gloucestershire, UK.

There are several useful guides to completing particular parts of applications, such as writing your philosophy of teaching and learning and your educational leadership philosophy (Berenson and Kenny 2016; Chism 1998; Kenny, Jeffs, and Berenson 2015; Schönwetter et al. 2002). The sponsors of teaching awards and fellowships often provide guidance of their own, though advice from others may also be available. For an example on applying for an NTF, see the relevant page of the Advance HE website, but also look at the advice given by people who have supported successful applicants (e.g., Healey and Healey 2019). For some reflections on excellence and scholarship in teaching see Healey (2011). Advice on applying for an HEA Fellowship follows.

Applying for a HEA Fellowship: Meeting the Requirements of the UKPSF

Although HEA Fellows originated in the UK, there is an increasing number of them around the world: at the end of 2019 there were over 125,000 HEA Fellows, 6,500 of them outside the UK. Being awarded a fellowship is a clear indication that you value professional development in your higher education career, and it demonstrates your commitment to teaching, learning, and the student experience through engagement in a practical process that encourages research, reflection, and development. You can apply directly to Advance HE, or you can apply through an institutionally based program, if your institution has been accredited.

The UK Professional Standards Framework is core to the process. It provides a comprehensive set of professional standards and guidelines for those involved in teaching and supporting learning in higher education, which can be applied to personal development programs at the individual or institutional level to improve teaching quality.

The framework identifies the diverse range of teaching and support roles and environments. These are reflected and are expressed in the Dimensions of Professional Practice, with higher education teaching and learning support defined as:

- areas of activity undertaken by teachers and those that support learning
- core knowledge needed to carry out those activities at the appropriate level
- professional values that individuals performing these activities should exemplify.

There are four fellowship descriptors, each of which has its own criteria and application process—Associate Fellowship, Fellowship, Senior Fellowship, and Principal Fellowship. There is a self-assessment tool to help you select the most appropriate category based on your recent experiences of teaching, supporting learning, and leadership. The categories are not sequential, and it may be very appropriate for someone providing learning support to retire with an Associate Fellowship and a head of department to finish their career with a Senior Fellowship. Most people apply for fellowship in writing, although some obtain Associate Fellowship or Fellowship through successfully passing part or all of an accredited postgraduate certificate in teaching and learning. Some institutions integrate dialogue as part of their accredited application process, usually as an option and based on a presentation and some documentation (Pilkington 2017; Smart et al. 2019).

In addition to the resources available on the Advance HE website, John Lea and Nigel Purcell provide a useful overview of applying for an HEA Fellowship (Lea and Purcell 2015; Purcell and Lea 2015), while the collection of chapters edited by Jackie Potter and Rebecca Turner gives a helpful discussion of how to become recognized as an experienced professional teacher (i.e., Senior Fellow) (Potter and Turner 2018). Among the points they emphasize is the importance of choosing a limited selection of examples of your practices and strategies to discuss how your experiences meet the dimensions and descriptor criteria; the need to go beyond description to reflect on and evidence the impact you have had on students and colleagues by answering the "so what?" and "then what?" questions; and, where appropriate, putting your practices and strategies in the context of the scholarly literature (Brown 2018). A series of podcasts on making a successful application for Principal Fellow is also available. Purcell and Lea (2015) provide some sound advice on how to make your application personal, individual, reflective, scholarly, evidence-based, aligned (with the UKPSF), current, and sufficient. Peter Scales (2017) maps the activities, knowledge, and values of the UKPSF in each chapter of his book, *An Introduction to Learning and Teaching in Higher Education*.

Preparing Your Application

Preparation for a teaching award, fellowship, or promotion can begin several years before you apply (Healey and Healey 2019; Pritchard, Wisker, and Potter 2018; Winter et al. 2018). So, you should begin assembling evidence and materials along the way and look for opportunities that will enhance your applications as part of your CPD and publication plans (see chapter 29). As Ruth Healey (personal communication, July 2, 2019) notes, there are "several different ways you may demonstrate 'excellence' without arrogance (e.g., collecting a 'happy' file of quotes from people about your work, student course evaluations, and grade improvements)." There are also recommendations for institutions as to how they can support the preparation of applicants (Healey and Healey 2019), ensure that their promotion practices take full account of education-focused scholarship (Fung and Gordon 2016), and consider how they can contribute to a culture of teaching enhancement beyond the recognition of individual practice (Seppala and Smith 2019).

Over to You

In this chapter we have explored writing an application for a teaching award, fellowship, or promotion based, at least in part, on your excellence as a teacher, supporter, and leader of learning. Success in these applications can be a turning point in the development of your career as our opening quote illustrates, and as Mick has also experienced (Healey 2019). Questions to address about teaching award, fellowship, and promotion applications include:

- In the next three years, which teaching award, fellowship, and promotion opportunities will you consider putting in an application for?
- What can you do to develop experiences and evidence that will support your applications for these and other opportunities as they arise?
- Which of the four dimensions of the Professional Standards Framework provide the best fit for your experiences of teaching, supporting learning, and leadership in learning?

PART 5

WRITING EFFICIENTLY, EFFECTIVELY, AND ENERGIZINGLY

The When, Where, and How of Writing

Introduction to Part 5

The overarching theme of this part of the book is how you might write about learning and teaching in efficient, effective, and energizing ways that strike a balance between, on the one hand, working within established structures and expectations for writing and, on the other, pushing beyond those structures and expectations. Through the stages of beginning, developing, and refining a text, you need to create an approach that is efficient, effective, and energizing *for you*. As we have maintained throughout this book, that approach will depend on what conversations about learning and teaching you hope to contribute to and create, who you are and want to become as a learning and teaching scholar, what values you embrace as a writer, and how you use writing to learn.

The set of chapters in this part of the book pose questions and offer recommendations for how to develop such an approach. It includes a discussion of allotting time and choosing space to write (chapter 23); writing and rewriting your draft (chapter 24); becoming an engaging writer (chapter 25); and seeking networks, critical friends, and feedback as a social and developmental process (chapter 26). These steps toward writing in ways that are efficient, effective, and energizing might not unfold in such a linear sequence; indeed, they are far more recursive and interactive than this list suggests. Although this section might be seen as the most practical of the guidelines we offer, we urge you to keep in mind how these more technical considerations are informed and guided by the threads we name in part 2 and weave throughout this book: contributing to and creating conversations with fellow learning and teaching scholars, shaping and building your identity and values as a learning and teaching scholar, and using writing to learn.

As you read the chapters in part 5, you might want to reconsider the questions we posed in the introduction to part 2, reframed here in terms of what is efficient, effective, and energizing for you. By "efficient" we mean that you have considered and made an informed judgment about how best to use your time. By "effective" we mean that the choices you have made allow you to succeed in meeting your goals. By "energizing" we mean that the choices you have made allow you to experience, generate, and benefit from, not just "use," energy.

- Is your approach efficient and effective in preparing you to engage in conversation with particular learning and teaching communities?
- Does your approach capture your commitments as a writer and convey them to others in a way that is efficient, effective, and energizing for you?
- Does your approach allow you to address in an efficient, effective, and energizing way what matters to you about writing?
- In what ways does your approach allow you to engage in writing to learn in a way that is efficient, effective, and energizing?
- Is your overall approach "active and energizing" (Sword 2017a, 206)?

After you address these questions, you might want to return to your responses to the parallel questions in part 2 and look for interesting echoes or new sounds in and of your voice.

CHAPTER 23

ALLOTTING TIME AND CHOOSING SPACE TO WRITE

*The Importance of Figuring Out
What Works for You*

> *I urge my colleagues and students to leave behind their hair
> shirts of scholarly guilt when they enter the house of writing.
> Productivity, it turns out, is a broad church that tolerates many
> creeds. (Sword 2016, 320-21)*

As Helen Sword implies in the above quote, everyone experiences the conditions for and processes of writing in a different way, and productivity can result from all of them. Building on this earlier work, Sword identifies the "BASE" habits of successful writing practice: discipline and persistence (behavioral); craftsmanship and care (artisanal); collegiality and collaboration (social); and positivity and pleasure (emotional) (Sword 2017b).

While all these habits are important, which ones need to be foregrounded may depend on the genre you are writing in. As Ruth Healey (personal communication, July 2, 2019) notes, the genre you are writing in at any given time may affect both where and how you write:

> In approaching something that is more of a personal experience, I can smash out ideas in relatively short time frames and come back to it easily as it's all in my head already, but when I'm trying to comprehend/

communicate more complex theoretical ideas or interpret empirical evidence, I need longer time frames.

Time and space are dimensions of reality in which we all live,
yet we each experience different kinds and degrees of choice and
control over them, depending on our current positions, goals, life
circumstances and responsibilities, and more. Therefore, this chapter
poses a series of questions that will help you discern which time
frames, spaces, and habits work best for you as a writer.

Allotting Time to Write

Whether you are a senior academic with lots of institutional
responsibilities, a newer academic trying to develop a teaching and
writing persona, a professional staff member, or a student scholar
managing an undergraduate or graduate workload, creating time for
writing can be a challenge.

As Paul Silvia (2018) argues, you need to *allot*—rather than *find*—
time for writing by prioritizing and being creative, and that takes
dedication and discipline. You may find helpful a highly structured
set of steps for designating time and being productive, such as that
provided by Robert Boice (1990). Chris Smith (2019) more recently
found that productive writers have a system for writing, and what
the system is does not matter as much as deliberately having one. As
Helen Sword (2016, 320-21) reminds us, there is no one right way to
make time for and manage your writing. Instead, she suggests reading
books and attending workshops or courses that will make you feel
more confident in your writing style and "forming collaborative relationships premised on emotional support rather than on disciplinary
sanctions" (321)—points she reinforces in the "S" of her "BASE."
To help yourself get clear on what might work for you in terms of
allotting time to write in a regular way, consider these questions:

Are you, by nature, a morning, afternoon, or evening person?

Some people (like Alison) wake up on their own every day long
before the sun comes up and are most alert and energetic at that time.
Other people are "night owls" and no amount of coffee can clear

their heads for writing before midnight. What time of day is best for you? If possible, try to write at a time of day when you are at your most alert and energetic.

What is the ideal stretch of time for you to get substantive writing done?

Are you most productive and satisfied with your work when you write in short, regular bursts, do you need longer, uninterrupted stretches, or can you mix and match these options? Do you need "warm-up time" or can you jump right in? Can you do some writing tasks (e.g., checking sources and references) in short bursts (15–30 minutes between other responsibilities) and focus in longer stretches on other aspects of writing (e.g., composing, revising)? No amount of time is too small to help form yourself into a writer, provided that it is taken up regularly so that you are making steady progress week by week.

What kind of flexibility do you have in your schedule?

If you have flexibility, can you arrange your schedule so that you can designate certain, regular times for writing that fall during your most alert and energetic times and that fit with the rest of your responsibilities? If you do not have flexibility, can you identify and protect some regular times for writing?

How will you keep track of your writing?

How do you maintain the thread of writing over time if you can't write in one concentrated period? Margy MacMillan (personal communication, July 25, 2019) suggests that, at the end of periods where you have gotten a lot done, it is helpful to use a journal with entries that recap what you accomplished for when you can return to the project. What kind of weekly calendar or planner can you keep in which you commit (in writing!) to writing? How will you reward yourself for making progress? Positive psychology tells us that this is important. Promising yourself little rewards, such as a cup of coffee or a walk, when you have completed a particular task, for example, writing a page or drafting a section, can be self-motivating. Beyond daily planning, what kind of longer-term publication plan can you create for yourself (see chapter 29)?

How you respond to all these questions will help you clarify who you are as a writer (and, perhaps, how you might need to evolve), how who you are intersects with what else you need to do, and what kinds of structures you need to put into place to ensure that you find time for writing. As Pat Hutchings (personal communication, June 10, 2019) notes, "I have increasingly heard people talking about writing as a practice—i.e., something with routines and rituals, like yoga or Tai Chi or prayer perhaps." This point links to several of the points of Helen Sword's (2017b) "BASE," including the behaviors of discipline and persistence, the artisanal habits of craftsmanship and care, and the emotional habits of positivity and pleasure. What does or could your writing practice look like?

Choosing Space to Write

How your writing space feels matters, unless you are like Kelly with two young children (see Our Perspectives 23.1), in which case time is more important than space. Some people write best in bustling cafés and others in secluded silence, but there is more to what makes a space conducive to writing than noise level. Also, if you have the luxury of choice, consider aesthetics, temperature, lighting, and other atmospheric qualities when you choose a space to write.

To help yourself get clear on what might work for you in terms of choosing space to write, consider these questions:

What qualities of space do you need for writing?

Which spaces draw you, make you feel able to focus, inspire you, or otherwise are conducive to writing? Do you have access to your own space, or do you carve out an area within a larger shared space?

What else is in the space?

Does clutter bother you and, if so, can you clear it out? Can you decorate the space to make it your own? Do you have a comfortable chair? A desk at the right height? How a space is filled can support or hinder your writing efforts.

What kind of lighting helps you write?

A space that has insufficient light to illuminate what you are reading or composing is obviously not conducive to writing, but neither is a space that is too bright or has artificial lighting that makes a buzzing sound or some such distraction. Helen Sword (2016, 321; see also 2017b) has long argued for seeking out writing venues "filled with light and air."

How you respond to all these questions will help you clarify what you need in terms of physical environment as a writer. Having some choice in creating your writing space is part of a larger sense of agency you need to develop as a writer, even if you have to carve out a space that is less than ideal.

Our Perspectives 23.1

Times and spaces we find for writing

Kelly: My life is crazy with two small kids at home and a work schedule filled with weekly meetings and teaching blocks. So long spans of time for writing or week-long writing retreats/vacations are not possible. All I need for writing is myself and something to write on. For example, I once wrote an editorial using a basic note-pad app on my phone in between infant feedings. After a month, I had the bones of the piece drafted. If I had waited for the right lighting and ambience, well, I would still be waiting. For years, I harbored the dream of place, space, and time for writing, and it was not helpful for me. Now, I prioritize writing—not planning the space and time for writing. I also accept that it is not possible for me to write every day, yet I can write almost anywhere when I have the time. I do schedule one work day per week for writing (taken over by other tasks 60% of the time), and I can sit for six hours straight writing before hunger and bathroom breaks disrupt me.

Mick:Throughout my career I've always done my writing at home. Now that I am independent, I am based at home. I rarely start work before 9am and contrary to many of the time management guides,

I like to clear as many emails as possible before I start reading or writing. Sometimes that means waiting until after lunch. I appreciate a late afternoon siesta, as this gives me the energy to work for three or four more hours in the evening. Weekends are often the most productive times as there are fewer emails! However, it's not all work. I also take the dogs for a walk and play tennis when I am at home. I work best in my study at my desk where I overlook the garden, though on a nice summer day I'll take my laptop and work in the garden. I travel a lot, and I find that train journeys can be quite productive, as long as I remember to take my headphones to listen to classical music and block out distracting noise. I keep mundane tasks, such as preparing a list of references, for while I watch TV.

Alison: I do my best writing in the (very) early mornings, in the solitude of any silent space I can sit with my laptop computer. I am a morning person, and I often spend a couple of hours between 5:00 (or even 4:00) and 7:00 working on my writing before the sun rises and before my daughter wakes up. I can also spend full days writing and need to remind myself to take breaks, walk outside, eat something. I need absolute silence to write (well, wind and rain don't bother me, but almost everything else does), so busy times of day and loud places like cafés or airports really don't work for me.

Your perspective: What times and spaces do you find for writing?

Over to You

Time and space are dimensions over which you will have varying degrees of control. What can you do to maximize your use of the time and space available to you? Keep in mind that writing for different genres might affect where and how you write. For example, if you are writing about more personal experiences that are in your head already, you might need less time; if you are trying to comprehend or communicate more complex theoretical ideas or interpret empirical evidence, you might need more time. Consider, too, where you are based—in a single- or multi-campus university—or whether you want to connect with colleagues at nearby campuses. Do you want to share space or work on a non-home campus in a pre-booked room nice and quietly where no one can find you?

Addressing the following questions may help inform your decisions about allotting time and making space to write:

- What do you know about yourself as a writer? Are you, by nature, a morning, afternoon, or evening person? What is the ideal stretch of time for you to get substantive writing done?
- How does who you are as a writer intersect with your life and how you keep track of your writing?
- How can you make steady progress week by week?
- What qualities of space do you need for writing, and what is or could be in your writing space?

CHAPTER 24

WRITING AND REWRITING YOUR DRAFT

The Writing Process as Iterative

When we write we not only produce text, we also produce ourselves as scholars. (Thomson 2015)

In this opening quote, Pat Thomson reminds us that writing produces both texts and selves. As with many dimensions of writing, there are numerous texts, including those we reference repeatedly throughout these chapters, to guide you through the various and multiple steps of drafting. We do not reiterate all or even much of that kind of detailed guidance because doing so is both unnecessary (since others have already done an excellent job, for example, in the works authored and co-authored by Pat Thomson) and impossible (in the space we have). Instead, we focus in this chapter on the key considerations that you, as a new or experienced author, should keep in mind when writing for the different genres we include in this book and as you strive to produce yourself as a particular kind of scholar.

Below we offer some general recommendations for drafting texts about learning and teaching that should apply across all genres, and then we discuss the importance of clearly articulating your argument. Then, we move through each genre, offering questions you might ask yourself as you draft. These questions are intended to help you keep in mind how, in your drafting process, you are working toward engaging in conversation with fellow learning and teaching scholars, clarifying and shaping your values and identities as a learning and teaching scholar, and using writing to learn.

Recommendations for Drafting across All Kinds of Genres

As we noted in the introduction to part 5 of this book, we hope that, as you develop and refine your writing, you will strive for the most generative balance between, on the one hand, working within established structures and expectations for writing and, on the other, pushing beyond those structures and expectations. The reason for this is both to stretch yourself as a writer and as a scholar of learning and teaching and to help the structures and expectations of the various genres become more accommodating of a diversity of authors. When you set out to draft a text, no matter what genre you are working within, we recommend that you do the following:

Familiarize or Re-familiarize Yourself with the Expectations for the Genre

- Which of the expectations is it essential that you meet (e.g., including components such as a literature review for an empirical research article; achieving a particular word count; referencing other work that has been published in that journal or outlet)?
- Which of the expectations might be more flexible (e.g., methods; voice [passive or active]; person [first or third])?
- With which of the expectations are you most comfortable and familiar? Do you want to start with writing toward meeting those, to give you a boost in energy and confidence, or save those for when you need a boost?

Capture Your Ideas Informally

- Consider keeping a diary, journal, or document on your computer or smartphone with you at all times and jot down thoughts as they come to you—or speak them into a smartphone or other recording device. If you wait until you get to your regular writing place and time, you may have forgotten them.
- When you are ready to sit down and write, you may also want to speak first. Writing can feel like a real risk or a commitment

for some people. So, as Margy MacMillan (personal communication, July 25, 2019) suggests: "Talk it through with your phone set to record. Sometimes we can be freer in getting the ideas out in speaking rather than writing—even better if you use something that can convert voice to text automatically."

- As Kathryn Sutherland describes in Reflection 7.1 (The experience of using Thomson and Kamler's (2013) three types of collaborative writing), you might try the "type-talk" technique with a colleague or critical friend, whereby one person talks and the other types, and then you switch roles.

Make an Outline

- Consider making an outline that includes the required sections of the genre or, if there are not required sections, the order in which you want to make your points.
- To structure your outline, you can use the Guiding Questions included in chapters 12-22; these questions also appear in the online resources.
- To start with, simply jot notes or write/paste in bits and pieces you want to be sure to include. It can be helpful to see them organized in outline form like this before you start writing.
- It can be helpful to make an outline at any stage of the drafting process, including part way through or even at the end. As staff at almost any university writing center will contend, writing an outline allows you to see the bigger picture to more easily identify lack of flow and logic. Outlines serve different functions and help you address different writing questions at different stages of writing.

Give Yourself Permission to Fill in Text in Whatever Order Works for You

- Some people work best if they make their way through from the beginning to end of a draft, starting by writing an introduction (even if they know it will likely change), then mapping out the subsequent sections.

- Other people can get more writing accomplished if they plug in bits and pieces of different parts of their draft when they feel inspired or have the time. For instance, you might have done some reading of literature that you want to be sure to include, so you work on that part of the draft first. Or, you might have some key insights or lessons that you know you want to emphasize in a discussion section, so you can start with articulating preliminary versions of those.

Revise but Do Not Perfect as You Draft

- There is an important difference between revising, rethinking, and redrafting, on the one hand, and putting pressure on yourself to capture exactly what you want to say in each sentence or section as you go. Many good writers write what Anne Lamott (1994, 21) calls "shitty first drafts," and she reminds us that "this is how they end up with good second drafts and terrific third drafts." Let the drafting be iterative, organic if you prefer, or even messy.
- Keep copies of each draft, giving each document a clear file name, such as with a short title and date or v1, v2, which will help you keep track of which is the most recent (rather than "latest draft," which will not be helpful).
- Consider preparing a version that is under the word limit, because reviewers almost always ask for more—more explanation, more references, more supporting data, more implications. Having a manuscript under the word count gives you a little wiggle room (or else you will have to cut as you add in responses to reviewer requests).

Seek Input and Feedback at Key Points

While it makes sense to spend some time gathering, drafting, rethinking, and revising your work on your own, it is also helpful to seek input and feedback from critical friends at various points. As we discuss in chapter 26, it is essential to develop networks and groups of critical friends whom you can ask for feedback.

- How might it be helpful to you to talk through your ideas with a critical friend before starting to draft?
- Which of your critical friends might be best suited to reading a very rough and messy draft when you are in the early stages in order to help you shape it and give it direction?
- Which of your critical friends is particularly good at getting you unstuck when you are stuck on a writing project?
- How do you decide when your draft is nearly finished and would benefit from a critical read to help you complete or polish it?

These general guidelines should be helpful to you across genres. In Reflection 24.1, we quote a blog post by Pat Thomson (2019f) in which she outlines how she goes about drafting a paper.

Reflection 24.1

Writing a draft paper

"I write in chunks. I'm doing it right now as I'm book writing under deadline pressure. . . .

"Here's how I do it. To begin, I spend time writing an initial road map—a tiny text [Thomson 2019g]—for the paper or chapter. I then amass the various bits and pieces that I think I'm going to use—quotations, bits of data (my writing mise-en-place [Thomson 2012]). I often have various books and PDFs open on my desktop and on the floor. At this point I'm ready to write chunks. I always start with the introductory chunk, as this sets the tone and argument thread for the whole piece. After I have the intro done I revisit my tiny text and make any adjustments I need to. I then work out how many steps there are in the argument to come. Each step is a section of the paper with heading. Each step is a chunk. . . .

"Writing in chunks is not the same as writing to a word count or writing to time. Chunk writing usually looks and feels a bit stop-and-startish while it's happening. I work consistently at the screen but swap between referencing, copying, or cutting and pasting.

Sometimes it becomes obvious that I need something not at hand and I'll either stop and find it, or leave a marker that I can come back to at the end of the chunk-writing. I do a clean-up at the end.

"Chunk writing always seems quite creative, seeing the various elements come together. I like to keep the flow going so that, in reality, I spend more time on writing new text than in inserting or hunting and gathering. I also try not to edit what I've done too much as I know that this is a first draft. I'll get another go. And another. Writing a chunk of text, of variable length, but usually between one and two thousand words—sometimes a bit shorter or longer—usually takes me the best part of a morning. . . .

"For me, the magic trick in writing in chunks comes from focusing on one step in the argument at a time. I keep the current step at the forefront of my mind. I don't worry about what's come before or what is to come next. I don't get distracted by the whole. I just focus on this bit. Here. Now. You write a whole [chunk], not a part. You stop when you're done. And it's very satisfying to make the last full stop knowing that you have advanced the chapter by taking that one more step."

(Source: Pat Thomson 2019f. Reproduced by permission of the author.)

Pat Thomson is a professor of education at the University of Nottingham, UK.

The Importance of Clarifying Your Argument

Writing produces text and selves, as Pat Thomson notes in the quote at the beginning of this chapter. It does this through intentional and iterative processes of shaping and reshaping arguments. As the term suggests, an argument is a single, clear reason or a more complex set of reasons presented with the goal of convincing or persuading someone of a way of thinking or a way of being. An argument might contend that a particular idea or approach is right or wrong, but as genres expand, so too must the notion of an argument to include not only "over against" points but also "yes, and" discussions. For some genres, for instance, such as reflective essays and stories, an argument might be a demonstration or narrative that aims to convince readers of the importance of considering something they had not thought about previously—not to replace but to expand existing perceptions. The iterative process of writing allows you to clarify and convey your argument. Ron Barnett provides a useful discussion of this in our online resource, "The Distinction between Thesis, Argument, and Argumentation."

As with all aspects of writing, your identities and values will shape what you argue, as will having a sense of the audience you aim to persuade, present with a particular perspective, or encourage to build on and expand previous understandings. Ensure that your argument is clear, strong, and compelling by being aware of how dimensions of your identity inform your perspective and what you argue, and by considering the logic, line of reasoning, or narrative that will convey your argument to a particular audience. In keeping with our metaphor of conversation, imagine that you are actually in dialogue with someone or with a particular group, and consider how you might best communicate with them.

The way you develop your argument and the evidence you use to support it depends in part on the genre in which you are writing. An argument can be a perspective (as in an opinion piece); it can be a call for a change in practice based on evidence of the outcomes of such a revision (as in an empirical research article); or, as noted above, it can be more of a demonstration of an important experience. The basic questions you want to address here include whom you are trying to convince of what and why, or whether your writing is striving instead to communicate an understanding rather than convince.

Recommendations for Drafting by Kinds of Genre

Below we offer recommendations for each genre, which can be downloaded in a table format in the online resource, "Overview of the Eleven Genres to Support Writing Drafts."

Empirical Research Articles

Use the Guiding Questions on page 121 or in the online resources to create an outline for yourself.

What to keep in mind while drafting: While the strict requirements of an empirical research article might seem constraining to some, they can also be seen as providing a clear structure that you can work, and even wiggle, within. In particular, they afford you the flexibility to jump around among the sections, as we suggest in our general guidelines above, filling in different parts when you have time and are in that frame of mind (to describe methods, for instance, which is more technical, or to work on the discussion, which requires more creativity and analysis).

Questions you might ask yourself as you draft: What particular contribution do my data, argument, and implications have to offer? How am I situating those within larger, ongoing conversations or positioning them to start a new conversation?

Theoretical and Conceptual Articles

Use the Guiding Questions on page 136 or in the online resources to create an outline for yourself.

What to keep in mind while drafting: Your theoretical or conceptual article aims to provoke, deepen, or expand thinking about learning and teaching, so you should ensure that you keep front and center in your mind how your draft is doing that.

Questions you might ask yourself as you draft: How does the point I am making here provoke, deepen, or expand thinking? Of course, every point you make does not need to do that in, of, and by itself, but if you endeavor to address the question repeatedly, you might find interesting patterns or themes that help clarify your argument as you write.

Literature Reviews

Use the Guiding Questions on page 148 or in the online resources to create an outline for yourself.

What to keep in mind while drafting: Because a freestanding literature review is primarily an analysis of what has already been published, albeit within a new frame and possibly opening new directions for thinking, it gives you an opportunity to join a conversation about learning and teaching from your particular perspective as a new, experienced, or student scholar without having to generate new data or a new conceptual model. Your synthesis should go beyond summarizing the literature and produce new insights and often a new framework.

Questions you might ask yourself as you draft: How does the point I am making here help readers understand in a new way what has already been presented or argued?

Case Studies

Use the Guiding Questions on page 158 or in the online resources to create an outline for yourself.

What to keep in mind while drafting: Contributing a discussion of a particular approach in your own practice affords you an opportunity to present yourself as a learning and teaching scholar and also invites potential dialogue and collaboration around the practice you present.

Questions you might ask yourself as you draft: What is this a case study of? What is most compelling and important about this case study to me as an author? What might readers find most compelling and inspiring?

Books and Edited Collections

Use the Guiding Questions on page 174 (for books) or 177 (for edited collections) or in the online resources to create an outline for yourself.

What to keep in mind while drafting: For a book proposal ensure your passion for the subject matter comes through as well as the need for the book and the potential market.

As an author or authors drafting a book, among your principle concerns will be organization, breadth, and depth. You are telling a larger and longer story than in any other genre we discuss, and so you need to map out and regularly check whether you are achieving the best balance between breadth and depth as you work within a word limit. Regularly return to the theme or focus of the text and ask yourself if you are still addressing that theme or focus and how you can ensure coherence.

As an editor of a collection, you will also need to consider organization, breadth, and depth, but in terms of other people's writing rather than your own. When you invite chapters, consider providing a template or outline that asks authors to address the same points as all other authors in the collection, but of course in their own ways and focused on their own contributions. As you offer feedback and guidance to chapter authors, consider ways in which you can ensure a coherent experience for your readers, reminding authors to address the sections of the outline provided.

Questions you might ask yourself as you draft: Have I articulated or invited a sufficiently diverse set of perspectives? Are the chapters organized in the best order to build into an engaging and coherent whole?

For a book proposal: Why is there a need for this book? What is the overarching argument?

For a book: Am I deepening, expanding, or otherwise developing the argument as I move through the book, or, alternatively, offering a logical series of perspectives from different angles?

For an edited collection: Are we ensuring that each chapter has integrity but also that there is consistency across chapters?

Conference and Workshop Presentations

Use the Guiding Questions on page 187 or in the online resources to create an outline for yourself.

What to keep in mind while drafting: Many people find it best to avoid writing out your presentation, as reading from a script is rarely effective. Drafting some outline notes in bullet format that you memorize and use as prompts when you talk to your audience is much better than attempting to read a script, because how we talk and how we write are significantly different, for example, in terms of length and construction of sentences. You need to make sure the connections and transitions are clear and be prepared to respond to real-time input and feedback—questions and suggestions from participants. For a workshop devote as much time to designing the activities as designing the presentation portion of the workshop. For posters the layout and design are as important as the content.

Questions you might ask yourself as you draft: Will this [statement, activity] be clear and accessible on a first hearing? Is the series of steps I am moving through/asking participants to move through logical and compelling and will they lead them to engage productively with the topic?

Reflective Essays

Use the Guiding Questions on page 199 or in the online resources to create an outline for yourself.

What to keep in mind while drafting: Reflective essays are not necessarily trying to prove or convince but rather to convey the particulars of a lived experience and their significance.

Questions you might ask yourself as you draft: In what ways am I conveying the lived experience I am describing and analyzing?

Opinion Pieces

Use the Guiding Questions on page 212 or in the online resources to create an outline for yourself.

What to keep in mind while drafting: In an opinion piece you are conveying your own particular perspective, so you need to consider how best to make that "hearable" and compelling to readers who may not have thought of what you address or may disagree.

Questions you might ask yourself as you draft: What is my main argument? What voice or perspective am I adding to the ongoing conversation about learning and teaching and why is it important?

Stories

Use the Guiding Questions on page 225 or in the online resources to create an outline for yourself.

What to keep in mind while drafting: Since a story is a narrative, an attempt to capture and convey something you have experienced or witnessed but without the necessity to prove or convince, your focus can be on the details that will bring the experience most vividly alive for readers. Stories might be the most challenging genre in which to gain enough distance from the content to convey it effectively to readers, so try to be cognizant of that challenge as you are drafting.

Questions you might ask yourself as you draft: In what ways am I moving from writer-based to reader-based prose—from writing for myself as audience to work through my ideas to writing for an external audience, someone not inside my own head?

Social Media

Use the Guiding Questions on page 238 or in the online resources to create an outline for yourself.

What to keep in mind while drafting: Social media, including blog posts, listserv messages, or tweets, allow you to play with the format in creative ways and to write outside of narrow academic constraints. Drafting involves writing text along with consideration of the format, images, and hyperlinks to other outlets.

Questions you might ask yourself as you draft: What do I want readers to take away from my social media contribution and how do I want to express myself as a writer using social media?

Teaching Award, Fellowship, and Promotion Applications

Use the Guiding Questions on page 246 or in the online resources to create an outline for yourself.

What to keep in mind while drafting: Drafting such applications is an iterative process that has to focus on the criteria. Kelly's drafting approach consists of: claim (of "excellence") + example (of what you do in your teaching) + evidence (data supporting excellence claim). She gets people to write these in outline form first and then to think through the flow. Don't forget the role critical friends can play in this genre, because they will see your practices and praise you in ways that you might not see.

Questions you might ask yourself as you draft: As I draft my application, how can I keep to the forefront my compelling argument as to how I meet the criteria?

Over to You

Drafting is an iterative process that should take into consideration your own goals and your audience's interests; as you draft, you are producing yourself as well as your argument, as Pat Thomson notes in the quote with which we open this chapter. Questions to address about writing and rewriting your draft include:

- How might you use structures, guiding questions, outlines, and dialogue with critical friends to help ensure that you clarify and embrace your values as a writer and use the drafting process to learn?
- With which expectations are you already familiar in any given genre and with which do you need to familiarize yourself?
- What structures or questions might be most useful to you in your drafting process?
- At what points in the drafting process might you use outlining and why?
- In what order might you fill in different sections of the texts and why?
- Which of your critical friends might you consult at different stages of drafting and why?
- At what point do you feel your texts are ready for submission?

CHAPTER 25

BECOMING AN ENGAGING WRITER

How to Compel and Inspire

Pick up a peer-reviewed journal in just about any academic discipline and what will you find? Impersonal, stodgy, jargon-laden, abstract prose that ignores or defies most of the stylistic principles [I have] outlined. (Sword 2012, 3)

Becoming an engaging writer requires working against what Helen Sword describes in the quote above. It is a combination of asserting your own voice and ensuring that you write in ways that are accessible and compelling to your intended audience. How you achieve this depends in part on which genre you choose, but we suggest that accessibility should be a goal across genres. Among the three of us, we have different levels of comfort and confidence regarding our writing capacities, but we agree in principle, as we argue in this chapter, that writing should be clear, have a strong voice, and strive to be stylish.

Engaging Writing Is Clear to the Reader

Think about what the word "clear" means. Its primary definitions focus on the experience people have if something is clear: it is easy to perceive, understand, or interpret; it is comprehensible and coherent. A secondary and equally important definition refers to the thing itself, the substance: it is transparent, unclouded—one can see through it. It's worth thinking about these definitions in relation to writing, which strives to create an experience for people, and which uses the medium, the substance, of words.

William Zinnser (1998) has argued that the secret of good writing is clarity—stripping every sentence to its cleanest components. Robert Harris (2017) concurs, as the title of his book, *Writing with Clarity and Style*, suggests. The words, sentences, and paragraphs should not only be comprehensible, they should also compel and provoke in productive ways rather than hinder understanding or distract from or obscure what you as a writer are addressing. A mistake many writers make is to try to sound fancy, to mistake unnecessary complexity for sophistication, but such efforts usually obfuscate rather than clarify. Simple, direct language is typically most effective and certainly most accessible to a wide range of readers. And sentences and paragraphs should not be too long, a tendency in some writing that reveals lack of clarity in the argument.

Consider the following excerpt from Alise de Bie's (2019) article on how "Mad students" come to be abandoned as knowers and learners, and practice loneliness as a form of Mad knowing:

> When I politicize and spend time with loneliness, rather than attempt to contain or resolve it, it has a lot to teach me about what I want from "justice," and I have come to consider it an essential quality of how I approach knowing Madly and creating Mad knowledge (de Bie 2019). Fricker (2007) argues that epistemic injustices lead to a literal loss and erosion of knowledge, and prevent knowledge from coming into existence, and I confirm and grieve that this occurs in the ways already described and a host of other ways. At the same time, so much of my knowledge has been developed in the presence of, in desperation over, and in reaction and contrast to the loneliness that I experience as a Mad knower and learner; many Mad experiences (especially those related to abandonment and loneliness) and ways of knowing are sharply tied to oppression, although oppression is not all that we are (Nicolazzo 2017). To consider getting rid of loneliness or sending it away breaks my heart, as this only sustains the treatment of loneliness (and myself

as someone living loneliness) as a problem, and further facilitates hermeneutical injustice by failing to recognize this emergent loneliness as a form of Mad knowledge.

In this excerpt Alise de Bie employs a style that is clear—writing in direct ways—and that contrasts with what Helen Sword (2012) critiques in the opening quotation: de Bie's writing is personal rather than impersonal; compelling rather than stodgy; and concrete rather than abstract. Note, too, that they come into conversation with other scholars while clearly holding their own voice and sharing their lived experience. This example of de Bie's writing seeks to change the conversation in learning and teaching scholarship through inviting a different way of understanding the process and experience of knowledge creation and legitimating them. Their writing illustrates how the style of writing and the substance of what they are communicating through words work together.

One way of checking your writing to make sure it is clear is to ask yourself the simple question: Have I written this in the most direct way possible? Try writing a sentence several different ways and see which one is clearest. Try reading sentences, paragraphs, and even whole papers out loud. You might be surprised to find how hearing words spoken can quickly reveal lack of clarity and coherence. Also, as Ronald Barnett (personal communication, July 28, 2019) recommends, "Try to imagine yourself in a café with 3–4 other people, representative of different groups and interests, and imagine yourself speaking to them, and trying to take each of them with you, all at the same time."

Engaging Writing Has a Strong Voice

"Voice" is a contested term in virtually every arena. It certainly references sound, typically in relation to speaking, but it has been used more metaphorically to mean opinion or, as Alison has argued, to signal presence and power (Cook-Sather 2006). The excerpt from Alise de Bie (2019) above shows a form of power and presence in their writing, one example of a strong voice. bell hooks (1994, 12) suggests that the feminist focus on "coming to voice" emphasizes "moving from silence into speech as a revolutionary gesture." She notes that African American women in particular "must work against speaking as 'other'" (hooks 1994, 16) and embrace coming to voice "as a gesture of resistance, an affirmation of struggle" (hooks 1994, 18). hooks' points link to our contention in chapter 3 that not everyone has the same standing, the same voice, in any given context or discourse community, and speaking and writing carries different stakes for different people.

"Voice" has been debated as a term in writing since at least the 1980s, first in the grammatical sense of whether to use passive or active voice, although most scholars agree that active voice "makes your meaning clear for readers" (Purdue Online Writing Lab n.d.). The more important debate is over how an author establishes an authentic voice. While the "sound" or quality of a writer's voice is mediated by identity, context, and intended readers, ideally voice conveys a writer's identity, experiences, values, and perspectives. Through developing voice rather than using jargon and stock phrases, you can achieve an authenticity in your writing and be committed to what you are saying. It is your own voice and no one else's.

Writing scholar Peter Elbow (2007) argues that there are good reasons to attend to voice in writing and good reasons to ignore it, and over the last ten years, while the concept of voice continues to be debated among writing scholars, it has been taken up by linguists, particularly in relation to constructing an identity in academic discourse (Flowerdew and Wang 2015). We suggest that it is a useful concept both for what it signals regarding the human being behind the words (not necessarily that the person is knowable through their words) and what it signals regarding the intentional construction of an identity in any given piece of writing.

The voice in which you present your ideas will have a powerful impact on how people "hear" them. As we note in relation to the excerpt from Alise de Bie's article above, clearly locating authority both in theory and in lived experiences can often make an argument more "hearable." The following sentences from the abstract of Tara Yosso's (2005, 69) highly influential article "Whose Culture Has

Capital? A Critical Race Theory Discussion of Community Cultural Wealth" calls for a profound shift in how we understand culture and the cultural capital of learners:

> This article conceptualizes community cultural wealth as a critical race theory (CRT) challenge to traditional interpretations of cultural capital. CRT shifts the research lens away from a deficit view of Communities of Color as places full of cultural poverty disadvantages, and instead focuses on and learns from the array of cultural knowledge, skills, abilities and contacts possessed by socially marginalized groups that often go unrecognized and unacknowledged.

Through use of clear assertions such as "shifts the research lens away from a deficit view" and through modelling the alternative, recognizing and valuing "the array of cultural knowledge, skills, abilities and contacts possessed by socially marginalized groups," Yosso's voice positions her as authoritative and allows her to make a compelling argument for a profound change of mindset and values. The shift for which she argues has informed the work Alison and colleagues have done in SoTL, specifically in recognizing students, particularly underrepresented students, as partners in explorations and co-creation of learning and teaching (Cook-Sather and Agu 2013; de Bie et al. 2019).

The voice a writer uses for each different genre can be equally strong but sound different. Consider, for instance, this student's voice in the opening lines of "Leaping and Landing in Brave Spaces," a reflective essay:

> It is hard to describe in words the feeling of deciding to speak or raise my hand in a classroom. It is a crucial moment, the moment between silence and sound, closed and open. It can happen in many different ways: I can feel it as I write, as I make any kind of art, tell a story, or do something that breaks the boundary between myself and the world around me. This feeling of exposure to

others can lead to hurt or rejection or great joy and growth. (Abbott 2016, 1)

Clara Abbott's voice is strong because she is so present in it; there is an immediacy, a vividness, an honesty to her words, and they create a multi-sensory experience for readers, drawing us in and making us feel that Abbott is in an informal, even intimate, conversation with us about the experience of learning.

While voice in publications is typically in the form of written words, it can be very helpful to read your written words out loud to make sure that they will be both readable and compelling to others. Linking our emphasis on voice (in this section) and style (in the next), Pat Hutchings (personal communication, June 10, 2019) notes: "For me, voice, and style too, have a lot to do with rhythm. I always find it useful to read what I've written out loud. And if I'm writing with someone, we read it back and forth to each other. Takes a while, but [it's] worth it."

We do recognize though that the ingredients of becoming an engaged writer vary culturally, as Nadya Yakovchuk states clearly in Reflection 25.1.

Reflection 25.1

Engaging writing and cultural context

For me, authorial voice is inextricably linked to authorial identity—how you see yourself as a writer and where you position yourself within your academic community on a spectrum from novice to expert. It is also influenced by the disciplinary and cultural context you come from. I remember writing my first assignment on a Masters course in the UK back in 2000 and using "we" throughout (as in "we suggest" or "our approach") to indicate my position on the topic and signal my presence as an author. This was a common way of writing in Belarus, the post-Soviet country I come from, even for single-authored papers and coursework. I'd imagine this was because of the reluctance to emphasize the individual "I" in a still predominantly collectivist society and perhaps also to acknowledge the "behind the scenes" work of supervisors or academic advisors that may have gone into the final product. My UK tutor queried me good-naturedly at the time—"Who are 'we'? Is this the royal we?"—and we discussed the conventions of academic writing in the UK context. This memory stayed with me because the approach to and the underlying assumptions around expressing oneself in academic writing were so different in the two contexts I was operating in at the time.

Dr Nadya Yakovchuk is a teaching fellow in academic writing, Doctoral College, at the University of Surrey, UK.

Engaging Writing Is Stylish Writing

While the word "stylish" might evoke the realm of fashion rather than academe, Helen Sword (2012) uses the term in a particular way (see chapters 2 and 6 of this book for further reference to her work). In the afterword to her book, *Stylish Academic Writing*, she argues that all stylish writers hold three ideals in common. The first is *communication*, which implies respect for your audience. The second is *craft*, which requires respect for language. The third is *creativity* or respect for the academic endeavor.

To these ideals, Sword adds three more. The first is *concreteness*, which she defines as a verbal technique: the use of "words that engage the senses and anchor your ideas in physical space" (2012, 173). The second is *choice*, which she asserts as an intellectual right: the intellectual right to choose which words you use and what effect they will have. She suggests that writers need to be what Donald Schön (1987) calls reflective practitioners in the realm of writing—always engaged in monitoring and adjusting methods. Finally, she adds *courage*, which she proposes is a frame of mind. While it is possible to always play safe and write in ways that conform to expectations out of fear that you might fail or disappoint, Sword (2012, 174) asks, "Why always assume the worst rather than aim for the best?"

Sword ends her book with an exhortation to writers to produce writing that "engages, impresses, and inspires" (2012, 175) through embracing the six ideals she discusses in her afterword. These ideals are consistent with some of the other points we have made in this chapter about engaging writing and with the threads we weave throughout this book: engaging in conversation with fellow learning and teaching scholars, fostering your identities through a values-based approach to writing, and using writing to learn. In Our Perspectives 25.1, we share our own development in relation to clarity, voice, and style.

Our Perspectives 25.1

Clarity, voice, and style in our writing

Alison: I am heavily influenced by all the fiction and poetry I read as a college undergraduate and taught as an instructor of high school English. I chose to major in English literature and then teach it because I love language—how beautiful it can sound and how powerfully it can capture human experience and insight. So when I write, I try to keep in mind the clear prose, the strong voices, and the elegant arguments and stories that make up so much of what I have read, and I try to bring some version of those to my writing about learning and teaching.

Mick: This is the area of the book I feel least comfortable with. Although I strive to be clear in my writing, and I have become more used to writing in the first person, style is not something I would ever claim. One of the many benefits of working with Alison is that she has done much to turn my turgid text into something more presentable. This is an area I need to learn more about.

Kelly: Yeah, no. Of course I want to communicate through writing in ways that make sense to my audience. I don't want my terrible execution of English grammar to diminish the content of what I am communicating. Perhaps because I know I am not a wordsmith, I tend to write in simple, direct ways without fancy words. When I try to be more than I am as a writer, I fail, and am then reminded to write like Kelly Matthews. Writing is a journey of communication and if readers understand what I am communicating, then I feel successful as a writer.

Your perspective: What is your sense of clarity, voice, and style in your writing?

Over to You

Striving for clarity, strong voice, and stylishness will not only make your writing engaging to others but can also make it more engaging to you. If you feel you are writing in ways that are clear, true to yourself, and dynamic, you will feel energized rather than depleted by writing. This, we suggest, is because you are experiencing a connection with yourself as a person with meaningful experiences and insights, and you are experiencing the potential of connecting with other people. It is an area, though, that many of us find challenging. Pause and reflect on your answers to these questions:

- Is your writing clear? Have you selected precise, accurate, clear, accessible words and arranged them in an order that conveys your intended meaning?
- Is the voice you have constructed for your writing true to your identity? Does it seek to connect with readers who share dimensions of your identity as well as those who may have different identities?
- Does your writing achieve the six ideals—communication, craft, creativity, concreteness, choice, and courage—as well as rigor, insight, imagination, and largeness of vision?

CHAPTER 26

SEEKING NETWORKS, CRITICAL FRIENDS, AND FEEDBACK

The Social Aspect of Writing

> *The critical friend is a powerful idea, perhaps because it contains an inherent tension. Friends bring a high degree of unconditional positive regard. . . . Critics are, at first sight at least, conditional, negative and intolerant of failure. Perhaps the critical friend comes closest to what might be regarded as "true friendship"—a successful marrying of unconditional support and unconditional critique. (MacBeath and Jardine 1998, 41)*

If writing is part of a conversation, it is sensible to ask one or two critical friends to look at what you have written before you submit your ideas for publication. The combination of qualities John MacBeath and Stewart Jardine note in the quote above is indeed what you need in someone reading drafts and revisions of your work. We have mentioned the importance of critical friends at several different points in this book (e.g., in chapter 24). Some colleagues find it helpful to join a writing group, which provides not only dedicated time for writing but also the opportunity to give and receive feedback from colleagues (see chapter 7). This chapter explores different ways that you can establish a group of critical friends and how to encourage them to give you supportive but also critical feedback.

Networking

Although we recognize that for some the term "networking" sounds too business-y and instrumental and that the writing relationships you form should be about developing long-lasting relationships (Cheng 2019), others see such work as critical for a successful career in academia (Hubrath 2008). Networking is a common topic in researcher development workshops and programs. For example, the University of Bristol (n.d.) has produced a six-part guide to networking on their researcher development website. There, they note that: "In the academic sector, the increasing value placed on collaborative partnerships and the emergence of the impact agenda have heightened the need to have a broad professional network." Building networks through social media is also important to enhance learning and teaching, research, professional practice, leadership, and career development (Rowell 2019; see also chapters 21 and 29).

Communicating about your work with others through your professional networks is part of building your identity as a learning and teaching scholar. Mick recalls how his economic geography and geography in higher education networks were largely separate in the 1980s and 1990s, though he did persuade them to come together when he co-edited two symposia on teaching economic geography (Healey and Clark 1994a, 1994b). Then, at the turn of the century, he had to develop an additional, largely new network as he began to participate in general higher education conferences and write pieces for transdisciplinary higher education journals (e.g., Healey 2000, 2003b). It was in part through effective networking that he achieved success in winning teaching awards and grants for higher education research and development, receiving funding for travel and participation in conferences, and greatly extending his national and international networks, which included some who became his critical friends.

Critical Friends

Özek, Edgren, and Jandér observe, "The critical friend method, which entails being a friend as well as having one, has proven to be a powerful tool to facilitate the process of continuous improvement in teaching" (2012, 70). There is an extensive critical friend literature (e.g., Costa and Kallick 1993; Moore and Carter-Hicks 2014), much of it focused on the role of critical friends throughout a project (e.g., Kember et al. 1997). Here we focus on the role of a critical friend in supporting writing, particularly commenting on draft manuscripts.

Identifying potential critical friends can be quite daunting if you are new to scholarship of teaching and learning (SoTL) and pedagogic research. Such friends might come from several sources, depending on what role you want them to play. Unless your institution allocates you a mentor (e.g., if you have been chosen to apply for a national teaching award), most will come from your professional network and will be people you already know and whom you choose to approach. They may be colleagues or peers at your university; people you have met in courses or at seminars, workshops, and conferences (see chapter 17); academic friends you have met through social media (see chapter 21); or other friends or relations. Most frequently, they will be people working in the same field as you, and they will be able to identify gaps in your argument or key sources you have not mentioned. Some will be the kind of people whom journal editors might ask to referee your work; others may be potential readers who are new to the topic area. You may request some friends to help you primarily with the clarity and style of your writing. Critical friends made during doctoral studies often remain in this role in your later academic life, and what started as a face-to-face relationship may move online (Morris and Cudworth 2018). If you are co-writing a piece, your co-authors will usually provide the first round of critical comments, but because of their role, co-authors may be too close to the subject. It is therefore helpful to have other critical friends who are not familiar with the topic comment on your writing. Networks of critical friends are even more important if you are writing on your own.

Care is needed in choosing appropriate critical friends, as it is in choosing potential co-authors (see chapter 7). The critical friend relationship is an emotional one, and you need to respect each other and be prepared to give and receive critical comments, as Rebecca

Hogue notes in Reflection 26.1. Sometimes these relationships are reciprocal, and you will in turn act as a critical friend to someone who took on that role for you. Every so often the experience of working together as critical friends can lead to you becoming co-authors. To an extent this is how the three of us came to write together. Sometimes this iterative process of being critical friends can lead to long-term writing partnerships, such as Mick developed with Alan Jenkins over twenty-five years, and Pat Thomson has experienced with Barbara Kamler (see chapter 7).

Reflection 26.1

What makes a good critical friend?

"I didn't really understand what it meant to have a critical friend or really what type of person makes a good critical friend until I found one. So I thought I'd share a little more about what makes a good critical friend.

"First and foremost, you need to find someone whose opinion you respect. If you don't respect their opinion, then you are wasting both their time and your time.

"Second, you must feel comfortable sharing your naked writing with your critical friend. Sharing first drafts can make you feel rather vulnerable, as you are exposing your unpolished work. You need to be comfortable enough to *accept feedback from this person without emotional attachments*. Anyone who is responsible for evaluating your work does not make a good critical friend.

"Third, you cannot be in a competitive relationship with this friend. This is why peers in the same academic year or program are not always your best choice for critical friends. When there is even the slightest sense of competition, then the review process becomes about comparing, rather than about providing authentic feedback (even if it is subconscious). You must both feel that there is no sense of competition for the critical friend relationship to work.

"And finally, your critical friend must be willing to be critical of your work and you must be willing to take the feedback (see my second comment about accepting feedback without emotional attachments). In an academic setting, it is often useful to have a critical friend who is from a different field, that way they can point out when you are making assumptions in your writing (this is always a concern when you are an expert in your field).

"I am lucky to have found the perfect critical friend. I deeply respect her and I am grateful for all the help she has given me. She helps me see the weaknesses in my arguments, and pushes me to improve. And although I am not emotionally attached to the feedback she provides, I feel a huge sense of accomplishment when she compliments my writing. Thank you critical friend!"

Source: Hogue (2012). Reproduced by permission of the author.

In writing this book our most important critical friends have been each other, as well as those whom we asked to read drafts of our text. Our experiences of writing are, of course, not transferable to all. You may be writing on your own, and you may not yet have developed an extensive network of critical friends. If that is the case, joining a writing group may be an attractive alternative (see chapter 7).

Giving Developmental Feedback

A theme running through this chapter is the desire to enhance our writing through giving and receiving developmental feedback. This feedback may be oral or written, but the challenge is the same: how to give critical feedback in a way that will help the recipient develop as a writer and not be perceived as criticizing them personally.

The context in which the feedback is given varies with the role you are playing. In some forms of the critical friend model, it is more like a mentor-mentee relationship (Johnson 2007), in which an experienced individual mentors a less experienced person; such relationships are highly individual and need to be negotiated between each pair (Carmel and Paul 2015). In contrast, in the context of a writing group, the role has more in common with a peer-support model (Healey et al. 2014), albeit in a group context. In both cases the providers of feedback need to be sensitive to how their feedback is being received. A good place to start is to ask the recipient where they are with their writing and what kind of feedback would be helpful to them at that stage in the process.

Keep in mind that it is very difficult for experienced writers to imagine what it is like "not knowing." Therefore, you want not only expert advice but also insights from those who are less experienced and who may use your work. Keep in mind, also, how tough some people find getting challenging feedback, especially when they've worked hard to write what they think is a final draft. There is also a lesson here in seeking feedback early rather than waiting until you feel you've almost finished.

Barbara Grant (2008, 61-2) suggests that when providing feedback to another writer, the following questions might help you to devise helpful responses:

- What is your immediate impression after reading this piece? Pick a few key words or images to describe your response.
- What are the immediate strengths you see in the piece? List at least two, and be as specific as possible.
- Is the focus/thesis clear? Are you able to tell the writer succinctly what the focus is?
- How well is the focus/thesis developed? Is supporting information clear, relevant, and presented in an orderly fashion? How well does the writer integrate primary/secondary source material, data analysis, and so forth?
- Where might there be problems?
- Has the writer's intent been clearly communicated such that non-specialists in the area might understand it?
- Has the writer's voice come to life for you? Can you describe where their voice is most alive and powerful? Where is it weak? Every writer must find their voice in their words. It is often difficult to create an appropriate tone in academic writing, given the constraints on the form.

We present in Table 26.1 some advice offered by several authorities, integrated with our own perspectives, regarding what to do, and what to avoid, when *giving* feedback and what to do when *requesting and receiving* feedback (a copy is also available in the online resources). If you are asked to give feedback to a colleague on their writing, or if you request that someone gives you feedback, this guidance may help you have a thoughtful dialogue. Sometimes you may give each other feedback and it may be iterative rather than a one-off occurrence. We include further discussion of responding to feedback in chapter 28.

Table 26.1: Giving and receiving effective developmental feedback

What to do when giving feedback
When possible, ask what the author would like feedback on, and what stage of development the manuscript is in.
Start by identifying what you think is working well and why and acknowledging what you think the writer is intending to do.
Give specific and substantiated praise and criticism and be precise regarding how you think the text might be enhanced.
Distinguish between macro-level issues (e.g., the clarity and consistency of the argument, and structure of the piece) and micro-level concerns (e.g., grammar and punctuation).
Suggest areas that might be cut or condensed as well as what to add; this is important when the piece is close to, or exceeding, the word limit.
Always respect the author, adopt a developmental approach, and make recommendations rather than judgments; consider how you would feel if you received this feedback.

What to avoid when giving feedback

Avoid concentrating on what is not in the piece; although it might be necessary to point out critical omissions, focus on improving what is in the piece.

Avoid making general or vague judgments to which it is difficult to respond; rather, be specific and action-oriented.

Avoid being obsessive about the author's bibliographic sources; although it is helpful to point out missing voices and perspectives, no one can cite everything on a topic, nor should you expect them to cite lots of your references!

What to do when you are requesting and receiving feedback

Tell the reviewer what kind of feedback you need and what stage you are at in the writing process.

When appropriate, offer to provide feedback on their writing.

Separate the delivery from the message; stay calm and avoid taking any comments personally.

Listen, don't talk; avoid defending your work instead of listening.

Reflect carefully on the advice received; take advantage of the opportunity to clarify your ideas.

Take ownership of your own writing; only make changes that make sense to you.

Source: Drawn in part on material in Belcher (2009, 223-8); Grant (2016, 87); Moore (2018, 123-4); Murray (2009, 163); Murray and Moore (2006, 49); and Thomson and Kamler (2013, 173-5); from where further guidance may be sought.

Over to You

Developing a network of critical friends is key to making your writing both more effective and more enjoyable. As you learn from your critical friends, expect in turn to provide critical but supportive feedback to others. Consider the questions below as you think about the role networking, critical friends, and feedback play in your writing process:

- Whom among your professional network do you respect and trust to act as critical friends? Which of these people could you approach to comment on drafts of your writing?
- Which of your critical friends might you consider co-authoring with?
- How do you give developmental feedback to colleagues, and how can you encourage them to do the same for you?

PART 6

SUBMITTING, RESPONDING TO REVIEWERS, AND PROMOTING YOUR WORK

Introduction to Part 6

Before you submit your writing for publication there are many important checks to undertake. Our experience as editors is that too many people submit manuscripts that are still in draft form. This does not give a good impression to hard-pressed, usually voluntary editors. Some people, of course, are the opposite, and in seeking perfection never get around to pressing the submit button. As Wendy Belcher (2009, 268) points out, "There are diminishing returns to perfecting your work. After all, the peer reviewers must have something to criticize. . . . Your biggest enemy at this point is fear of finishing." There is, though, no excuse for failing to follow the author guidelines and keeping to the word limit (unless the editor has agreed to an exception), and it is essential to put the references in the house style and check them against those cited in the text. We include a pre-submission checklist to help you try to avoid these traps.

It is rare for manuscripts to be accepted without reviewers or editors requesting changes, and rejection letters are common. Responding to these experiences can be emotionally draining. A request for minor changes is a cause for celebration. In this part of the book, we offer advice regarding how to join in a conversation with editors and how to respond to requests to revise and resubmit. We also discuss how to deal with the rejection email, which we have all experienced.

Once your writing is accepted you need to think strategically about how to promote your work and what your next publication will be. With the exponential increase in the number of works being published, a significant proportion of papers do not get cited. Given all the effort you have put in to researching and writing your pieces, it is sensible that you do what you can to make potentially interested readers aware of your work. We review the principal ways you can promote your work (without boasting) and how you could develop a publication plan to build a body of related work written across a range of genres.

Before you embark upon reading part 6, consider addressing the following questions, and then revisit your responses as you work your way through this final section of the book:

- How can you develop a mindset that ensures you are thorough without being overly perfectionistic in preparing to submit a piece of writing?
- How can you best prepare yourself for and manage the emotional, intellectual, and logistical demands of revision in response to reviewer comments?
- What strategies might you develop for ensuring that your writing is noticed and contributes to the unfolding conversations constituted by scholarship on learning and teaching?

CHAPTER 27

PREPARING FOR SUBMISSION

Polish and then repolish your work after you consider your manuscript finally written. (Sadler 2006, 32)

[There is a] common tendency both to procrastinate (by not writing) and to perfect (by endlessly revising). To get published, you have to train yourself to get over both tendencies. (Belcher 2009, 271)

Rewriting, revising, and refining make for good writing (see chapter 24). However, as editors and reviewers, we observe that all too often our colleagues submit work before it is ready. In this chapter we review some of the checks that you should undertake before you press the submit button. As the two quotes above indicate, authors need to find a balance between striving for perfection and letting go. We offer a checklist for final steps to take prior to submission; discuss the function of keywords, which are commonly used in journal publications and can maximize the likelihood that readers interested in your topic will find your work; and remind you of the role critical friends (see also chapter 26) can play at this final stage of preparing a manuscript.

Checking Your Manuscript

As well as checking the title, abstract, and text, you will need to sort tables, figures, illustrations, copyright permissions, references, keywords, acknowledgments, and biographics, and you must ensure that everything is in the right format and style for your chosen outlet. A brief checklist is provided in Table 27.1.

Table 27.1: Checklist before submitting your manuscript

Reread the guidelines for authors for your chosen outlet and check that you have complied with all of them, including, unless otherwise stated:
The text adheres to the stylistic and bibliographic requirements outlined in the author guidelines.
The layout and placing of tables, figures, and illustrations follow the publisher's guidelines and you provide titles and sources. Check that you can obtain any copyright permissions needed if your manuscript is accepted for publication.
The references in the text align with those in the list of references and vice versa.
The number of words is included at the end of the manuscript and it is fewer than the publisher's maximum for the genre you are submitting.
Ensure your email account is set to receive messages from the publisher, as notification emails can sometimes be sent to spam or junk folders.
Check quoted material against the original source (include page numbers where appropriate).
Ensure that you have properly cited all information taken from outside sources and that you have not inadvertently plagiarized.
Proofread and spell-check one last time (and if you don't feel strong in this area, have someone else proofread your text, or read it aloud—this will catch a lot of missing words and typos).
For journal publications
The manuscript has not been published previously, is not currently under review by another publisher, and represents new, unpublished findings or arguments (or an explanation has been provided in comments to the editor).

The abstract aligns with the text (i.e., you do what you say you do).

The keywords supplement rather than repeat those used in the title.

A copy of this checklist is available in the online resources.

If your manuscript will go out for double-blind review, ensure that you also submit an anonymized version of the manuscript with all identifying names and institutional affiliations removed. Use "Anon (date)" or "Author (date)" for references to your own work, exclude other details, and put these under "A" in the list of references. Exclude acknowledgments and biographies that may identify you or your institution.

If the contribution includes reporting on research that you have undertaken with human participants, include a statement in the methods section or at the end of the text that the research was successfully reviewed according to your institution's research ethics committee guidelines. Don't forget to omit the institution's name in the anonymized version of the paper.

Though you should always be consistent in following the publisher's guidance regarding layout and style, don't try to seek perfection in the content of your piece of writing. You will never be able to prepare for every possible point that reviewers may raise; they will usually surprise you regardless of how much you try to anticipate. You need to make a judgment regarding what you think the reader *needs* to know to understand your argument, methods, and conclusions, and what it *would be nice* for them to know in the space you have available. The phrase "beyond the scope of this article" (Belcher 2009, 272) is a very useful one to help you keep a clear focus, indicate what cannot be included because of that focus or length restrictions, and avoid over-claiming what your writing is contributing.

Editors are busy people and in the case of learning and teaching journals usually undertake the task on a voluntary basis. Making their lives easier by following to the letter the publisher's instructions for layout and style is both sensible and considerate. Submitting manuscripts that show little attention to these guidelines signals disrespect and laziness and may give the impression that your manuscript was prepared for, and rejected by, another outlet. Your aim should be to submit a manuscript that makes a good initial impression. Take particular care to ensure that the references are in the house style. As seasoned editors, we spend a significant amount of time correcting the style of references. Upon receipt of your manuscript, the editor should think, "This looks publishable in this journal."

Selecting Keywords

Most journals require keywords, at least for their research articles. Keywords are used by journal publishers, search engines, and indexing and abstracting services to categorize papers. Most proprietary databases default to only searching the title, author, abstract, and keywords, not the full text of the article, so ensuring a range of words appears in these (including alternative words that readers may use in search engines) will help prospective readers find your paper and increase the probability of it being read and cited (Margy MacMillan, personal communication, July 25, 2019). Unfortunately, as James Hartley (2008, 37) notes, there are "no rules for formulating them [keywords], little guidance on how to write them, and no instructions for reviewers on how to assess them." The kinds of words used vary by discipline, so pragmatically it is probably best to begin by looking at the guide for authors for the journal you are targeting, as well as the keywords used by other papers in that journal and in works you cite. The function of keywords is to supplement the words used in the title, and as the words in the title will be picked up automatically by indexing services, there is no point repeating them (Kate, Kumar, and Subair 2017), although it might be useful to include common synonyms for your title words. To select keywords, read through your manuscript and identify words and phrases that are used repeatedly. You may also consider, when appropriate, including the discipline, the educational sector, the institution or country, and the method used, as well as words that relate to the topic (Hartley 2008; Kate, Kumar, and Subair 2017). The aim in choosing suitable keywords, as well as using precise and evocative words in your title and abstract, is to maximize the discoverability of your work and facilitate search engine optimization, so that your work appears in a high-ranking placement in search results pages (Taylor & Francis, "A Researcher's Guide to Search Engine Optimization").

Seeking the Fresh Perspective of Critical Friends

We emphasize throughout this book that writing is contributing to or creating a conversation. If you proofread a manuscript alone, you are likely to miss stylistic and formatting errors, and so critical friends have a role at this final stage, too. They can catch errors and omissions that you might have missed from overfamiliarity with the text and ensure that your manuscript will be as ready as it can be to enter the wider conversation in the field. We recommend that you ask a critical friend to give your manuscript a final scan before you submit it. This may be someone outside academia, such as a friend or relation who comes to the text fresh and focuses on clarity and grammar. Some writers, particularly those for whom English is not their first language, use the services of a professional editor to copyedit (not just proofread) their manuscript to catch errors in their written English (Flowerdew 1999; Moreno et al. 2012).

Submitting Your Piece

When you submit to a journal, you may want to include a short (half-page) cover letter that makes the case for why the editor should consider sending your article out for review. According to Aijaz Shaikh (2016), "A good cover letter first outlines the main theme of the paper; second, argues the novelty of the paper; and third, justifies the relevance of the manuscript to the target journal."

Most publication venues have online submission processes. These are not necessarily straightforward or intuitive, and they vary across platforms. It is therefore a good idea to explore and practice with the system well before a deadline. You can also contact the managing editor if you are having trouble because they can clarify or help, or as a last resort, you could attach a copy of your full submission, and if appropriate, the anonymized version, to an email explaining the trouble you are having submitting through the online system.

Over to You

Once you have completed the final check of your manuscript, you have come up with some appropriate and complementary keywords, and your critical friend has caught any stylistic issues that remain, it is time to let go and press the submit button. Doing so rarely constitutes the end of the conversation. In relation to this phase of the writing process, we recommend that you address these questions:

- Have you gone through the checklist in Table 27.1 to ensure your manuscript is ready for submission?
- Have you devised a list of keywords that complement those in the title and abstract, if the genre in which you are writing calls for those?
- Have you asked a critical friend to read through for a final check of the readability of the manuscript?

CHAPTER 28

RESPONDING TO REVIEWERS AND DEALING WITH REJECTION

You cannot control what the reviewers say. But you can control how you respond to their comments. (Annesley 2011)

When you get a rejection letter, do not take it personally. Be resilient. Be persistent. Be patient with yourself. Keep your sense of proportion. Above all, do not take the publication game too seriously. Along the way, enjoy every success. (Sadler 2006, 54)

Because writing is entangled with our identities as scholars, the inherently judgmental nature of peer review can contribute to our professional growth but can also be emotionally taxing. In this chapter, we extend the metaphor of creating and contributing to conversations to discuss the peer-review process as a dialogic one between colleagues—an exchange that shapes us and that we can, in turn, shape. We begin by unpacking the academic peer-review process, and we share some stories of how colleagues have experienced that process. We then address ways to make sense of reviewer comments and offer suggestions for revising your work and responding to editors, bearing in mind Thomas Annesley's assertion above of what we can control—our response. Finally, we focus on dealing with rejection, noting the advice of Royce Sadler that we should not take it personally.

The Academic Peer-Review Process

Submitting your work for publication means submitting it for review, either formal peer review, as we focus on in this section, or informal evaluation by readers. Peer review is often framed as a form of quality control organized within scholarly communities. It is defined as:

> a process of subjecting an author's scholarly work, research or ideas to the scrutiny of others who are experts in the same field. It functions to encourage authors to meet the accepted high standards of their discipline and to control the dissemination of research data to ensure that unwarranted claims, unacceptable interpretations or personal views are not published without prior expert review. (Kelly, Sadeghieh, and Adeli 2014, 277)

The peer-review process is highly contested, however (Hirshleifer 2014; Rose and Boshoff 2017; Nature peer review web debate), because while it may ensure quality in some cases, it can also limit or preclude creativity, innovation, and productive development, and, like many structures, practices, and processes in academia, it was designed by and for a small subset of people. We do not delve into the peer-review debate here, but we note it so that you can keep it in mind as you join the peer-review conversation. For the foreseeable future, publishing in academic outlets will mean engaging in the inherently evaluative process through which colleagues make judgments—and, in some cases, decisions—about one another's written work. Such decisions have real consequences for careers, identities, and positions in scholarly communities. Consider, therefore, not only the experience of being reviewed by your peers but also how you approach reviewing others' work.

If you come to writing about learning and teaching from another scholarly discipline of research, you will have experience with peer review. A "double blind" review process is common in many disciplines where neither the authors nor the reviewers are known to each other—many journals publishing learning and teaching work use this approach. You might have experience with a single blind review where the author details are not hidden from reviewers (common in some PhD assessment processes, for example). Finally, "open peer review" is gaining traction—an approach through which reviewer names and reports are published along with the work. While this practice is emerging in some scientific publications, we are not aware of it in learning and teaching journals yet. In the journal we co-edit along with others, Kelly recently employed a dialogic peer-review process that involved a reviewer, an editor, and the author communicating in an iterative process of feedback that included naming the reviewer in the publication (Yahlnaaw/Aaron Grant, 2019, 9).

When you submit a manuscript for consideration, an editor can reject or decline it before it is even sent out for peer review if the editor decides that the submission is not *in the conversation* of the journal or outlet or does not align with its aims and scope. Papers that make it past this initial screening to the review stage will likely receive one of the following responses:

1. Unconditional acceptance: No changes are required and the paper is ready for publication.
2. Minor revisions: The paper is accepted pending minor changes.
3. Major revisions / Revise and resubmit: The reviewers and editors require significant changes to the work that will determine if the paper is publishable.
4. Rejection: The paper is declined for publication.

In some cases, editors request changes without distinguishing between major or minor revisions. When substantial revisions are requested, the editor is likely to send the paper back to reviewers (either the same or new ones) to evaluate whether the authors have sufficiently addressed the requested revisions, though sometimes the editor may make this judgment.

Each journal is different, so the exact wording of decisions and the process will vary. Overall, unconditional acceptances of submissions are extremely rare (Brookfield 2011). It is more likely that you will be asked to make minor or major revisions, if your submission is not declined or rejected. Many established and top-rated journals linked to publishing companies (e.g., Taylor & Francis, Springer) have high rejection rates: commonly rejecting over 80–90% of manuscripts submitted. For these reasons, Thomson and Kamler (2013, 128) suggest that "minor revisions are, or ought to be, a cause for celebration." While these statistics and reminders can offer some solace, particularly when you receive what could be perceived as negative feedback, Stephen Brookfield (2011, 252) notes that reviews often trigger "a familiar cycle of emotions" that influences the confidence of both new and experienced writers. Even very widely published authors get rejected quite often, so this is an experience everyone has and should expect.

Some common reasons for journal submissions to be rejected are highlighted in Table 28.1. If you are aware of these, you can try to avoid them as you write.

Table 28.1: Reasons for reviewers recommending rejection or substantial revision for articles submitted to *Higher Education Research and Development*

Reason for rejection or substantial revision	Out of 24 reviewers' reports
Weakness with regard to the conclusions and argument, including unsubstantiated assertions	22
Lack of methodological soundness or weakness in analysis	19
Absence of any important critical or analytical insight, including unfocused discussion	18
Failure to read well and engage a broad (i.e., international) higher education audience; lack of clarity on contribution to knowledge	18
Weakness in situating in appropriate literature	15
Weakness in quality and clarity of writing and structuring	13

Source: Based on Soliman (2008)

The Stories We Tell about Peer Review

Understanding the peer-review process is one thing; experiencing it is another. Kate Chanock (2008) has written about "surviving the review process"—a struggle through which we persist despite hardships and even "danger." Peer review can feel dangerous because our writing is entangled with our identities: we have invested emotionally and intellectually in a piece of work, and then we have to submit it for judgment by other people who are positioned as experts in the scholarly community. Thus, comments on our written work, regardless of genre, have a profound impact on how we see ourselves as members of a learning and teaching scholarly community.

Kate Chanock (2008, 1) urges us to share our experiences of peer review, because "many more things get rejected than accepted, and nearly everything gets sent back to be rewritten." By sharing these experiences we can come to understand that even though it's not "ever going to be easy . . . at least it doesn't have to be mysterious." Martin Haigh (2012) usefully includes the reviews he obtained, and his responses to them, in the article he wrote on writing successfully for a learning and teaching journal. Kenneth Moore shares his first experience of peer review, capturing how it can be a complex emotional and intellectual process, in Reflection 28.1. Importantly, Moore sought the perspectives and support of colleagues and had time to make sense of the reviewer comments and the decision of the editor.

Reflection 28.1

My first peer-review experience

My first peer-review story was traumatising but ultimately very gratifying. I have the review framed . . . not the paper. No joke. The reviewer response was about as many words as my paper. I saw it and thought, my god, is this normal? Colleagues assured me it was not normal. Importantly, the paper was not rejected. The reviewer liked the kernel of the idea and liked the methods, just didn't like anything about the way it was presented. They had me change everything under the sun (e.g., starting a sentence with "But"). I tried to find some humour in how painfully candid this person was. Luckily, I had the time and support of colleagues, so I did the work to revise the paper. To be quite frank, it was inspiring that the person had invested so much time. The end result is something I know I can be prouder of. Knowing that my work would not have been accepted into that journal without passing a significant check on quality served to instil my confidence in the peer-review system. It has motivated me to give more thoughtful reviews to others—while hopefully avoiding snarky remarks! The review stoked some negative emotions and set me on a difficult personal journey, but I now respect the process more as a whole.

Kenneth Moore reflects on his first experience of peer review as a PhD student in the area of higher education studies at The University of Melbourne, Australia.

Moore's reflection suggests he took seriously the "revise and resubmit" (or R and R) request from the editor. Pat Thomson (2019h) explains the work required in a major revisions decision:

> The key word in R and R is **REVISE—re-vision, re-imagine, re-think**. This may well be more than simply adding in a few sentences here or there or a new section. An R and R [is] not always going to be a "tinkering around" leaving most of the paper intact. Just adding and deleting a few things is a correction, not a re-imagining. In fact, most of the time, when reviewers recommend R and R they are looking for some pretty big changes. Gah—it's likely to be a pretty substantial **re-write**.

It's OK to take the time you need to process the experience of receiving a detailed peer review. You need to process both the emotions and the intellectual challenges reviews can pose. Mills Kelly (2019), an experienced history professor in the US and recent president of ISSOTL, has had to set aside harsh reviewer comments for weeks before he could process them productively and "take the high road" in responding to reviewers. Sometimes a good laugh is the perfect medicine for harsh reviews. Following Alison receiving a particularly noxious review, Mick shared with her the link to a Facebook group called "Reviewer 2 Must Be Stopped." She laughed and laughed.

As with all dialogic exchanges with others, you have a choice in how you engage in the process of peer review. In chapter 26, we write about ways to give feedback through writing groups and as critical friends. Consider carefully how you review others so that the stories we all tell can be more gratifying than traumatizing and lead to more productive, less destructive conversations.

Based on his experience with peer review, Mike Duncan (2018) describes three types of reviewers; his classification can both prepare you for potential reviews and invite consideration of the type of reviewer you want to be.

- Type 1: Reviewers who are a credit to the profession by offering helpful and constructive reviews
- Type 2: Reviewers who do not read or engage with the entire work and offer misguided and brief reviews
- Type 3: Reviewers who trash a paper, whether in a single sentence or pages of text

Making Sense of Reviewer Comments and Responding to Editors

While it might be easier in some cases than others, try to tell yourself as you read reviewer comments that *this person is trying to enhance your work*. Sally Brown attests to that interpretation in Reflection 28.2. It can be especially challenging to understand and respond when you receive two or three reviews (from reviewers and editors) that are contradictory. This can feel overwhelming and confusing.

Reflection 28.2

Don't burn the reviews: It is so easy to misunderstand reviewers

In the days before electronic journal submission, I submitted a paper copy of an article which I received back with some very heavy critique requiring a lot of changes. Disheartened and a bit angry, I ripped it up, set fire to it and stamped on the ashes. Six months later I met the editor at a conference and he said to me, "Where is that good article on peer assessment?" I said, "You didn't say it was a good article, you gave me so many negative comments I thought you were saying it was rubbish!" And he said, "But I and the two reviewers had spent hours writing those comments and we had a slot saved for you in the very next edition of the [very eminent] journal!" Of course, because of what I had done, all the reviewer comments were gone!

Sally Brown is an emerita professor at Leeds Beckett University, UK.

If you think about the reviewers as colleagues with whom you are in conversation, you can respond in kind. After you have a sense of all the requests being made and if you decide to resubmit to the same journal, you will need not only to revise the paper but also to draft a letter to the editor outlining the changes you have made. Therefore, it is a good idea to keep a running list of those revisions as you make them. While you might not be certain to whom the letter will be sent, write it as if the reviewers will be reading it, and be specific about how your revisions address each of the reviewers' suggestions. Kelly has a standard template for responding to reviewers, which she created following a writing collaboration with a colleague. In responding to reviewers after a major revisions request, her collaborator drafted a letter and copied in every comment and then responded to each. It was long but it showed respect for the reviewers because the approach acknowledged everything they said. See the following online resources for examples of Kelly's approach: "Template for

Writing Reviews," "Example of a Review Using the Template," and "Example of Response to Reviewers."

Reviews that accompany a reject decision can still be important to inform your revisions prior to submitting to another journal. Keep in mind, too, that if you submit the manuscript to another journal, the editor may send it to one of the same reviewers who responded to it originally. Imagine how a reviewer might feel seeing again basically the same manuscript upon which they already spent considerable time offering feedback. In the process of responding to reviewers, you gain another opportunity to practice your writing. Table 28.2 lists decisions to make when responding to reviewer requests. It is a good practice to express your appreciation for a suggested revision, whether or not you follow it (Annesley 2011). Phrases such as "Thank you for bringing this to my attention" or "I appreciate your raising this point" can precede whatever you write subsequently. Reviewers are also human, and they too value respectful and constructive responses as much as authors do.

If you have not considered being a reviewer, you might want to. Reviewing others' submissions will expose you to the range of conversations unfolding around learning and teaching, including the most current literature being published on your own topic and related topics. It will also afford you insights into the review process and help you develop into a respectful and constructive reviewer—one who takes seriously people's efforts and offers thoughtful, useful feedback and suggestions. Revisit the advice we offered for delivering feedback in chapter 26. Offering thoughtful, useful, respectful feedback takes time and patience, but it helps build a more welcoming and inclusive community, and it can even sometimes be recognized. For instance, Alison spends a great deal of time on writing supportive, detailed reviews, and she was awarded the American Educational Research Association (AERA) Outstanding Reviewer Award for outstanding contribution to AERA's journals. Contact editors of your favorite learning and teaching journals to ask how you can become a reviewer. Most editors welcome new reviewers.

Table 28.2: Decisions for revising and responding to reviewers

Decision	Response
Agree with request	Say you can see how the request will enhance the work and indicate how you have revised
Disagree with request	Explain why you do not agree with the request and have therefore not made the suggested change
Reviewers make contradictory requests	Acknowledge their requests and explain why you have responded as you have

Responding to Rejection

"Rejection . . . is never nice, but you learn to manage by having alternative strategies" (Pells 2018, quoting Janet Ward). Everyone who submits their work to journals, with rare exceptions, has dealt with a reject decision. And we do, as Janet Ward points out, develop strategies to deal with that reality. Our Perspectives 28.1 demonstrates the different ways the three of us have handled rejection and how those strategies evolve with experience.

Our Perspectives 28.1

How do you deal with rejection in the peer-review process?

Kelly: "Welcome to the club, Kelly" was the response from a mentor when I admitted I had a paper rejected for publication. "You are in the academic club now. We all have had that experience." It was oddly comforting for me. To this day, when I get a rejection decision, I remember it is part of being an academic.

However, the more I get into the academic game of peer review, the more I want to push back against aspects of it. If I think a decision is unfair, I will contact the editor to discuss it. If I think a reviewer is being nasty, I'll contact the editor. Authors also need to be careful how they respond to reviewer comments. Recently, in reading an author's response to my and another reviewer's comments following a major revision decision, I wrote in my comments to the authors that I found their dismissive tone toward the other reviewer troublesome and not in the spirit of collegiality. At this stage, I am okay with a rejection decision and have the agency to engage in discussion with editors as I think the review process should be a collegial one.

Mick: Here are extracts from two reviews from a paper I submitted to a highly rated geography journal in 1999. *Reviewer 1:* "I find the argument about 'scholarship of teaching' highly unconvincing and lacking intellectual rigour and substance. . . . The paper is really about the status of university teachers, i.e. there is a political agenda here which gets very close to a self-serving personal manifesto which is, despite the occasional lip service to the situation in the US, very parochial." *Reviewer 2:* "The paper does not succeed in its claim that 'developing the scholarship of teaching can make an important contribution to the progress of geography'. All it does is to rehearse arguments about the relatively lower status of teaching without providing a convincing intellectual case. . . . The first paragraph under II contains a lot of platitudinous statements. The quotation from Prosser and Trigwell strikes me as being especially banal."

A few months later, after tending to my bruises, I began to consider other possible publication venues. I was invited to submit a paper to a special issue of *Higher Education Research and Development (HERD)* on scholarship of teaching and learning (SoTL). I revised the paper (with a changed introduction, conclusion, and title—critically as noted in chapter 9, dropping reference to geography and instead referring to "a discipline-based approach," but otherwise making only minor changes) and it was accepted (Healey 2000). It has since been recognized as having an important impact and been widely cited. On reflection, I realize that the geography journal was not yet ready for an article on SoTL, but there may also have been an element of misfortune in who was allocated to review the article. By a strange coincidence the editor of the special issue of *HERD* was Keith Trigwell (the source of the "banal" quotation), though I did not tell him about the geography reviewer's comment!

Alison: When I first started submitting manuscripts for publication, I hadn't really developed a sense of how to write for an audience unfamiliar with the work I was doing, and I took rejections of my writing about it deeply personally. Over the years, I came to see rejections less as personal attacks and more as indicators that I hadn't found the best way to frame and present what I was trying to share—as a failure of communication rather than a failure of self. After nearly twenty years of publishing, almost all of my submissions are judged to need either major or minor revisions—cause for celebration, as Thomson and Kamler (2013) suggest, but I still occasionally forget how unfamiliar my work is in some circles. Recently, for instance, a colleague and I had a paper rejected because we had made too many assumptions about our reviewers' familiarity with pedagogical partnership, the main area of research and practice for both of us. One of the reviewer comments was so unrelated to what we were writing about that we thought maybe the editor had sent a review for someone else's paper! Then we realized that the reviewer was evoking the closest thing they knew to our work, trying to make sense of it. So, we revised to include more context for and explanation of what we had assumed would be obvious but clearly wasn't. This was an important reminder not to make assumptions, to start where the reader is in the way Jerome Bruner (1977, xi) famously argued that one must start "where the learner is." This is not a matter of condescension or dumbing down; it's a matter of being in conversation in the right key.

Your perspective: How do you or will you deal with rejection in the peer-review process?

Over to You

The peer-review process is itself in a process of evolution, but publication will always involve contributing to or creating a conversation, and none of us wants to be rejected or excluded from a conversation we want to join or develop. As you are joining the conversation constituted by the peer-review process, we hope you will think about the type of reviewer, as well as the type of writer, you want to be. As Tom Lowe (2019) has observed, reviewers have a choice: they can go in thinking, "What can I find wrong with this paper[?]" or they can ask themselves, "How can I help this person publish and succeed[?]" Some of the questions that you may want to think about following receipt of comments from reviewers include:

- How do you think you will respond to a rejection decision?
- Whom in your support network can you contact if you get a rejection decision?
- If revisions are requested, what changes are reviewers arguing for in your work?
- Are any of these requested changes at odds? Do any overlap?

Then you may want to decide a few things for yourself and with any co-authors:

- Can you see how making the suggested changes will enhance your paper?
- Are some requests moving the work in a direction you are not comfortable with?
- Are some requests unclear to you?
- Do some requests seem irrelevant, because you have addressed them elsewhere in the paper or because they are more comments rather than suggested changes, for example?
- How, and to what extent, will you retain the integrity of your text while also responding to the reviewers' comments?

CHAPTER 29

PROMOTING YOUR PUBLISHED WORK AND DEVELOPING A PUBLICATION PLAN

We have been astonished by the wide number of learning and teaching "wheels" that are reinvented on an annual basis due to lack of dissemination. (Cleaver, Lintern, and McLinden 2018, 98)

Once your work is published, you need to share it so others can read it, learn from it, and include it in scholarly conversations, and in so doing help avoid some of the reinventing of wheels that Elizabeth Cleaver and colleagues mention above, which are too common in the learning and teaching field. However, your work can easily go unnoticed given the explosion of higher education publications in the past decades (Tight 2018b). There is a reason "publish or perish" has been joined by the cliché "achieve visibility or vanish." A third of social science articles included in Web of Science are not cited within five years of publication (Larivière, Gingras, and Archambault 2009). Melissa Terras (2012) found that when some of her papers were tweeted and blogged, these publications "had at least more than eleven times the number of downloads than their sibling paper which was left to its own devices in the institutional repository." More systematic research, however, indicates little relationship between social media interventions and readership (Davis 2019), though increasing awareness of your work may have other benefits, such as invitations to speak or contribute to related projects (Green 2019). In this chapter we share strategies for collegial promotion of your work, including developing publication plans to generate a coherent body of work.

Promoting Your Published Work

Self-promotion does not come easily to most of us, as we discuss in Our Perspectives 29.1. However, there are over three million journal articles published every year, and this number is increasing annually (Johnson, Wilkinson, and Mabe 2018)—a trend also evident in the broad field of higher education (Tight 2018b). If you want your paper to be noticed, you need to help it along, and this can be done without appearing to boast (see also chapter 22).

Our Perspectives 29.1

How do you feel about promoting your own work?

Alison: I try to think of promoting my work as offering what I have learned in order to support others' efforts and showing how both my own work and theirs are part of an ongoing conversation. So actually I think of it less as promoting and more as connecting—showing continuity of ongoing explorations, inviting new directions that build on those and also that take off from them. I have found such self-promotion/connecting most important when moving from one area of scholarship and practice to another, as I did in shifting from education to SoTL, when I realized that colleagues in the latter arena had little or no familiarity with the work I had done in the former arena.

Mick: Self-promotion goes against the grain. However, particularly since I became an independent consultant, I have realized some is necessary. I try to keep our website up to date and provide links to it from my email signature and handouts I use in workshops. Rather than promote individual publications or workshops, I encourage people to visit the website by providing resources (handouts and bibliographies), most of which are regularly updated, and hope visitors may look at other pages, such as the list of recent publications, while they are there, and, of course, the photos of our dogs!

Kelly: I have a contradictory range of emotions about promoting my own work. I want to share a sense of achievement and contribution, yet the "look at me" part of it feels like shameless self-promotion and makes me want to hide away. I have a love-hate relationship with social media when it comes to promoting my own work. My university now includes Twitter metrics in our researcher dashboards, so I live in a vexing state of discomfort with my role in the metrics/look-at-me game. My current strategy is to log into Twitter at designated times 2–3 times a week to share new publications from myself or others and interact with people who have interacted with me.

Your perspective: How do you feel about promoting your own work?

Making your writing easy to find starts well before you submit it for publication. Choosing a suitable title (see chapter 9), writing an informative abstract (see chapter 10), and selecting appropriate keywords (see chapter 27) are critical in making your work visible, if those are required for the genre you select. Raising awareness of your work also occurs prior to writing when you make presentations about what you are working on at conferences (see chapter 17).

Once your writing is published, you should also be active in ensuring potentially interested readers are made aware of its existence. Most higher education conferences will allow you to present recently published work. Nearly all the major publishers provide useful advice on promoting your work (e.g., Elsevier 2019). Several strategies are appropriate at this stage. These include:

1. **Make your research open.** Add a pre-print copy of journal publications to academic databases, such as ResearchGate and Academia.edu, as well as your own institutional repository. Ensure that you include a link to the final published version by including its DOI (Digital Object Identifier). If your paper is published in an open access (OA) journal, then a direct link to the published version is easy to include. OA papers are not only downloaded more than non-OA papers, they are also cited more (Hitchcock 2011; Piwowar et al. 2018).

2. **Create a Google Scholar profile.** If you have not already done so, register for a Google Scholar account. It creates a profile of your publications and the number of citations each has received, though you should check the profile for accuracy, particularly if you have the same name as other academics. You can set your account to email you automatically when a new citation is found. It is a great way to keep up with new literature that cites your work (always a nice email to receive), and to see what else authors in your field have written (Konkiel 2014).

3. **Ensure your web pages are up to date.** Check that your latest publications are listed on your institutional web pages and, if you have one, your own website.

4. **Provide a link from your email signature and profiles.** Adding a link to your most recent publications in your email signature is an obvious way of increasing awareness of your work.

5. **Create a video abstract.** Most large commercial journal publishers, such as Taylor & Francis, are beginning to encourage authors of journal articles to produce short video abstracts to promote their articles. They are "easy to share via social media, include in an email, or link to from a web page, [and] they can be a quick and easy way to tell others your research story" (Taylor & Francis "Video Abstracts").

6. **Post on social media.** Make links to your work via any social media accounts you have, such as LinkedIn, Twitter, and Facebook. For Facebook, consider opening a "professional" account, separate from your social account, to which you invite fellow researchers. Encourage a colleague or the editor to tweet a link to your publication. You could also focus your Twitter promotion around conferences that are relevant to your research topic, by using the event's hashtag and clarifying how your work may be of interest. Your postings may be better received if you include information about interesting publications other than just your own; this may also help you

attract more followers. Melissa Terras (2012), as we noted in chapter 21, suggests that the best time to tweet in the UK is between 11am and 5pm GMT, Monday to Thursday of a working week, though this may differ depending where in the world your target audience is based.

7. **Contribute to a multi-author blog or start your own.** "If you've devoted months to writing the paper, dealing with comments, doing rewrites and hacking through the publishing process, why would you not spend the extra couple of hours crafting an accessible blogpost?" (Dunleavy 2016). There are plenty of multi-author blogs available, or you may wish to consider starting your own blog and regularly post about your ideas (Crick and Winfield 2013; Thesis Whisperer 2018; see also chapter 21).

8. **Register for an ORCID iD.** Ensure that you have registered for ORCID (Open Researcher and Contributor Identifier). It provides you with a unique identifier and gives a record of your scholarly work.

9. **Send publications to scholars you have cited.** Consider sending a copy of your publication to scholars you cite while also thanking them for their contributions to the scholarly community (Sutherland, personal communication, August 18, 2019). Some may already be aware of your work through citation notifications they receive from Google Scholar or ResearchGate.

Making a Publication Plan

At many universities, we are increasingly being encouraged to plan our activities more systematically so that we can manage our time and meet institutional targets. This is a common topic covered in doctoral programs, and many universities require that their research-active staff and faculty produce publication plans for their research (e.g., University of Manchester 2018; Sheffield Hallam University 2016).

A sample writing plan is given in Table 29.1. When creating your publication plan, it is important to be as specific as you can in terms of

Table 29.1: A sample three-year writing-for-publication plan

Genre	Outlet	Year 1				Year 2				Year 3			
		Q1	Q2	Q3	Q4	Q1	Q2	Q3	Q4	Q1	Q2	Q3	Q4
Empirical research article on … for …	Journal	■	■										
Research paper presentation on … at …	Conference		■										
Teaching award	Application			■									
Case study on … for …	Chapter				■		■						
Presentations on … at …	Workshop					■							
Opinion piece on … for …	Blog							■					
Poster presentation on … at …	Conference							■	■				
Empirical research article on … for …	Journal								■	■	■		
Edit a collection of articles	Book									■	■	■	■
Conceptual article on … for …	Report										■	■	
Promotion	Application												■

what topics you'll write about, where each item may be published (including whether the outlet will be generic or discipline-based), and whether the publications will be sole- or co-authored. You are likely to be less specific the longer in advance you are planning, in part because your writing plans will depend on the progress of your research and on your success in obtaining funding. Most of the outputs should normally, at least in the short run, cover a limited number of related topics, so that your body of work is making a significant contribution to a broad research area and you are not seen as jumping around among too many different subjects. You will also need to build in some flexibility to allow time to respond positively to interesting requests to, for example, co-author an article or essay, write a book chapter, or present a keynote. Similarly, you may be active in promoting a co-authored publication with a colleague or someone you meet at a conference or on social media. Hence you will probably need to update the plan every quarter or so. A blank version of the "Sample Three-Year Writing-for-Publication Plan" is available in the online resources.

However, it is important to remember that what is reasonable for you to achieve is dependent on your motivations, stage of career, kind of institution, and other contextual factors that affect the opportunities available to you. Planning for two or three outputs over a three-year period may be just as appropriate as planning for fifteen to twenty outputs. You may also consider keeping a publication diary that helps you keep track of key deadlines or target dates for different stages in the writing and publication process for the multiple, overlapping projects you may have on the go (Salter 2016). As we noted in chapter 23, writing in some genres, such as preparing a blog post or an opinion piece, takes considerably less time than writing an empirical research article or a book.

The plan in Table 29.1 is one approach, and we freely admit that none of us maintains a plan like this (although we know people who do!). Indeed, Kelly's reaction on seeing this plan was:

> I have never in my life used a publication plan like
> the one we show—it would stress me out! For me, the

weight of all that work would shut me down. I almost need to agree to a writing project with a sense of un-estimating the work or I would never agree to any!

The important point is to maintain a running record, backwards and forwards, of your writing accomplishments and ventures. Each of us has a less formalized list of commitments, which we regularly update and reprioritize as new opportunities arise. Kelly uses a template for planning group projects, which helps to clarify each participant's planned contribution from start to finish of the project (see "Simple Publication Plan for Getting Started" and "Project Plan for Research" in the online resources). In planning you should recognize the overlapping nature of writing timelines. For example, writing an 800-word blog post within two weeks may overlap with a two-month deadline for revisions requested from a journal article submitted six months prior as well as the need to return proofs of another article that had been accepted for publication several months ago within three days. In short, writing requires juggling differing yet overlapping time frames.

You will notice that examples of many of the genres we discuss in this book are included in our sample plan. Few people would write in all these genres in a three-year period. We would encourage you, however, as we have argued in several places in this book, to consider writing in a wide range of genres over your career, because many of the genres will address different audiences and engage you in varied, though related, conversations.

There are, of course, many reasons why we write, and these reasons may be extrinsic as well as intrinsic (see chapter 6). Pat Thomson (2014), who is a highly prolific author, breaks down her writing tasks into:

- stuff she has to write (e.g., reporting on research projects);
- stuff she gets asked to write (such as book chapters);
- stuff related to supervision (writing with her students); and
- stuff she wants to write (projects that interest her).

She has several of these kinds of "stuff" going on at the same time. Notably, she leaves out writing her weekly blog (*Patter*), describing it as "part of everyday activity, a bit like brushing your teeth."

For many people, ourselves included, much writing is responsive to openings as they appear, whether these are a result of chance conversations, ideas that have arisen from our reading, or invitations. Furthermore, we have each experienced different forms of continuity in topic areas in the short and the long run, and we have all experienced shifting our interests in relation to external stimuli as well as internal commitments.

Kelly, for example, experienced a shift from discipline-based to more general higher education publication outlets that started from a locally based project informing institutional curriculum development. Her early research in learning and teaching explored how science students experienced learning in their undergraduate programs. Naturally, her inquiry was in a specific disciplinary (life sciences), institutional (large, comprehensive research-intensive university), and geographical context (Australia). She employed methods that privileged numeric data gathered via surveys to capture large numbers of students, because using quantitative data is common in the sciences. Yet her research spoke to different conversations that were unfolding in the science higher education community and more broadly. While it might appear daunting if you are new to writing, Kelly's cascading "plan" over a seven-year period signals how writing can contribute to different scholarly communities and be translated across social media and traditional research outlets (and involve students as co-authors):

1. **Starting with a national and discipline-specific contribution:** Kelly's conference talk at a national, discipline-based conference became a publication (in the *International Journal for Science and Mathematics Education*) on capturing science students' perceptions of learning outcomes (Matthews and Hodgson 2012).

2. **Joining a discipline-specific, international conversation:** An article for the *International Journal of Science Education* explored science students' perceptions of learning outcomes

with broader implications for undergraduate science curriculum development (Varsavsky, Matthews, and Hodgson 2014).

3. **Informing local curriculum development:** An institutional report for a seven-year curriculum review cycle of the Bachelor of Science degree program focused on students' perceptions of their learning gains and outcomes to guide ongoing curriculum planning (Faculty of Science 2015).

4. **Connecting to a broader higher education conversation:** A publication for *Studies in Higher Education* contributed to a broader, cross-disciplinary conversation in higher education about student and lecturer perceptions of learning outcomes linked to ongoing debates about "graduate attributes" (Matthews and Mercer-Mapstone 2018).

5. **Linking to a higher education, topic-specific conversation:** An article on comparative assessment of student learning outcomes was published in *Assessment and Evaluation in Higher Education* (Dvorakova and Matthews 2017).

6. **Reaching new audiences through different genres**: Kelly contributed focused pieces through blog posts for a national science teaching centre (Australian Council of Deans of Science New Ideas in TL), professional society newsletter contributions (*Higher Education Research and Development Society of Australasia News*), and an article in *The Conversation* (Matthews 2018).

This example shows how engaging in writing about learning and teaching is a journey through conversations over many years with different scholarly communities (see chapter 8) that span local, national, and international knowledges (see chapter 1). We would readily admit, however, that looking back, our writing appears more strategic and ordered than it was at the time, when things appeared messier and more responsive. Nevertheless, preparing writing plans can be valuable in managing time and mapping out a strategic direction, as long as they are flexible and allow for the uncertainties and opportunities, disappointments and delights that arise in a learning and teaching scholar's academic life.

Over to You

Although they do not necessarily come naturally, promoting your publications and developing a writing plan for publication are important skills to acquire and cultivate, if you are going to be a productive writer who has an impact on scholarly conversation about learning and teaching in higher education. As with everything we recommend in this book, we suggest that you need to develop versions of these strategies that work for you and that are consistent with the writing self you want to be. Thinking about your answers to these questions might help:

- Which of the suggested ways of promoting your published work do you use? Which could you see yourself using?
- Do you keep a writing-for-publication plan that you regularly update? If not, you might try completing the "Sample Three-Year Writing-for-Publication Plan" available in the online resources (but do not feel guilty if this is not your thing).
- What kind of publication plan might you develop to reach varied audiences through a range of genres?

CHAPTER 30

CONCLUSION

*Reflecting on the Potential of Writing
about Learning and Teaching*

*We revisit the key issues we have raised, speaking again of the
principles, and end with an invitation for those who read this
book. (Phillips and Bunda 2018, 89)*

The Latin roots of the word conclusion are "to shut" (*claudere*) and
"to convince." A conclusion is, in both senses, a closing. While some
things, such as events, come to a close simply because they are over, the
conclusion of an academic text draws to an intentional close. At the
same time, as Louise Phillips and Tracey Bunda note in their book on
storying as research, a conclusion is an opportunity to revisit, to speak
again, and to invite readers into ongoing dialogue. In this final chapter,
we conclude intentionally—deliberately and with awareness—in the
same way we have endeavored to write throughout this text, to name
and to make visible the process in which we are engaged: a writing
process that is a learning process and an act of communication. Due
to its length, a book requires a more extensive revisiting than some
other genres of what has carried us to this conclusion. And so, we
begin with the beginning.

Revisiting, Reviewing, and Reinterpreting Our Overarching Themes

We argued in our introduction that contributing to and creating
scholarly conversations and fostering identities are best achieved by

publishing in a wide range of genres. Our own stories and those of the many writers we include throughout the chapters of this book illustrate that there is no one right way to join, contribute to, benefit from, or create scholarly conversations about learning and teaching, and the identity—or identities—you develop through your engagement will evolve over time. Indeed, the richness of the opportunities afforded by the expanding set of acceptable writing genres and the increasing recognition of the validity of different identities mean that academic writing is a more open and inclusive process than it has been in the past.

Who you are as a scholar and what and how you choose to write will influence the ways that scholarly writing about learning and teaching continue to evolve. That reality will affect you personally, and it will shape the world of scholarly publication. Every choice you make as a scholar both reflects your values and builds values-based practice, and conceptualizing writing as a learning process ensures that both you and those who read your writing continue to learn. These dynamic, dialogic processes can support your particular process of "self-authoring a professional identity as an educator" (Gunersel, Barnett, and Etienne 2013, 35) and, concurrently, your identity as a scholar of learning and teaching.

Throughout this book we have both offered advice and posed questions, alternating between informing and querying in an attempt to enact a dynamic, dialogic process that we capture in the metaphor of conversation. Writing is contributing to and creating conversations, but of course not everyone has equal access to every conversation, and even once in, not everyone is attended to with the same respect as everyone else. Our hope is that, by legitimating and advocating a wider range of genres for academic writing, we can open conversations about learning and teaching to a wider range of participants—a widening that is more inclusive and equitable as well as more educative for everyone.

Because identity is a complex intersection of how you see yourself and how you are seen by others, it is never fixed; it is, rather, contextual, relational, and evolving. Likewise, what and how we write for any given publication is never the final iteration; it is one in a series of versions of what matters to us and what we want to share with others. This is partly why writing is always a learning process. But writing to learn also means taking risks, composing texts that take you beyond where you might feel you are. These forays may inspire new internal realizations as well as new connections with others.

Revisiting, Reviewing, and Reinterpreting Our Practical Advice

Interwoven with these larger themes of contributing to and creating conversations and fostering identities, explored in part 2 of this book, are more practical questions, addressed in part 3: What are your motivations for writing? Will you write alone or with others? How will you decide what outlet is the best venue for any given piece of writing? How will you prepare for your writing process? Intersecting with these questions are decisions about genre, some of which you can choose to write in and some of which will be required of you. How to make even the required writing joyful and fulfilling is important for sustaining your own energy and for making academic writing a more engaging and affirming experience for everyone.

The when, where, and how of writing, which we address in part 5, has similarities and differences across genres and across writers. The advice we offer and the questions we pose about allotting time and choosing space to write, writing and rewriting your draft, becoming an engaging writer, and developing a network of critical friends are meant to offer a set of considerations but also signal that you may make your own choices about these aspects of writing. Our conclusion, then, in relation to these practical aspects of writing, is that it is *your process that matters*. It's not that you can work entirely in isolation; rather, it is that you can be intentional and idiosyncratic even while being an engaged member of a community.

The final phase of your writing journey (for any given piece of writing)—which includes preparing for submission and submitting the piece, responding to reviewers and dealing with rejection, and promoting your published work and developing a publication plan—is one you will experience over and over: a mini version of the larger cycle of writing for publication. Part 6, then, in addition to addressing a particular form of conclusion, is also a reminder that each conclusion precedes another commencement: every closure makes way for a new exploration or analysis to begin.

Part 4, the section of the book that deals with the "across genres" component of our book's title, addresses selected phases and aspects of writing in different genres. Conclusions across genres vary and may include one or more of these forms of intentional closure:

- Restating and reinforcing the main points of your argument
- Proposing possible directions for future research
- Re-delineating a new conceptual frame for analyzing literature
- Naming the implications of your findings for others in different contexts
- Specifying what you learned from which others could benefit
- Articulating the call to action or advice that arises from your expressed opinion
- Inviting reflections from others regarding what they are taking away from your presentation
- Stating clearly the message you want readers to take from your story or blog
- Reiterating why readers should believe the argument you have made.

What all these different kinds of conclusions have in common, though, is that they guide readers in how to think about what they just read. They close and aim to convince, and they do so in a way consistent with the genre. Dolores Black, Sally Brown, Abby Day, and Phil Race (1998, 116) offer a helpful reminder about conclusions:

> **Take particular care with the wording of your conclusions.** These are the parts of your work which may be most likely to be quoted by others, and you need to protect yourself from the position of having to live with words which you would prefer to have been different.

Multiple Conclusions and Final Thoughts

Looking at the list above of the various forms conclusions might take, we strive here to enact a version of as many of them as we can. Thus far we have restated and reinforced the main points of our argument, attempting to follow Wendy Belcher's (2009, 217-8) advice:

> A good conclusion is one that summarizes your argument and its significance in a powerful way. The conclusion should restate the article's relevance to the scholarly literature and debate. Although the conclusion does not introduce new arguments, it does point beyond the article to the larger context or the more general case. It does not merely repeat the introduction, but takes a step back, out of the bigger picture and states why the argument matters in the larger scheme of things.

In terms of possible directions for future research, we hope scholars will both engage in systematic studies and gather more stories of the range of purposes, strategies, and lived experiences of academic writers. As signaled in chapters 1 and 11, we encourage scholars to share and publish writing in genres on learning and teaching we have not covered in this text. For example, pieces on writing teaching portfolios, annotated syllabi, how-to guides, and grant proposals. We also encourage you to experiment with podcasts and vodcasts. All of these are also part of ongoing conversations about learning and teaching.

Our conceptual frame, which brings together the concepts of writing as contributing to and creating scholarly conversations, writing as fostering identities, and writing as a learning process, highlights the mutually informing nature of the professional and the personal. Every choice you make, or how you proceed when you do not have a choice, will influence who you become as a scholar and as an author about learning and teaching.

In writing our conclusion as a deliberate and self-aware enactment of and reflection on conclusions, we endeavored to follow the advice of Black et al (1998, 116):

Decide which one impression you would like your readers to go away with. Ask yourself "If there's only one thing they will remember, what do I want it to be?" This is likely to be the most suitable basis for your final words.

The one thing we hope you will remember after having read or dipped into this book is that writing for publication is not simply producing a text but is, rather, a complex process of contributing to and creating conversations, forging an identity aligned to your values, and embracing an opportunity for ongoing learning.

We have noted throughout how much we have learned through writing this book together and inviting the wisdom of so many other writers to bring these ideas to life. We knew that we knew something about academic writing, but mapping what we knew and having to write our way toward understanding what we didn't know was at once an invigorating, humbling, sometimes exhausting, but ultimately inspiring experience. We hope you will be encouraged and emboldened by the advice we offer and the questions we pose to self-author and re-write yourself as you, in turn, offer and explore understandings of learning and teaching in higher education. The possibilities are endless. Thank you for reading (and writing!).

Over to You

That is all from us. We are turning it over to you one last time with these final questions:

- What conclusions do you draw from having read this book, and what are the main messages that you take away?
- What themes guide—or could guide—your writing practice?
- What was reaffirmed for you about the way you approach writing about learning and teaching?
- What changes will you make to the way you write about learning and teaching in higher education?
- How will you ensure that you continue to grow as a writer, both creating and contributing to ongoing and new conversations?

Remember that the discussion questions are also posted on the book's website. We hope that you will use them to continue this conversation with others!

REFERENCES

Abbott, Clara. 2016. "Leaping and Landing in Brave Spaces." *Teaching and Learning Together in Higher Education* 1 (18). http://repository. brynmawr.edu/tlthe/vol1/iss18/4.

Academy of Management Learning & Education Editorial Team. 2018. "From the AMLE Editorial Team: Disciplined Provocation: Writing Essays for AMLE." *Academy of Management Learning and Education* 17 (4): 397–400. https://doi.org/10.5465/amle.2018.0245.

ACRL (Association of College and Research Libraries). 2016. "Framework for Information Literacy for Higher Education." Chicago: Association of College and Research Libraries. http://www.ala.org/acrl/files/issues/infolit/framework.pdf.

Adichie, Chimamanda Ngozi. 2009. "The Danger of a Single Story." TED Talk. https://www.ted.com/talks/chimamanda_ngozi_adichie_the_danger_of_a_single_story?language=en.

Adom, Dickson, Emad Kamil Hussein, and Joe Adu Agyem. 2018. "Theoretical and Conceptual Framework: Mandatory Ingredients of a Quality Research." *International Journal of Scientific Research* 7 (1): 438–41. https://doi.org/10.36106/ijsr.

Advance HE. n.d. "National Teaching Fellowship Scheme 20th Anniversary." Accessed May 13, 2020. https://www.advance-he.ac.uk/awards/teaching-excellence-awards/NTFSis20.

Aitchison, Claire, Barbara Kamler, and Alison Lee. 2010. *Publishing Pedagogies for the Doctorate and Beyond*. London: Routledge.

Albert, Tim. 2000. *The A–Z of Medical Writing*. London: BMJ Books.

American Psychological Association. 2010. *Publication Manual of the American Psychological Association (6th edition)*. Washington, DC: American Psychological Association.

Amundsen, Cheryl, and Mary Wilson. 2012. "Are We Asking the Right Questions? A Conceptual Review of the Educational Development Literature in Higher Education." *Review of Educational Research* 82 (1): 90–126. https://doi.org/10.3102/0034654312438409.

Anderson, Kent. 2012. "Bury Your Writing—Why Do Academic Book Chapters Fail to Generate Citations?" *The Scholarly Kitchen.* August 28, 2012. https://scholarlykitchen.sspnet.org/2012/08/28/bury-your-writing-why-do-academic-book-chapters-fail-to-generate-citations/.

Annesley, Thomas M. 2011. "Top 10 Tips for Responding to Reviewer and Editor Comments." *Clinical Chemistry* 57(4): 551–4. https://doi.org/10.1373/clinchem.2011.162388.

Anonymous. 2014. "Silence in the Classroom." *Teaching and Learning Together in Higher Education* 1 (11). https://repository.brynmawr.edu/tlthe/vol1/iss11/10.

Arendt, Hannah. 1970. *Men in Dark Times.* London: Cape.

Arnold, Lydia, and Lin Norton. 2018. *HEA Action-Research: Sector Case Studies.* York: Higher Education Academy. https://www.advance-he.ac.uk/knowledge-hub/hea-action-research-sector-case-studies.

Ashwin, Paul, and Keith Trigwell. 2004. "Investigating Educational Development." In *Making Sense of Staff and Educational Development*, edited by David Baume and Peter Kahn, 117–31. London: Kogan Page.

Association of National Teaching Fellows. 2018. "What Do People Get Out of Being a National Teaching Fellow?" February 5, 2018. http://ntf-association.com/national-teaching-fellows/what-do-people-get-out-of-being-a-national-teaching-fellow/.

Baaijen, Veerle M., and David Galbraith. 2018. "Discovery Through Writing: Relationships with Writing Processes and Text Quality." *Cognition and Instruction* 36 (3): 199–223. https://doi.org/10.1080/07370008.2018.1456431.

Bain, Ken. 2013. "Introduction: Growing Deep Learning." *Teaching and Learning Together in Higher Education* 1(8). https://repository.brynmawr.edu/cgi/viewcontent.cgi?article=1054&context=tlthe.

Barnett, Ronald. 2019a. "Supercomplexity and Education Research: Six Scholarships." In *Emerging Methods and Paradigms in Scholarship and Education Research*, edited by Lorraine Ling and Peter Ling, 231–43. Sydney: IGI Global.

Barnett, Ronald. 2019b. "Scholarship in the University: An Ecological Perspective." In *The Oxford Handbook of Higher Education Systems and University Management*, edited by Gordon Redding, Antony Drew, and Stephen Crump, chapter 18. Cambridge: Oxford University Press.

Barnett, Ronald. 2004. "Learning for an Unknown Future." *Higher Education Research & Development* 23 (3): 247–60. https://doi.org/10.1080/0729436042000235382.

Barnett, Ronald. 1990. *The Idea of Higher Education*. Buckingham, UK: Open University Press.

Barr, Robert B., and John Tagg. 1995. "From Teaching to Learning—A New Paradigm for Undergraduate Education." *Change: The Magazine of Higher Learning* 27 (6): 12–26. https://doi.org/10.1080/00091383.1995.10544672.

Barrineau, Sanna, Alexis Engström, and Ulrike Schnaas. 2019. *An Active Student Participation Companion*. Uppsala: Uppsala University. http://www.diva-portal.org/smash/get/diva2:1286438/FULLTEXT02.pdf.

Bass, Randy. 1999. "The Scholarship of Teaching: What's the Problem?" *Inventio: Creative Thinking about Learning and Teaching* 1 (1). https://my.vanderbilt.edu/sotl/files/2013/08/Bass-Problem1.pdf.

Bauman, Zygmunt. 2013. *What Use is Sociology? Conversations with Michael Hviid Jacobsen and Keith Tester*. London: Polity Press.

Baume, David. 1996. Editorial. *International Journal for Academic Development* 1 (1): 3–5. https://doi.org/10.1080/1360144960010101.

Baxter, Denise, and Kelly Donohue-Wallace. 2016. "Getting Beyond the Anecdote: Research and Art History Pedagogy." *Art History Teaching Resources*. May 11, 2016. http://arthistoryteachingresources.org/2016/05/getting-beyond-the-anecdote-research-and-art-history-pedagogy/.

Bazerman, Charles, Arthur Applebee, Virginia W. Berninger, Deborah Brandt, Steve Graham, Paul Kei Matsuda, Sandra Murphy, Deborah Wells Rowe, and Mary Schleppegrell. 2017. "Taking the Long View on Writing Development." *Research in the Teaching of English* 51: 351–60.

Beall's List of Predatory Journals and Publishers. n.d. Accessed May 13, 2020. https://beallslist.net/standalone-journals/.

Becher, Tony. 1994. "The Significance of Disciplinary Differences." *Studies in Higher Education* 19 (2): 151–61. https://doi.org/10.10 80/03075079412331382007.

Becher, Tony, and Paul R. Trowler. 2001. *Academic Tribes and Territories.* London: SHRE and Open University Press.

Belcher, Wendy. 2009. *Writing Your Journal Articles in 12 Weeks.* Thousand Island, California: SAGE Publishing.

Bennett, Dawn, Lynne Roberts, and Subramaniam Ananthram. 2017. "Teaching-Only Roles Could Mark the End of Your Academic Career." *The Conversation.* March 27, 2017. https://theconversation. com/teaching-only-roles-could-mark-the-end-of-your-academic-career-74826.

Berenson, Carol, and Natasha Kenny. 2016. "Preparing an Educational Leadership Philosophy Statement." Calgary, Alberta: Taylor Institute for Teaching and Learning.

Bernstein, Dan, and Randy Bass. 2005. "The Scholarship of Teaching and Learning." *Academe* 91 (4): 37–43.

Berthiaume, Denis. 2008. "Teaching in the Disciplines in Higher Education." In *The Effective Academic: A Handbook of Enhanced Academic Practice*, edited by Steve Ketteridge, Stephanie Marshall, and Heather Fry, 215–25. London: Kogan Page.

Bialka, Christa. 2018. "College Students with Disabilities Are Too Often Excluded." *The Conversation.* November 5, 2018. https:// theconversation.com/college-students-with-disabilities-are-too-often-excluded-105027.

Biesta, Gert, Mark Priestley, and Sarah Robinson. 2017. "Talking about Education: Exploring the Significance of Teachers' Talk for Teacher Agency." *Journal of Curriculum Studies* 49 (1): 38–54. https://doi.org/10.1080/00220272.2016.1205143.

Bindra, Gagandeep, Kirthika Easwaran, Lamia Firasta, Monika Hirsch, Aakriti Kapoor, Alexandra Sosnowski, Taleisha Stec-Marksman, and Gizem Vatansever. 2018. "Increasing Representation and Equity in Students as Partners Initiatives." *International Journal for Students as Partners* 2 (2): 10–15. https://doi.org/10.15173/ijsap.v2i2.3536.

Black, Dolores, Sally Brown, Abby Day, and Phil Race. 1998. *500 Tips for Getting Published*. London: Kogan Page.

Boice, Robert. 1990. *Professors as Writers: A Self-help Guide to Productive Writing*. Stillwater, OK: New Forums.

Boote, David, and Penny Beile. 2005. "Scholars before Researchers: On the Centrality of the Dissertation Literature Review in Research Preparation." *Educational Researcher* 34 (6): 3–15. https://doi.org/10.3102/0013189X034006003.

Booth, Shirley, and Lorenzo C. Woollacott. 2018. "On the Constitution of SoTL: Its Domains and Contexts." *Higher Education* 75: 537–51. https://doi.org/10.1007/s10734-017-0156-7.

Boud, David, Rosemary Keogh, and David Walker. 1985. *Reflection: Turning Experience into Learning*. London: Routledge.

Boyer, Ernest. 1990. "Scholarship Reconsidered: Priorities of the Professoriate." Princeton University Press, Carnegie Foundation for the Advancement of Teaching. https://depts.washington.edu/gs630/Spring/Boyer.pdf.

Bozalek, Vivienne, Arona Dison, Melanie Alperstein, and Veronica Mitchell. 2017. "Developing Scholarship of Teaching and Learning through a Community of Enquiry." *Critical Studies in Teaching and Learning* 5 (2): 1–15. https://doi.org/10.14426/cristal.v5i2.106.

Brande, Dorothea. 1934. *Becoming a Writer*. New York: J. P. Tarcher.

Brennan, Emma. 2016. "Framing and Proposing an Edited Volume for Publication." *Manchester University Press*. February 17, 2016. https://www.manchesteruniversitypress.co.uk/articles/framing-and-proposing-an-edited-volume-for-publication/.

Breslow, Lori, Linda Drew, Mick Healey, Robert Matthew, and Lin Norton. 2004. "Intellectual Curiosity: A Catalyst for the Scholarship of Teaching and Learning and Education." In *Exploring Academic Development in Higher Education: Issues of Engagement,* edited by Liz Elvidge, 83–96. Cambridge: Jill Roger Associates.

Brew, Angela. 2011. "Higher Education Research and the Scholarship of Teaching and Learning: The Pursuit of Excellence." *International Journal for the Scholarship of Teaching and Learning* 5 (2). https://doi.org/10.20429/ijsotl.2011.050203.

Brew, Angela. 2006. *Research and Teaching: Beyond the Divide.* London: Palgrave Macmillan.

Brookfield, Stephen. 2011. "Addressing Feedback from Reviewers and Editors." In *The Handbook of Scholarly Writing and Publishing,* edited by Tonette S. Rocco and Tim Hatcher, 251–61. San Francisco: Jossey-Bass.

Brost, Christel, Christelle Lauture, Karen Smith, and Saskia Kersten. 2018. "Reflections on That-Has-Been: Snapshots from the Students-as-Partners Movement." *International Journal for Students as Partners* 2 (1): 130–35. https://doi.org/10.15173/ijsap.v2i1.3366.

Brown, Sally. 2018. "Opportunities for Recognition for Experienced Staff Linked to Descriptor 3 of the UKPSF." In *Doing a Good Job Well - Being Recognised as an Experienced, Professional Teacher in HE,* edited by Jackie Potter and Rebecca Turner, 11–15. London: SEDA.

Bruner, Jerome. 1977. *The Process of Education.* Cambridge: Harvard University Press.

Callahan, Jamie. 2010. "Constructing a Manuscript: Distinguishing Integrative Literature Reviews and Conceptual and Theory Articles." *Human Resource Development Review* 9 (3): 300–304. https://doi.org/10.1177/1534484310371492.

Campbell, Fiona, and Celia Popovic. 2018. "Ensuring Learning through Session Formats and Networking Opportunities." In *Learning from Academic Conferences,* edited by Celia Popovic, 110–38. Leiden, Netherlands: Brill.

Cargill, Margaret, and Patrick O'Connor. 2013. *Writing Research Articles: Strategies and Steps*. Oxford: Wiley-Blackwell.

Carlton College. 2016. "How to Write an Op-Ed Article." https://apps.carleton.edu/media_relations/about/op_ed_guidelines/.

Carmel, Roofe G., and Miller W. Paul. 2015. "Mentoring and Coaching in Academia: Reflections on a Mentoring/Coaching Relationship." *Policy Futures in Education* 13 (4): 479-91. https://doi.org/10.1177/1478210315578562.

Carnegie Foundation for the Advancement of Teaching. 2006. "Opportunities for Scholarship." Presentation to Hong Kong University Grants Committee, Hong Kong, January 23-24, 2006.

Case, Jennifer M. 2015. "Knowledge for Teaching, Knowledge about Teaching: Exploring the Links Between Educational Research, Scholarship of Teaching and Learning (SOTL) and Scholarly Teaching." *Journal of Education* 61: 53–72. http://joe.ukzn.ac.za/Libraries/No_61_2015/Joe_61_case.sflb.ashx.

Cashmore, Annette, Chris Cane, and Robert Cane. 2013. *Rebalancing Promotion in the HE Sector: Is Teaching Excellence Being Rewarded*. York, UK: Higher Education Academy. https://www.advance-he.ac.uk/knowledge-hub/rebalancing-promotion-he-sector-teaching-excellence-being-rewarded.

Cassidy, Alice L. E.V. 2018a. "Submitting a Proposal." In *Learning from Academic Conferences*, edited by Celia Popovic, 43–58. Leiden, Netherlands: Brill.

Cassidy, Alice L. E.V. 2018b. "Preparing and Presenting Your Session." In *Learning from Academic Conferences*, edited by Celia Popovic, 59-78. Leiden, Netherlands: Brill.

Cassidy, Alice L. E.V. n.d. "Alice Cassidy's In Review Educational Development." Accessed October 15, 2019. https://cassidyinview.wordpress.com/.

Cerejo, Clarinda. 2013. "A 10-Step Guide to Make Your Research Paper Abstract More Effective." *Editage Insights*. https://www.editage.com/insights/a-10-step-guide-to-make-your-research-paper-abstract-more-effective.

Chakravarthi, Srikumar, and Priya Vijayan. 2010. "Analysis of the Psychological Impact of Problem Based Learning (PBL) towards Self Directed Learning among Students in Undergraduate Medical Education." *International Journal of Psychological Studies* 2 (1): 38–43. http://citeseerx.ist.psu.edu/viewdoc/download?doi=10.1.1.614.9584&rep=rep1&type=pdf.

Chalmers, Denise. 2011. "Progress and Challenges to the Recognition and Reward of the Scholarship of Teaching in Higher Education." *Higher Education Research & Development* 30 (1): 25–38. https://doi.org/10.1080/07294360.2011.536970.

Chanock, Kate. 2008. "Surviving the Reviewing Process and Getting Published." *Journal of Academic Language and Learning* 2 (1): E1–E4.

Chapnick, Adam, and Christopher Kukucha. 2016a. "The Other Side of the Desk: Advice from a University Press Editor." *University Affairs: The Scholarly Edition.* July 25, 2016. https://www.universityaffairs.ca/career-advice/the-scholarly-edition/side-desk-advice-university-press-editor/.

Chapnick, Adam, and Christopher Kukucha. 2016b. "The Pros and Cons of Editing a Collection of Essays." *University Affairs: The Scholarly Edition.* May 10, 2016. https://www.universityaffairs.ca/career-advice/the-scholarly-edition/the-pros-and-cons-of-editing-a-collection-of-essays/.

Chen, Julie, and John Ho. 2020. "A Medical Humanities Curriculum in Medical School: Unexpected Partnerships and Unintended Consequences." In *Building Courage, Confidence, and Capacity in Learning and Teaching through Student-Faculty Partnership: Stories from across Contexts and Arenas of Practice,* edited by Alison Cook-Sather and Chanelle Wilson. Lanham, MD: Lexington Books.

Cheng, Christine (@cheng_christine). 2019. "Some advice for attending big discipline-wide academic conferences." Twitter, March 22, 2019. https://twitter.com/cheng_christine/status/1109027320126423042.

Chick, Nancy. 2019. "SoTL as Public Scholarship." *ChickChat* (blog). March 28, 2019. https://nancychick.wordpress.com/2019/03/28/sotl-as-public-scholarship/.

Chick, Nancy, Sarah Bunnell, Peter Felten, Bettie Higgs, Aaron Long, Karen Manarin, Beth Marquis, Katarina Mårtensson, Kelly Matthews, Jessie L. Moore, and Lauren Scharff. 2017. "ISSOTL Conference Pedagogy." https://www.issotl.com/issotl-conference-pedagogy.

Chick, Nancy, La Vonne Cornell-Swanson, Katina Lazarides, and Renee Meyers. 2014. "Reconciling Apples & Oranges: A Constructivist SoTL Writing Program." *International Journal for the Scholarship of Teaching and Learning* 8 (2): Article 13. https://doi.org/10.20429/ijsotl.2014.080213.

Chick, Nancy, and Peter Felten. 2018. "How to Tell a True SoTL Story." In *ISSOTL18 Toward a Learning Culture: Program and Book of Abstracts*: 193. https://www.dropbox.com/s/n7rn6wgxeolpyy2/ISSOTL18_program_book.pdf?dl=0.

Chism, Nancy. 1998. "Developing a Philosophy of Teaching Statement." *Essays on Teaching Excellence* (3): 1–3. http://podnetwork.org/content/uploads/V9-N3-Chism.pdf.

Chng, Huang Hoon, and Peter Looker. 2013. "On the Margins of SoTL Discourse: An Asian Perspective." *Teaching & Learning Inquiry* 1 (1): 131–45.

Cleaver, Elizabeth, Maxine Lintern, and Mike McLinden. 2018. *Teaching and Learning in Higher Education: Disciplinary Approaches to Educational Enquiry*. London: SAGE.

Colquhoun, Heather L., Danielle Levac, Kelly K. O'Brien, Sharon Straus, Andrea C. Tricco, Laure Perrier, Monika Kastner, and David Moher. 2014. "Scoping Reviews: Time for Clarity in Definition, Methods, and Reporting." *Journal of Clinical Epidemiology* 67 (12): 1291–94. https://doi.org/10.1016/j.jclinepi.2014.03.013.

Convery, Andy, and Andrew Townsend. 2018. "Action Research Update: Why Do Articles Get Rejected from EARJ?" *Educational Action Research* 26 (4): 503–12. https://doi.org/10.1080/09650792.2018.1518746.

Cook-Sather, Alison. 2019. "Becoming: Realizing Selves through Participating in Pedagogical Partnership." *Teaching and Learning*

Together in Higher Education 26: 1–2. https://repository.brynmawr. edu/cgi/viewcontent.cgi?article=1204&context=tlthe.

Cook-Sather, Alison. 2018a. "Developing 'Students as Learners and Teachers': Lessons from Ten Years of Pedagogical Partnership that Strives to Foster Inclusive and Responsive Practice." *Journal of Educational Innovation, Partnership and Change* 4 (1) https://journals.studentengagement.org.uk/index.php/ studentchangeagents/article/view/746.

Cook-Sather, Alison. 2018b. "Tracing the Evolution of Student Voice in Educational Research." In *Radical Collegiality through Student Voice*, edited by Roseanna Bourke and Judith Loveridge. London: Springer Publishers.

Cook-Sather, Alison. 2018c. "Perpetual Translation: Conveying the Languages and Practices of Student Voice and Pedagogical Partnership across Differences of Identity, Culture, Position, and Power." *Transformative Dialogues: Learning and Teaching Journal* 11 (3): 1–7. http://www.kpu.ca/sites/default/files/Transformative%20 Dialogues/TD.11.3_Cook-Sather_Perpetual_Translation.pdf.

Cook-Sather, Alison. 2015. "Dialogue across Differences of Position, Perspective, and Identity: Reflective Practice in/on a Student-Faculty Pedagogical Partnership Program." *Teachers College Record* 117 (2). http://repository.brynmawr.edu/edu_pubs/32.

Cook-Sather, Alison. 2011. "Teaching and Learning Together: College Faculty and Undergraduates Co-Create a Professional Development Model." *To Improve the Academy* 29: 219–32. https://doi. org/10.1002/j.2334-4822.2011.tb00633.x.

Cook-Sather, Alison. 2008. "'What You Get Is Looking in a Mirror, Only Better': Inviting Students to Reflect (on) College Teaching." *Reflective Practice* 9 (4): 473–83. https://doi. org/10.1080/14623940802431465.

Cook-Sather, Alison. 2006. "Sound, Presence, and Power: 'Student Voice' in Educational Research and Reform." *Curriculum Inquiry* 36 (4): 359–90. https://doi.org/10.1111/j.1467-873X.2006.00363.x.

Cook-Sather, Alison. 2002. "Authorizing Students' Perspectives: Toward Trust, Dialogue, and Change in Education." *Educational Researcher* 31 (4): 3–14. https://doi.org/10.3102/0013189X031004003.

Cook-Sather, Alison, and Sophia Abbot. 2016. "Translating Partnerships: How Faculty-Student Collaboration in Explorations of Teaching and Learning Can Transform Perceptions, Terms, and Selves." *Teaching & Learning Inquiry* 4 (2). https://doi.org/10.20343/teachlearninqu.4.2.5.

Cook-Sather, Alison, Sophia Abbot, and Peter Felten. 2019. "Legitimating Reflective Writing in SoTL: 'Dysfunctional Illusions of Rigor' Revisited." *Teaching & Learning Inquiry* 7 (2): 14–27. https://doi.org/10.20343/teachlearninqu.7.2.2.

Cook-Sather, Alison, and Praise Agu. 2013. "Students of Color and Faculty Members Working Together Toward Culturally Sustaining Pedagogy." In *To Improve the Academy: Resources for Faculty, Instructional, and Organizational Development,* edited by James E. Groccia and Laura Cruz, 271–85. San Francisco: Jossey Bass.

Cook-Sather, Alison, and Zanny Alter. 2011. "What Is and What Can Be: How a Liminal Position Can Change Learning and Teaching in Higher Education." *Anthropology & Education Quarterly* 42 (1): 37–53. https://doi.org/10.1111/j.1548-1492.2010.01109.x.

Cook-Sather, Alison, Catherine Bovill, and Peter Felten. 2014. *Engaging Students as Partners in Learning and Teaching: A Guide for Faculty.* San Francisco: Jossey-Bass.

Cook-Sather, Alison, and Heather Curl. 2014. "'I Want to Listen to My Students' Lives': Developing an Ecological Perspective in Learning to Teach." *Teacher Education Quarterly* 41 (1): 85–103.

Cook-Sather, Alison, and Crystal Des-Ogugua. 2018. "Lessons We Still Need to Learn on Creating More Inclusive and Responsive Classrooms: Recommendations from One Student-Faculty Partnership Programme." *International Journal of Inclusive Education* 23 (6): 594-608. https://doi.org/10.1080/13603116.2018.1441912.

Cook-Sather, Alison, Kelly E. Matthews, Anita Ntem, and Sandra Leathwick. 2018. "What We Talk about When We Talk about

Students as Partners." *International Journal for Students as Partners* 2 (2): 1–9. https://doi.org/10.15173/ijsap.v2i2.3790.

Cook-Sather, Alison, and Olivia Porte. 2017. "Reviving Humanity: Grasping Within and Beyond Our Reach." *Journal of Educational Innovation, Partnership and Change* 3 (1). https://journals.gre.ac.uk/index.php/studentchangeagents/article/view/638.

Cook-Sather, Alison, and Chanelle Wilson. 2020. *Building Courage, Confidence, and Capacity in Learning and Teaching through Student-Faculty Partnership: Stories from across Contexts and Arenas of Practice.* Lanham, MD: Lexington Books.

Cooper, Harris. 2003. "Editorial." *Psychology Bulletin* 129 (1): 3–9. http://dx.doi.org/10.1037/0033-2909.129.1.3.

Cooper, Harris. 1988. "Organizing Knowledge Syntheses: A Taxonomy of Literature Reviews." *Knowledge in Society* 1 (1): 104–26. https://doi.org/10.1007/BF03177550.

Corrigan, Mark. 2019a. "Writing a Second Edition Is Much Harder than I Realised" *Patter.* December 16, 2019. https://patthomson.net/2019/12/16/writing-a-second-edition-is-much-harder-than-i-realised/.

Corrigan, Mark. 2019b. *Social Media for Academics.* 2nd edition. London: Sage.

Corrigan, Paul T. 2010. "Listservs on Teaching and Learning." *Teaching and Learning in Higher Education* (blog). May 13, 2013. https://teachingandlearninginhighered.org/2013/05/13/listservs-on-teaching-and-learning/.

Costa, Arthur L., and Bena Kallick. 1993. "Through the Lens of a Critical Friend." *Educational Leadership* 51 (2): 49-51. http://www.ascd.org/publications/educational-leadership/oct93/vol51/num02/Through-the-Lens-of-a-Critical-Friend.aspx.

Cotton, Debby R. E., Wendy Miller, and Pauline Kneale. 2017. "The Cinderella of Academia: Is Higher Education Pedagogic Research Undervalued in UK Research Assessment?" *Studies in Higher Education* 43 (9): 1625–36. http://doi.org/10.1080/03075079.2016.1276549%20%20.

Cousin, Glynis. 2009. *Researching Learning in Higher Education: An Introduction to Contemporary Methods and Approaches.* London: Routledge.

Cranton, Patricia. 2011. "A Transformative Perspective on the Scholarship of Teaching and Learning." *Higher Education Research & Development* 30 (1): 75–86. https://doi.org/10.1080/07294360.2011.536974.

Crick, Tom, and Alan Winfield. 2013. "Academic Blogging – 10 Top Tips." *The Guardian.* December 13, 2013. https://www.theguardian.com/higher-education-network/blog/2013/dec/13/how-to-academic-blogging-tips.

Critical Studies in Education. n.d. "Aims and Scope." Accessed May 13, 2020. https://www.tandfonline.com/action/journalInformation?show=aimsScope&journalCode=rcse20.

Critical Studies in Education. n.d. "Instructions for Authors." Accessed May 13, 2020. https://www.tandfonline.com/action/authorSubmission?journalCode=rcse20&page=instructions.

Daniel, Ben Kei, and Tony Harland. 2017. *Higher Education Research Methodology: A Step-by-Step Guide to the Research Process.* London: Routledge.

Daviduke, Natasha. 2018. "Growing into Pedagogical Partnerships Over Time and Across Disciplines: My Experience as a Non-STEM Student Consultant in STEM Courses." *International Journal for Students as Partners* 2 (2): 151–6. https://doi.org/10.15173/ijsap.v2i2.3443.

Davis, Phil. 2019. "Can Twitter, Facebook, and Other Social Media Drive Downloads, Citations?" *The Scholarly Kitchen.* May 23, 2019. https://scholarlykitchen.sspnet.org/2019/05/23/can-twitter-facebook-and-other-social-media-drive-downloads-citations/.

Day, Abby. 2016. *How to Get Research Published in Journals.* Abingdon, UK: Routledge.

de Bie, Alise. 2019. "Finding Ways (and Words) to Move: Mad Student Politics and Practices of Loneliness." *Disability & Society* 34 (7–8): 1154–79. https://doi.org/10.1080/09687599.2019.1609910.

de Bie, Alise, Elizabeth Marquis, Alison Cook-Sather, and Leslie Luqueño. 2019. "Valuing Knowledge(s) and Cultivating Confidence: Contributing to Epistemic Justice via Student-Faculty Pedagogical Partnerships." In *Strategies for Fostering Inclusive Classrooms in Higher Education: International Perspectives on Equity and Inclusion*, edited by Jaimie Hoffman, Patrick Blessinger, and Mandla Makhanya, 35–48. West Yorkshire, UK: Emerald Publishing Limited. https://doi.org/10.1108/S2055-364120190000016004.

Deitering, Anne-Marie, Robert Schroeder, and Richard Stoddart. 2017. *The Self as Subject: Autoethnographic Research into Identity, Culture, and Academic Librarianship.* Atlanta, GA: American Library Association.

Dewey, John. 1933. *How We Think.* New York: D. C. Heath.

Dowse, Renee, Jacqueline Melvold, and Kristine McGrath. 2018. "Students Guiding Students: Integrating Student Peer Review into a Large First Year Science Subject. A Practice Report." *Student Success* 9 (3): 79–86. https://doi.org/10.5204/ssj.v9i3.471.

Duke University. n.d. "Writing Effective Op-Eds." Accessed October 15, 2019. https://styleguide.duke.edu/toolkits/writing-media/how-to-write-an-op-ed-article/.

Duncan, Mike. 2018. "The 3 Types of Peer Reviewers." *The Chronicle of Higher Education.* June 19, 2018. https://www.chronicle.com/article/The-3-Types-of-Peer-Reviewers/243698.

Dunleavy, Patrick. 2016. "How to Write a Blogpost from Your Journal Article in Eleven Easy Steps." *LSE Impact Blog.* January 25, 2016. https://blogs.lse.ac.uk/impactofsocialsciences/2016/01/25/how-to-write-a-blogpost-from-your-journal-article/.

Dunleavy, Patrick. 2014. "Why Do Academics Choose Useless Titles for Articles and Chapters? Four Steps to Getting a Better Title." *LSE Impact Blog.* February 5, 2014. https://blogs.lse.ac.uk/impactofsocialsciences/2014/02/05/academics-choose-useless-titles/.

Dunne, Liz, Derfel Owen, Hannah Barr, Will Page, James Smith, and Sabina Szydlo. 2014. "The Story of Students as Change Agents at the University of Exeter: From Slow Beginnings to Institutional

Initiative." *Teaching and Learning Together in Higher Education* 13. http://repository.brynmawr.edu/tlthe/vol1/iss13/9.

Duquesne University Center for Teaching Excellence. n.d. "Writing to Learn." Accessed May 15, 2020. https://www.duq.edu/about/centers-and-institutes/center-for-teaching-excellence/teaching-and-learning-at-duquesne/writing-to-learn.

Dutta, Mohan J. 2018. "Autoethnography as Decolonization, Decolonizing Autoethnography: Resisting to Build Our Homes." *Cultural Studies Critical Methodologies* 18 (1): 94–96. https://doi.org/10.1177/1532708617735637.

Dvorakova, Lucie S., and Kelly E. Matthews. 2017. "Graduate Learning Outcomes in Science: Variation in Perceptions of Single-and Dual-Degree Students." *Assessment & Evaluation in Higher Education* 42 (6): 900–913. https://doi.org/10.1080/02602938.2016.1208804.

Dwyer, Alexander. 2018. "Toward the Formation of Genuine Partnership Spaces." *International Journal for Students as Partners* 2(1): 11–15. https://doi.org/10.15173/ijsap.v2i1.3503.

Eco, Umberto. 1984. *Postscript to the Name of the Rose*. New York: Harcourt.

Elbow, Peter. 2007. "Voice in Writing Again: Embracing Contraries." *College English* 7. https://scholarworks.umass.edu/cgi/viewcontent.cgi?article=1006&context=eng_faculty_pubs.

Elbow, Peter. 1975. *Writing Without Teachers*. Oxford University Press.

Elken, Mari, and Sabine Wollscheid. 2016. *The Relationship between Research and Education: Typologies and Indicators. A Literature Review.* Institute for Studies in Innovation, Research and Education (NIFU) 8. Oslo: Nordic. https://www.nifu.no/en/publications/1351162/.

Elsevier. 2019. "Get Noticed: Increase the Impact of Your Research." https://www.elsevier.com/__data/assets/pdf_file/0014/201326/ELS-GH-GetNoticed-Factsheet-A4-Mar19-Web.pdf.

Elton, Lewis. 1983. "Conferences: Making a Good Thing Rather Better?" *British Journal of Educational Technology* 14 (3): 200–15. https://doi.org/10.1111/j.1467-8535.1983.tb00462.x.

Faculty of Science. 2015. "Bachelor of Science Curriculum Review Submission." Brisbane: The University of Queensland. http:// espace.library.uq.edu.au/view/UQ:715983.

Fanghanel, Joelle. 2013. "Going Public with Pedagogical Inquiries: SoTL as a Methodology for Faculty Professional Development." *Teaching & Learning Inquiry* 1 (1): 59–70. https://doi. org/10.20343/teachlearninqu.1.1.59.

Fanghanel, Joelle. 2011. *Being an Academic*. Abingdon, UK: Routledge.

Fanghanel, Joelle, Susannah McGowan, Pam Parker, Catherine McConnell, Jackie Potter, William Locke, and Mick Healey. 2015. *Literature Review. Defining and Supporting the Scholarship of Teaching and Learning (SoTL): A Sector-Wide Study*. York, UK: Higher Education Academy. https://www.academia.edu/19942913/ Defining_and_Supporting_the_Scholarship_of_Teaching_and_ Learning_A_literature_review.

Faulkes, Zen. 2019. "Critique: The Morrison Billboard Poster." *Better Posters* (blog). April 11, 2019. https://betterposters.blogspot. com/2019/04/critique-morrison-billboard-poster.html.

Feldman, Daniel C. 2004. "The Devil Is in the Details: Converting Good Research into Publishable Articles." *Journal of Management* 30 (1): 1–6. https://doi.org/10.1016/j.jm.2003.09.001.

Felten, Peter. 2019. "How Do You Tell a True Partnership Story? Four Reflections." *Teaching and Learning Together in Higher Education* 27. https://repository.brynmawr.edu/tlthe/vol1/iss27/2.

Felten, Peter. 2016. "On the Threshold with Students." In *Threshold Concepts in Practice*, edited by Ray Land, Jan H. F. Meyer, and Michael T. Flanagan, 3–9. Rotterdam, The Netherlands: Sense Publishers.

Felten, Peter. 2013. "Introduction: Crossing Thresholds Together." *Teaching and Learning Together in Higher Education* 9. https://repository. brynmawr.edu/tlthe/vol1/iss9/1.

Felten, Peter, and Nancy Chick. 2018. "Is SoTL a Signature Pedagogy of Educational Development?" *To Improve the Academy: A Journal of Educational Development* 37 (1): 4–16. https://doi.org/10.1002/ tia2.20077.

Felten, Peter, Jessie L. Moore, and Michael Strickland. 2009. "Faculty Writing Residencies: Supporting Scholarly Writing and Teaching." *Journal on Centers for Teaching and Learning* 1: 39–55. http://openjournal.lib.miamioh.edu/index.php/jctl/article/view/101.

Flower, Linda. 1979. "Writer-Based Prose: A Cognitive Basis for Problems in Writing." *College English* 41 (1): 19–37. https://www.jstor.org/stable/376357.

Flowerdew, John. 1999. "Problems in Writing for Scholarly Publication in English: The Case of Hong Kong." *Journal of Second Language Writing* 8 (3): 243–64. https://doi.org/10.1016/S1060-3743(99)80116-7.

Flowerdew, John, and Simon Ho Wang. 2015. "Identity in Academic Discourse." *Annual Review of Applied Linguistics* 35: 81–99. https://doi.org/10.1017/S026719051400021X.

Foucault, Michel. 1972. *The Archaeology of Knowledge and the Discourse on Language.* New York: Pantheon.

Fraser, Gordon. 2019. "The Twitterization of the Academic Mind: Social Media Has Made Scholars Impatient, Vicious, and Dull." *The Chronicle of Higher Education.* March 22, 2019. https://www.chronicle.com/article/The-Twitterization-of-the/245965.

Fricker, Miranda. 2007. *Epistemic Injustice: Power and the Ethics of Knowing.* Oxford University Press.

Frison, Daniela, and Claudio Melacarne. 2017. "Introduction – Students-Faculty Partnership in Italy: Approaches, Practices, and Perspectives." *Teaching and Learning Together in Higher Education* 20. https://repository.brynmawr.edu/tlthe/vol1/iss20/1.

Fuller, Mary, Jan Georgeson, Mick Healey, Alan Hurst, Katie Kelly, Sheila Riddell, Hazel Roberts, and Elisabet Weedon. 2009. *Improving Disabled Student Learning in Higher Education: Experiences and Outcomes.* Abingdon, UK: Routledge.

Fulwiler, Toby, and Art Young. 1982. "Introduction." In *Language Connections: Writing and Reading across the Curriculum,* edited by Toby Fulwiler and Art Young, ix–xiii. Urbana, IL: National Council of Teachers of English.

Fung, Dilly. 2017. *Connected Curriculum for Higher Education*. London: UCL Press.

Fung, Dilly, and Claire Gordon. 2016. *Rewarding Educators and Education Leaders in Research-Intensive Universities.* York: Higher Education Academy. https://www.advance-he.ac.uk/knowledge-hub/rewarding-educators-and-education-leaders.

Geller, Anne Ellen, and Michele Eodice. 2013. *Working with Faculty Writers.* Logan, UT: Utah State University Press.

Geertsema, Johan. 2016. "Academic Development, SoTL and Educational Research." *International Journal for Academic Development* 21 (2): 122–34. https://doi.org/10.1080/1360144X.2016.1175144.

Germano, William. 2016. *Getting It Published: A Guide for Scholars and Anyone Else Serious about Serious Books*. Chicago, IL: University of Chicago Press.

Gibbs, Graham. 2000. "Are the Pedagogies of the Disciplines Really Different?" In *Improving Student Learning through the Disciplines*, edited by Chris Rust. Proceedings of the 1999 7th International Symposium: 41–51. Oxford: Oxford Centre for Staff and Learning Development, Oxford Brookes University.

Gibbs, Graham. 1988. *Learning by Doing: A Guide to Teaching and Learning Methods.* Further Education Unit. Oxford: Oxford Centre for Staff and Learning Development. https://thoughtsmostlyaboutlearning.files.wordpress.com/2015/12/learning-by-doing-graham-gibbs.pdf.

Glassick, Charles E., Mary Taylor Huber, and Gene I. Maeroff. 1997. *Scholarship Assessed: Evaluation of the Professoriate*. San Francisco: Jossey-Bass.

Gleason, Nancy W. 2018. *Higher Education in the Era of the Fourth Industrial Revolution*. Singapore: Palgrave Macmillan. https://link.springer.com/book/10.1007%2F978-981-13-0194-0.

Goldsmith, Meredith, Megan Hanscom, Susanna Throop, and Cody Young. 2017. "Growing Student-Faculty Partnerships at Ursinus College: A Brief History in Dialogue." *International Journal for Students as Partners* 1 (2). https://doi.org/10.15173/ijsap.v1i2.3075.

Golightly, Aubrey. 2018. "The Influence of an Integrated PBL Format on Geography Students' Perceptions of their Self-directedness in Learning." *Journal of Geography in Higher Education* 42 (3): 460–78. http://doi.org/10.1080/03098265.2018.1463974.

Grant, Adam. 2018. "What Straight-A Students Get Wrong." *The New York Times*. December 8, 2018. https://www.nytimes.com/2018/12/08/opinion/college-gpa-career-success.html?module=inline.

Grant, Barbara. 2017. "In Praise (Really!) of Academic Conferences: Selected Memories." *Conference Inference*. June 19, 2017. https://conferenceinference.wordpress.com/2017/06/19/guest-post-by-barbara-grant-in-praise-really-of-academic-conferences-selected-memories/.

Grant, Barbara. 2016. "Getting My Work Out There: Writing the Journal Article." In *Publishing and the Academic World: Passion, Purpose and Possible Futures*, edited by Ciaran Sugrue and Sefika Mertkan, 75–89. London: Routledge.

Grant, Barbara. 2008. *Academic Writing Retreats: A Facilitator's Guide.* Milperra: Higher Education Research and Development Society of Australasia.

Grant, Maria J., and Andrew Booth. 2009. "A Typology of Reviews: An Analysis of 14 Review Types and Associated Methodologies." *Health Information and Libraries Journal* 26: 91–108. https://doi.org/10.1111/j.1471-1842.2009.00848.x.

Gravett, Emily O., and Lindsay Bernhagen. 2018. "Ways of Doing: Feminist Educational Development." *To Improve the Academy* 37 (1): 17–29. https://doi.org/10.1002/tia2.20068.

Green, Toby. 2019. "Publication Is Not Enough, To Generate Impact You Need to Campaign." *LSE Impact Blog*. September 26, 2019. https://blogs.lse.ac.uk/impactofsocialsciences/2019/09/27/publication-is-not-enough-to-generate-impact-you-need-to-campaign/.

Greenfieldboyce, Nell. 2019. "To Save the Science Poster, Researchers Want to Kill It and Start Over." *NPR Health Shots*. June 11, 2019. https://www.npr.org/sections/

health-shots/2019/06/11/729314248/to-save-the-science-poster-researchers-want-to-kill-it-and-start-over.

Griffioen, Didi M. E. 2019. "The Influence of Undergraduate Students' Research Attitudes on their Intentions for Research Usage in their Future Professional Practice." *Innovation in Education and Teaching International* 56 (2): 162–72. https://doi.org/10.1080/14703297.2018.1425152.

Guest, Jon, and Elwyn Lloyd, eds. 2013. *Engaging Students in Active, Inquiry-based and Effective Learning.* Coventry: Faculty of Business, Environment and Society, Coventry University.

Gunersel, Adalet Baris, Pamela Barnett, and Mary Etienne. 2013. "Promoting Self-authorship of College Educators: Exploring the Impact of a Faculty Development Program." *Journal of Faculty Development* 27 (1): 35–44. http://citeseerx.ist.psu.edu/viewdoc/download?doi=10.1.1.448.5073&rep=rep1&type=pdf.

Haggan, Madeline. 2004. "Research Paper Titles in Literature, Linguistics and Science: Dimensions of Attraction." *Journal of Pragmatics* 36 (2): 293–317. https://doi.org/10.1016/S0378-2166(03)00090-0.

Haigh, Martin. 2012. "Writing Successfully for the *Journal of Geography in Higher Education.*" *Journal of Geography in Higher Education* 37 (1): 117–135. https://doi.org/10.1080/03098265.2012.692158.

Haley, Karen J., Colleen Aalsburg Wiessner, and E. Erin Robinson. 2009. "Encountering New Information and Perspectives: Constructing Knowledge in Conference Contexts." *The Journal of Continuing Higher Education* 57 (2): 72–82. https://doi.org/10.1080/07377360902964384.

Hall, Meegan, and Kathryn Sutherland. 2018. "He pī, ka rere: Māori Early Career Academics in New Zealand Universities." In *Early Career Academics in New Zealand: Challenges and Prospects in Comparative Perspective,* edited by Kathryn Sutherland, 137–56. Cham, Switzerland: Springer. https://doi.org/10.1007/978-3-319-61830-2_7.

Hall, Meegan, and Kathryn Sutherland. 2013. "Students Who Teach: Developing Scholarly Tutors." In *Effective Part-time Teachers in Contemporary Universities: New Approaches to Professional*

Development, edited by Fran Beaton and Amanda Gilbert, 82–93. Abingdon, UK: Routledge.

Harris, Robert A. 2017. *Writing with Clarity and Style: A Guide to Rhetorical Devices for Contemporary Writers*. London: Routledge.

Harrison, Margaret. 2004. "'In Memorium': Preparing Obituaries on Key Geographers." In *Engaging Students in Active Learning: Case Studies in Geography, Environment and Related Disciplines*, edited by Mick Healey and Jane Roberts, 14–16. Cheltenham: Geography Discipline Network and School of Environment, University of Gloucestershire. https://gdn.glos.ac.uk/active/engagingstudents.pdf.

Hart, Chris. 2018. *Doing a Literature Review: Releasing the Research Imagination*. London: SAGE.

Hartley, James. 2008. *Academic Writing and Publishing: A Practical Handbook*. London: Routledge. http://inf.ucv.ro/~mirel/courses/MIAM114/docs/academicwriting.pdf.

Hattie, John. 2008. *Visible Learning*. London: Routledge.

Hay, Iain. 2011. *Inspiring Academics: Learning with the World's Great University Teachers*. Maidenhead, Open University Press.

Haynes, Anthony. 2010. *Writing Successful Academic Books*. Cambridge University Press.

Haynes, Anthony, Karen Haynes, Sue Habeshaw, Graham Gibbs, and Trevor Habeshaw. 2012. *53 Interesting Things to Do in Your Lectures*. Sydney: Allen & Unwin.

Healey, Mick. 2019. "'20 Years an NTF': Some Reflections." *Advance HE Blog*. December 5, 2019. https://www.advance-he.ac.uk/news-and-views/20-years-as-an-NTF-some-reflections.

Healey, Mick. 2011. "Excellence and Scholarship in Teaching: Some Reflections." In *Inspiring Academics: Learning with the World's Great University Teachers*, edited by Iain Hay, 198–207. Maidenhead, UK: Open University Press.

Healey, Mick. 2005. "Linking Research and Teaching Exploring Disciplinary Spaces and the Role of Inquiry-based Learning." In *Reshaping the University: New Relationships between Research,*

Scholarship and Teaching, edited by Ronald Barnett, 30–42. Maidenhead, UK: McGraw-Hill/Open University Press.

Healey, Mick. 2003a. "Trojan Horse Is Good Bet for All: Strategies to Improve Flexibility for Disabled Students Could Benefit Everyone." *The Times Higher Education Supplement.* September 19, 2003.

Healey, Mick. 2003b. "The Scholarship of Teaching: Issues around an Evolving Concept." *Journal on Excellence in College Teaching* 14 (1/2): 5–26.

Healey, Mick. 2000. "Developing the Scholarship of Teaching in Higher Education: A Discipline-Based Approach." *Higher Education Research and Development* 19 (2): 169–89. https://doi.org/10.1080/072943600445637.

Healey, Mick, and Mike Addis. 2004. "Use of Peer and Self-assessment to Distribute Group Marks among Individual Team Members: Ten Years Experience." In *Engaging Students in Active Learning: Case Studies in Geography, Environment and Related Disciplines*, edited by Mick Healey and Jane Roberts, 116–21. Cheltenham: Geography Discipline Network and School of Environment, University of Gloucestershire. https://gdn.glos.ac.uk/active/engagingstudents.pdf.

Healey, Mick, Trudy Ambler, Malin Irhammar, Wendy Kilfoil, and Judith Lyons. 2014. "International Perspectives on Peer Review as Quality Enhancement." In *Peer Review of Learning and Teaching in Higher Education*, edited by Judyth Sachs, and Mitch Parsell, 201–19. Dordrecht, Netherlands: Springer.

Healey, Mick, and Gordon Clark. 1994a. "Teaching Economic Geography: A *JGHE* Symposium (Part I—Course Content)." *Journal of Geography in Higher Education* 18 (1): 67–69. https://doi.org/10.1080/03098269408709238.

Healey, Mick, and Gordon Clark. 1994b. "Teaching Economic Geography: A *JGHE* Symposium, Part II: Teaching Methods." *Journal of Geography in Higher* Education 18 (2): 195–235. https://doi.org/10.1080/03098269408709257.

Healey, Mick, Abbi Flint, and Kathy Harrington. 2016. "Students as Partners: Reflections on a Conceptual Model." *Teaching & Learning Inquiry* 4 (2): 1–13. https://doi.org/10.20343/teachlearninqu.4.2.3.

Healey, Mick, Abbi Flint, and Kathy Harrington. 2014. *Engagement through Partnership: Students as Partners in Learning and Teaching in Higher Education.* York, UK: Higher Education Academy. https://www.advance-he.ac.uk/knowledge-hub/engagement-through-partnership-students-partners-learning-and-teaching-higher.

Healey, Mick, Mary Fuller, Andrew Bradley, and Tim Hall. 2006. "Listening to Students: The Experiences of Disabled Students of Learning at University." In *Towards Inclusive Learning in Higher Education: Developing Curricula for Disabled Students,* edited by Mike Adams and Sally Brown, 32–43. Abingdon, UK: RoutledgeFalmer.

Healey, Mick, and Ruth Healey. 2019. *Applying for a National Teaching Fellowship: This Year, Next Year or Sometime.* https://www.mickhealey.co.uk/download/applying-for-a-national-teaching-fellowship-this-year-next-year-or-sometime-2.

Healey, Mick, and Ruth Healey. 2018. "'It Depends': Exploring the Context-Dependent Nature of Students as Partners Practices and Policies." *International Journal for Students as Partners* 2 (1): 1–10. https://doi.org/10.15173/ijsap.v2i1.3472.

Healey, Mick, and Alan Jenkins. 2009. *Developing Undergraduate Research and Inquiry.* York, UK: Higher Education Academy. https://www.advance-he.ac.uk/knowledge-hub/developing-undergraduate-research-and-inquiry.

Healey, Mick, and Alan Jenkins. 2003. "Discipline-based Educational Development." In *The Scholarship of Academic Development*, edited by Heather Eggins and Ranald Macdonald, 47–57. Milton Keynes, UK: Open University Press.

Healey, Mick, Alan Jenkins, and Jonathan Leach. 2006. *Issues in Developing an Inclusive Curriculum: Examples from Geography, Earth and Environmental Sciences.* Cheltenham, UK: University of Gloucestershire, Geography Discipline Network. https://gdn.glos.ac.uk/icp/gdlist.htm.

Healey, Mick, Kelly E. Matthews, and Alison Cook-Sather. 2019. "Writing Scholarship of Teaching and Learning Articles for Peer-Reviewed Journals." *Teaching & Learning Inquiry* 7 (2): 28–50. https://doi.org/10.20343/teachlearninqu.7.2.3.

Healey, Mick, and Jane Roberts. 2004. *Engaging Students in Active Learning: Case Studies in Geography, Environment and Related Disciplines.* Cheltenham, UK: University of Gloucestershire, Geography Discipline Network and School of Environment. https://gdn.glos.ac.uk/active/engagingstudents.pdf.

Healey, Ruth L., Mick Healey, and Anthony Cliffe. 2018. "Engaging in Radical Work: Students as Partners in Academic Publishing." *Efficiency Exchange.* May 1, 2018. https://chesterrep.openrepository.com/handle/10034/621052.

Healey, Ruth L., and Jenny Hill. 2019. "Reflecting on 'Directions': Growing with the Times and Future Developments." *Journal of Geography in Higher Education* 43 (2): 125–130. https://doi.org/10.1080/03098265.2019.1599832.

Heidegger, Martin. 1962. *Being and Time.* Translated from German by John Macquarie and Edward Robinson. London: SCM Press.

Henderson, Emily. 2019. "Organising, Funding and Participating in Care-Friendly Conferences." *Conference Inference.* February 18, 2019. https://conferenceinference.wordpress.com/2019/02/18/organising-funding-and-participating-in-care-friendly-conferences/.

Henderson, Emily F., Xuemeng Cao, and Julie Mansuy. 2018. *In Two Places at Once: The Impact of Caring Responsibilities on Academics' Conference Participation: Final Project Report.* Coventry: Centre for Education Studies, University of Warwick. https://doi.org/10.31273/CES.06.2018.001.

Hill, Jennifer, Helen Walkington, and Helen King. 2018. "Geographers and the Scholarship of Teaching and Learning." *Journal of Geography in Higher Education* 42 (4): 557–72. https://doi.org/10.1080/03098265.2018.1515188.

Hirshleifer, David. 2014. "Cosmetic Surgery in the Academic Review Process." *The Review of Financial Studies* 28 (3): 637–49. https://doi.org/10.1093/rfs/hhu093.

Hitchcock, Steve. 2011. "The Effect of Open Access and Downloads ('Hits') on Citation Impact: A Bibliography of Studies." Research-Gate. https://www.researchgate.net/publication/261773651_The_effect_of_open_access_and_downloads_'hits'_on_citation_impact_A_bibliography_of_studies_OpCit_project.

Hogue, Rebecca. 2012. "What Makes a Good Critical Friend?" *Rebecca J. Hogue* (blog). November 14, 2012. http://rjh.goingeast.ca/2012/11/14/what-makes-a-good-critical-friend/.

Holmes, Trevor, and Kathryn Sutherland. 2015. "Deconstructive Misalignment: Reflections on Method and Theory in Academic Development." *The Canadian Journal for the Scholarship of Teaching and Learning* 6 (2): Article 11. http://dx.doi.org/10.5206/cjsotl-rcacea.2015.2.11.

hooks, bell. 2003. *Teaching Community: A Pedagogy of Hope.* New York: Routledge.

hooks, bell. 1994. *Teaching to Transgress: Education as the Practice of Freedom.* New York: Routledge.

hooks, bell. 1989. *Talking Back: Thinking Feminist, Thinking Black.* Boston, MA: South End Press.

Huber, Mary Taylor. 2009. "Teaching Travels: Reflections on the Social Life of Classroom Inquiry and Innovation." *International Journal for the Scholarship of Teaching and Learning* 3 (2). https://doi.org/10.20429/ijsotl.2009.030202.

Huber, Mary Taylor. 2000. "Disciplinary Styles in the Scholarship of Teaching: Reflections on the Carnegie Academy for Scholarship of Teaching and Learning." In *Proceedings of the 1999 7th International Symposium Improving Student Learning: Improving Student Learning through the Disciplines*, edited by Chris Rust, 20–31. Oxford Centre for Staff and Learning Development, Oxford Brookes University.

Hubrath, Margarete. 2008. "Networking for a Successful Career in Academia." Academics.com (blog). https://www.academics.com/guide/academic-networking-germany.

Huff, Anne Sigismund. 2008. *Designing Research for Publication*. New York: SAGE.

Hunt, Lynne, and Denise Chalmers. 2013. *University Teaching in Focus: A Learning-Centred Approach*. Abingdon, UK: Routledge.

Hutchings, Pat, Mary Tayler Huber, and Anthony Ciccone. 2011. *The Scholarship of Teaching and Learning Reconsidered: Institutional Integration and Impact*. San Francisco: Jossey-Bass.

Iber, Patrick. 2016. "A Defense of Academic Twitter." *Inside Higher Education*. October 19, 2016. https://www.insidehighered.com/advice/2016/10/19/how-academics-can-use-twitter-most-effectively-essay.

ICMJE (International Committee of Medical Journal Editors). 2017. "Recommendations for the Conduct, Reporting, Editing, and Publication of Scholarly Work in Medical Journals." http://www.icmje.org/icmje-recommendations.pdf.

Illeris, Knud. 2018. "An Overview of the History of Learning Theory." *European Journal of Education* 53: 86–101. https://doi.org/10.1111/ejed.12265.

Imel, Susan. 2011. "Writing a Literature Review." In *The Handbook of Scholarly Writing and Publishing,* edited by Tonette S. Rocco and Timothy Gary Hatcher, 145–60. San Francisco: Jossey-Bass.

International Journal for Students as Partners. n.d. "Submissions." Accessed May 13, 2020. https://mulpress.mcmaster.ca/ijsap/about/submissions.

International Journal of Sustainability in Higher Education. n.d. "Author Guidelines." Accessed May 13, 2020. https://www.emeraldgrouppublishing.com/products/journals/author_guidelines.htm?id=ijshe.

International Journal for the Scholarship of Teaching and Learning. n.d. "Policies – Areas of Submission." Accessed May 18, 2020. https://digitalcommons.georgiasouthern.edu/ij-sotl/policies.html#AOS.

ISSOTL. 2020. "Call for Proposals." https://issotl.com/call-for-proposals/.

James, Edward, and Farah Mendlesohn. 2005. "How to Give a Conference Paper." https://www.academia.edu/15569469/How_to_Give_a_Conference_Paper.

Johnson, Brad. 2007. *On Being a Mentor: A Guide for Higher Education Faculty*. Mahwah, NJ: Lawrence Erlbaum Associates.

Johnson, Rob, Anthony Wilkinson, and Michael Mabe. 2018. *The STM Report: An Overview of Scientific and Scholarly Journal Publishing*. 5th edition. STM: International Association of Scientific, Technical and Medical Publishers. https://www.stm-assoc.org/2018_10_04_STM_Report_2018.pdf.

Kahu, Ella R. 2013. "Framing Student Engagement in Higher Education." *Studies in Higher Education* 38 (5): 758–73. https://doi.org/10.1080/03075079.2011.598505.

Kamler, Barbara, and Pat Thomson. 2014. *Helping Doctoral Students Write: Pedagogies for Supervision*. London: Routledge.

Kara, Helen. 2019. "The Ethics of Working with Literature." *Helen Kara* (blog). September 18, 2019. https://helenkara.com/2019/09/18/the-ethics-of-working-with-literature/.

Kate, Vikram, S. Suresh Kumar, and Mohsina Subair. 2017. "Abstract and Keywords." In *Writing and Publishing a Scientific Research Paper*, edited by Subhash Chandra Parija and Vikram Kate, 27–37. Singapore: Springer Nature.

Kek, Megan, Lindy Kimmins, Jill Lawrence, Lindy Abawi, Courtney Lindgren, and Trent Stokes. 2017. "Students Enabling Students in a Student Partnership Project: A Case Study Emerging from the OLT Transforming Practice Project on Student Partnerships." *Student Success* 8 (2): 117–22. https://doi.org/10.5204/ssj.v8i2.389.

Kelley, Susan. 2016. "Diverse Faculty Shift National Discourse One Op-ed at a Time." *Cornell Chronicle*. April 11, 2016. http://news.cornell.edu/stories/2016/04/diverse-faculty-shift-national-discourse-one-op-ed-time.

Kelly, Jacalyn, Tara Sadeghieh, and Khosrow Adeli. 2014. "Peer Review in Scientific Publications: Benefits, Critiques, & a Survival Guide." *Journal of the International Federation of Clinical Chemistry and Laboratory Medicine* 25 (3): 227–43. https://www.ncbi.nlm.nih.gov/pmc/articles/PMC4975196/.

Kelly, Mills. 2019. "I set it aside for a month, then came back to it." Twitter, January 21, 2019. https://twitter.com/EdwiredMills/status/1087348397936443397.

Kember, David, Tak-Shing Ha, Bick-Har Lam, April Lee, Sandra NG, Louisa Yan, and Jessie C.K. Yum. 1997. "The Diverse Role of the Critical Friend in Supporting Educational Action Research Projects." *Educational Action Research* 5 (3): 463–81. https://doi.org/10.1080/09650799700200036.

Kenny, Natasha, Cheryl Jeffs, and Carol Berenson. 2015. "Preparing a Teaching Philosophy Statement." Calgary, AB: Taylor Institute for Teaching and Learning. https://natashakenny.files.wordpress.com/2017/05/preparing-a-teaching-philosophy-statement-handout-nov-2015.pdf.

Kern, Beth, Gwendolyn Mettetal, Marcia Dixson, and Robin K. Morgan. 2015. "The Role of SoTL in the Academy: Upon the 25th Anniversary of Boyer's *Scholarship Reconsidered*." *Journal of the Scholarship of Teaching and Learning* 15 (3): 1–14. https://scholarworks.iu.edu/journals/index.php/josotl/article/view/13623/25313.

Kimmerer, Robin Wall. 2014. *Braiding Sweetgrass: Indigenous Wisdom, Scientific Knowledge and the Teachings of Plants*. Minneapolis, MN: Milkweed Editions.

Kinash, Shelley, and Kayleen Wood. 2012. Workshop on research questions.

Kivunja, Charles. 2018. "Distinguishing between Theory, Theoretical Framework, and Conceptual Framework: A Systematic Review of Lessons from the Field." *International Journal of Higher Education* 7 (6): 44–53. https://doi.org/10.5430/ijhe.v7n6p44.

Kneale, Pauline, Debby Cotton, and Wendy Miller. 2016. *REF2014: Higher Education Pedagogic Research and Impact*. York, UK: Higher Education

Academy. https://www.advance-he.ac.uk/knowledge-hub/ref-2014-higher-education-pedagogic-research-and-impact.

Knowles, Malcolm. 1970. *The Modern Practice of Adult Education: From Pedagogy to Andragogy*. New York: Cambridge Books.

Knox, Katelyn. 2018. "The 7 Stages of Publishing Your First Academic Book, Challenges & Tips: Stage 3 Preparing and Submitting Your Proposal." *Katelyn Knox* (blog). March 6, 2018. https://katelynknox.com/writing-first-humanities-book/7-stages-publishing-first-academic-book/#stage3.

Konkiel, Stacy. 2014. "Impact Challenge Day 3: Create a Google Scholar Profile." *Our Research Blog*. November 5, 2014. http://blog.impactstory.org/impact-challenge-day-3-google-scholar/.

Kordts-Freudinger, Robert, Daniel Al-Kabbani, and Niclas Schaper. 2017. "Learning and Interaction at a Conference." *New Horizons in Adult Education and Human Resource Development* 29 (1): 29–38. https://doi.org/10.1002/nha3.20169.

Kornhaber, Rachel, Merylin Cross, Vasiliki Betihavas, and Heather Bridgman. 2016. "The Benefits and Challenges of Academic Writing Retreats: An Integrative Review." *Higher Education Research & Development* 35 (6): 1210–27. https://doi.org/10.1080/07294360.2016.1144572.

Krause, Kerri-Lee. 2019. "Scholarship and Supercomplexity: Policy Implications." In *Emerging Methods and Paradigms in Scholarship and Education Research*, edited by Lorraine Ling and Peter Ling, 263–82. Sydney: IGI Global.

Krause, Kerri-Lee. 2012. "Addressing the Wicked Problem of Quality in Higher Education: Theoretical Approaches and Implications." *Higher Education Research & Development* 31 (3): 285–97. https://doi.org/10.1080/07294360.2011.634381.

Kreber, Carolin. 2013. *Authenticity in and through Teaching in Higher Education: The Transformative Potential of the Scholarship of Teaching*. London: Routledge.

Kreber, Carolin. 2009. *The University and Its Disciplines: Teaching and Learning Within and Beyond Disciplinary Boundaries*. London: Routledge.

Lamott, Anne. 1994. *Bird by Bird: Some Instructions on Writing and Life.* New York: Anchor Books.

Larivière, Vincent, Yves Gingras, and Éric Archambault. 2009. "The Decline in the Concentration of Citations, 1900–2007." *Journal of the American Society for Information Science and Technology* 60 (4): 858–62. https://doi.org/10.1002/asi.210.

Larsson, Maria, Katarina Mårtensson, Linda Price, and Torgny Roxå, 2017. "Constructive Friction? Exploring Patterns between Educational Research and the Scholarship of Teaching and Learning." The 2nd EuroSoTL Conference, June 8-9, 2017, Lund, Sweden. https://www.researchgate.net/publication/316860423.

Lave, Jean, and Etienne Wenger. 1991. *Situated Learning: Legitimate Peripheral Participation.* Cambridge University Press.

Lea, John, ed. 2015. *Enhancing Learning and Teaching in Higher Education: Engaging with the Dimensions of Practice.* Maidenhead, UK: Open University Press.

Lea, John, and Nigel Purcell. 2015. "Introduction: The Scholarship of Teaching and Learning, the Higher Education Academy, and the UK Professional Standards Framework." In *Enhancing Learning and Teaching in Higher Education: Engaging with the Dimensions of Practice*, edited by John Lea, 1–17. Maidenhead, UK: Open University Press.

Lea, Mary, and Brian Street. 1998. "Student Writing in Higher Education: An Academic Literacies Approach." *Studies in Higher Education* 23 (2): 157–72. https://doi.org/10.1080/03075079812331 380364.

Leigh, Andrew. 2008. "A Few Tips for Opinion Piece Writers." http://andrewleigh.org/pdf/oped_tips.pdf.

Liatsis, Emily, Ethan Pohl, and Jessica Riddell. 2018. "Building Souls and CVs with a Student-Run Podcasting Course." *International Journal for Students as Partners* 2 (2): 115–24. https://doi.org/10.15173/ijsap.v2i2.3564.

Little, Brenda, William Locke, Jan Parker, and John Richardson. 2007. *Excellence in Teaching and Learning: A Review of the Literature for the Higher Education Academy.* York, UK: Higher Education Academy.

https://www.advance-he.ac.uk/knowledge-hub/excellence-teaching-and-learning-review-literature-higher-education-academy.

Little, Deandra, David Green, and Colette Hoption. 2018. "A Lasting Impression: The Influence of Prior Disciplines on Educational Developers' Research." *International Journal for Academic Development* 23 (4): 324–38. https://doi.org/10.1080/13601 44X.2018.1458617.

Litzinger, Thomas, John Wise, Sangha Lee, and Stephani Bjorklund. 2003. "Assessing Readiness for Self-directed Learning." In *Proceedings of the 2004 American Society for Engineering Education Annual Conference & Exposition.* https://www.researchgate.net/profile/Thomas_Litzinger/publication/228870484_Assessing_Readiness_for_Self-directed_Learning.

Locke, William. 2014. *Shifting Academic Careers: Implications for Enhancing Professionalism in Teaching and Supporting Learning.* York, UK: Higher Education Academy. https://www.advance-he.ac.uk/knowledge-hub/shifting-academic-careers-implications-enhancing-professionalism-teaching-and.

Looker, Peter. 2018. "Contextualising Contexts—Scholarship of Teaching and Learning and Cultural Difference." *SoTL in the South* 2 (1): 112–28. https://doi.org/10.36615/sotls.v2i1.32.

Louw, Ina, and Ortrun Zuber-Skerritt. 2011. "The Learning Conference: Knowledge Creation through Participation and Publication." *The Learning Organization* 18 (4): 288–300. https://doi.org/10.1108/09696471111132504.

Lowe, Tom (@TomLowe_). 2019. "I feel that there is a reviewer divide from my experience." Twitter, January 23, 2019. https://twitter.com/TomLowe_/status/1088330365104779264.

Lubicz-Nawrocka, Tanya, and Hermina Simoni. 2018. "Co-researching Co-creation of the Curriculum: Reflections on Arts-based Methods in Education and Connections to Health Care Co-production." *International Journal for Students as Partners* 2 (2): 157–65. https://doi.org/10.15173/ijsap.v2i2.3427.

Luey, Beth. 2011. *Handbook for Academic Authors*. Cambridge University Press.

MacBeath, John, and Stewart S. Jardine. 1998. "'I Didn't Know He Was Ill': The Role and Value of the Critical Friend." *Improving Schools* 11 (1) 41–47. https://doi.org/10.1177/136548029803010118.

Macfarlane, Bruce. 2011. "Prizes, Pedagogic Research and Teaching Professors: Lowering the Status of Teaching and Learning through Bifurcation." *Teaching in Higher Education* 16 (1): 127–30. https://doi.org/10.1080/13562517.2011.530756.

Macfarlane, Kirsty, Jarah Dennison, Pam Delly, and Damir Mitric. 2018. "Sailing Through a Storm: The Importance of Dialogue in Student Partnerships." *International Journal for Students as Partners* 2 (2): 144–50. https://doi.org/10.15173/ijsap.v2i2.3457.

Mackinlay, Elizabeth. 2016. *Teaching and Learning Like a Feminist: Storying Our Experiences in Higher Education*. Boston: Sense Publishers.

MacPherson Institute. 2019. *Preparing a Teaching Portfolio*. Hamilton: McMaster University. https://mi.mcmaster.ca/app/uploads/2019/11/Preparing-a-Teaching-Portfolio-Guidebook.pdf.

Manarin, Karen. 2017. "Reading the Stories of Teaching and Learning—ISSOTL 2016 Opening Keynote." *Teaching & Learning Inquiry* 5 (1): 1–8. https://doi.org/10.20343/teachlearninqu.5.1.13.

Manarin, Karen. 2016. "Interpreting Undergraduate Research Posters in the Literature Classroom." *Teaching & Learning Inquiry* 4 (1), 1–15. https://doi.org/10.20343/teachlearninqu.4.1.8.

Manarin, Karen, and Earle Abrahamson. 2016. "Troublesome Knowledge of SoTL." *International Journal for the Scholarship of Teaching and Learning* 10 (2): Article 2. https://doi.org/10.20429/ijsotl.2016.100202.

Manathunga, Catherine. 2018. "Decolonising the Curriculum: Southern Interrogations of Time, Place and Knowledge." *Scholarship of Teaching and Learning in the South* 2 (1): 95–111. https://doi.org/10.36615/sotls.v2i1.23.

Manjoo, Farhad. 2010. "The Joys of Listservs." *Slate*. August 5, 2010. https://slate.com/technology/2010/08/

the-listserv-one-of-the-internet-s-earliest-innovations-is-still-one-of-its-best.html.

Marquis, Elizabeth, Varun Puri, Stephanie Wan, Arshad Ahmad, Lori Goff, Kris Knorr, Ianitza Vassileva, and Jason Woo. 2016. "Navigating the Threshold of Student–Staff Partnerships: A Case Study from an Ontario Teaching and Learning Institute." *International Journal for Academic Development* 21 (1): 4–15. https://doi.org/10.1080/1360144X.2015.1113538.

Masters, Ken, Trevor Gibbs, and John Sandars. 2015. "How to Make an Effective e-Poster." *MedEdPublish* 1 (1). http://dx.doi.org/10.15694/mep.2015.004.0001.

Matthews, Kelly E. 2019a. "Rethinking the Problem of Faculty Resistance to Engaging with Students as Partners in Learning and Teaching in Higher Education." *International Journal for the Scholarship of Teaching and Learning* 13 (2): 2. https://doi.org/10.20429/ijsotl.2019.130202.

Matthews, Kelly E. 2019b. "What I Learned about Teaching from the President of the Academic Board." The University of Queensland Institute for Teaching and Learning Innovation (blog). February 4, 2019. https://itali.uq.edu.au/blog/2019/04/blog-post-%E2%80%93-what-i-learned-about-teaching-president-academic-board.

Matthews, Kelly E. 2019c. "How Do You Keep Up with Emails?" The University of Queensland Institute for Teaching and Learning Innovation (blog). August 2, 2019. https://itali.uq.edu.au/blog/2019/07/blog-post-%E2%80%93-how-do-you-keep-emails?.

Matthews, Kelly E. 2019d. "Prioritising Your Time: The Power of Saying No." The University of Queensland Institute for Teaching and Learning Innovation (blog). September 2, 2019. https://itali.uq.edu.au/blog/2019/08/blog-post-%E2%80%93-prioritising-your-work-time-power-saying-no.

Matthews, Kelly E. 2018a. "Simple Publication Pro Forma: A Heuristic Framework to Shape an Empirical Publication." Brisbane: The University of Queensland. May 31, 2018. https://espace.library.uq.edu.au/view/UQ:68aebe0.

Matthews, Kelly E. 2018b. "Publication Pro Forma: A Heuristic Framework to Support Scholarly Research into Teaching and Learning." Brisbane: The University of Queensland. May 31, 2018. https://espace.library.uq.edu.au/view/UQ:2f9b305.

Matthews, Kelly E. 2018c. "Stop Treating Students Like Customers and Start Working with Them as Partners in Learning." *The Conversation.* April 12, 2018. https://theconversation.com/stop-treating-students-like-customers-and-start-working-with-them-as-partners-in-learning-93276.

Matthews, Kelly E. 2017. "Students and Staff as Partners in Australian Higher Education: Introducing Our Stories of Partnership." *Teaching and Learning Together in Higher Education* 21. https://repository.brynmawr.edu/tlthe/vol1/iss21/1.

Matthews, Kelly E. 2016. "Students as Partners as the Future of Student Engagement." *Student Engagement in Higher Education Journal* 1 (1). https://sehej.raise-network.com/raise/article/view/380.

Matthews, Kelly E. 2013. "Learning of Doing? Science Degrees Need Reform and Students Can Help." November 20, 2013. *The Conversation.* https://theconversation.com/learning-or-doing-science-degrees-need-reform-and-students-can-help-20074.

Matthews, Kelly E., Carmen Garratt, and Doune Macdonald. 2018. "The Higher Education Landscape: Trends and Implications." Brisbane: The University of Queensland. https://itali.uq.edu.au/files/1240/Discussion-paper-Higher-Education-Landscape_%20Trends-and-Implications.pdf.

Matthews, Kelly E., and Yvonne Hodgson. 2012. "The Science Students Skills Inventory: Capturing Graduate Perceptions of Their Learning Outcomes." *International Journal of Innovation in Science and Mathematics Education (formerly CAL-laborate International)* 20 (1). https://openjournals.library.sydney.edu.au/index.php/CAL/article/view/6648.

Matthews, Kelly E., and Lucy D. Mercer-Mapstone. 2018. "Toward Curriculum Convergence for Graduate Learning Outcomes: Academic Intentions and Student Experiences." *Studies in Higher Education.* https://doi.org/10.1080/03075079.2016.1190704.

Matthews, Kelly E., Lucy Mercer-Mapstone, Sam Lucie Dvorakova, Anita Acai, Alison Cook-Sather, Peter Felten, Mick Healey, Ruth L. Healey, and Elizabeth Marquis. 2018. "Enhancing Outcomes and Reducing Inhibitors to the Engagement of Students and Staff in Learning and Teaching Partnerships: Implications for Academic Development." *International Journal for Academic Development* 24 (3): 246–59. https://doi.org/10.1080/1360144X.2018.1545233.

Matthews, Kelly E., Karen Moni, and Roger W. Moni. 2007. "Strategies for Enhancing Equity Practices in the Teaching, Learning and Assessment Priorities of Large First-Year Classes." Equal Opportunity Practitioners in Higher Education Australasia, Melbourne University, November 19-22, 2007. Conference proceedings, 127–37.

Maurer, Trent. 2017. "Guidelines for Authorship Credit, Order, and Co-inquirer Learning in Collaborative Faculty-Student SoTL Projects." *Teaching & Learning Inquiry* 5 (1): 1–17. http://dx.doi.org/10.20343/teachlearninqu.5.1.9.

Maxwell, Joseph. 2006. "Literature Reviews of, and for, Educational Research: A Commentary on Boote and Beile's 'Scholars Before Researchers'." *Educational Researcher* 35 (9): 28–31. https://doi.org/10.3102/0013189X035009028.

May, Helen. 2013. *Writing Up Your Case Study*. York, UK: Higher Education Academy. https://www.advance-he.ac.uk/knowledge-hub/writing-your-case-study.

McDrury, Janice, and Maxine Alterio. 2003. *Learning through Storytelling in Higher Education: Using Reflection and Experience to Improve Learning*. New York: Routledge.

McEwan, Hunter, and Kieran Egan. 1995. *Narrative in Teaching, Learning, and Research*. New York: Teachers College, Columbia University.

McKiernan, Erin, Juan Pablo Alperin, and Alice Fleerackers. 2019. "The 'Impact' of the Journal Impact Factor in the Review, Tenure and Promotion Process." *LSE Impact Blog*. April 26, 2019 https://blogs.lse.ac.uk/impactofsocialsciences/2019/04/26/

the-impact-of-the-journal-impact-factor-in-the-review-tenure-and-promotion-process/.

McKinney, Kathleen. 2012a. *The Scholarship of Teaching and Learning in and Across the Disciplines*. Bloomington, IN: Indiana University Press.

McKinney, Kathleen. 2012b. "Increasing the Impact of SoTL: Two Sometimes Neglected Opportunities." *International Journal for the Scholarship of Teaching and Learning* 6 (1). https://doi.org/10.20429/ijsotl.2012.060103.

McKinney, Kathleen. 2007. *Enhancing Learning through the Scholarship of Teaching and Learning: The Challenges and Joys of Juggling*. Boston: Anker Publishing.

McNay, Ian. 2010. "Start Well: Get the Abstract Right." *Presentation at SRHE Annual Conference*, Newport, UK.

Meishar-Tal, Hagit, and Efrat Pieterse. 2017. "Why Do Academics Use Academic Social Networking Sites?" *The International Review of Research in Open and Distributed Learning* 18 (1). https://doi.org/10.19173/irrodl.v18i1.2643.

Mendlesohn, Farah, and Edward James. 2015. "Some Short Additional Notes on How to Give a Conference Paper." https://www.academia.edu/16120577/2015_notes_and_additions_to_How_to_Give_a_Conference_Paper.

Mercer-Mapstone, Lucy, and Sophia Abbot, eds. 2020. *The Power of Partnership: Students, Staff, and Faculty Revolutionizing Higher Education*. Elon, NC: Elon University, Center for Engaged Learning Open Access Book Series. https://doi.org/10.36284/celelon.oa2.

Mercer-Mapstone, Lucy, Sam Lucie Dvorakova, Kelly E. Matthews, Sophia Abbot, Breagh Cheng, Peter Felten, Kris Knorr, Elizabeth Marquis, Rafaella Shammas, and Kelly Swaim. 2017a. "A Systematic Literature Review of Students as Partners in Higher Education." *International Journal for Students as Partners* 1 (1). https://doi.org/10.15173/ijsap.v1i1.3119.

Mercer-Mapstone, Lucy, Sam Lucie Dvorakova, Lauren Groenendijk, and Kelly E. Matthews. 2017b. "Idealism, Conflict, Leadership, and Labels: Reflections on Co-Facilitation as Partnership Practice."

Teaching and Learning Together in Higher Education 21. http://repository.brynmawr.edu/tlthe/vol1/iss21/8.

Mewburn, Inger, and Pat Thomson. 2013. "Why do Academics Blog? An Analysis of Audiences, Purposes and Challenges." *Studies in Higher Education* 38 (8): 1105–19. https://doi.org/10.1080/030 75079.2013.835624.

Meyer, Jan H.F., and Ray Land. 2005. "Threshold Concepts and Troublesome Knowledge (2): Epistemological Considerations and a Conceptual Framework for Teaching and Learning." *Higher Education* 49 (3): 373–88. https://doi.org/10.1007/s10734-004-6779-5.

Miller-Young, Janet, and Michelle Yeo. 2015. "Conceptualizing and Communicating SoTL: A Framework for the Field." *Teaching & Learning Inquiry* 3 (2): 37–53. https://doi.org/10.20343/teachlearninqu.3.2.37.

Miller-Young, Janice E., Michelle Yeo, and Karen Manarin. 2018. "Challenges to Disciplinary Knowing and Identity: Experiences of Scholars in a SoTL Development Program." *International Journal for the Scholarship of Teaching and Learning* 12 (1): Article 3. https://doi.org/10.20429/ijsotl.2018.120103.

Mintz, Evan. 2019. "Take Your Ideas Mainstream: An Opinion Pages Editor Offers Tips on Writing for a Broader Readership." *Association of American Colleges & Universities Liberal Education* 105 (1). https://www.aacu.org/liberaleducation/2019/winter/mintz.

Mistry, Virendra. 2018. "Waving Not Drowning: Reflections from an In-house Journal." *Educational Developments* 19 (4): 22–25. http://researchonline.ljmu.ac.uk/id/eprint/10333/.

Mistry, Virendra. 2017. "Publishing or Perishing? The Scale and Scope of Open Access Institutional Teaching and Learning Journals in the UK." *Innovations in Practice* 11 (2): 100–122. http://openjournals.ljmu.ac.uk/index.php/iip/article/view/179/193.

Monash University, n.d. "Reflective Writing in Education." Melbourne: Monash University. Accessed October 15, 2019. https://www.monash.edu/rlo/assignment-samples/education/education-reflective-writing.

Moon, Jennifer. 2013. *A Handbook of Reflective and Experiential Learning*. London: Routledge Falmer.

Moon, Jennifer. 2006. "Reflective Writing: Some Initial Guidance for Students." University of Exeter. http://efs.weblogs.anu.edu.au/files/2018/01/Moon-on-Reflective-Writing.pdf.

Moore, Jessie L. 2018. "Writing SoTL: Going Public for an Extended Audience." In *SoTL in Action: Illuminating Critical Moments of Practice*, edited by Nancy L. Chick, 119–26. Sterling, VA: Stylus.

Moore, Julie A., and Joya Carter-Hicks. 2014. "Let's Talk! Facilitating a Faculty Learning Community Using a Critical Friends Group Approach." *International Journal for the Scholarship of Teaching and Learning* 8 (2): Article 9. https://doi.org/10.20429/ijsotl.2014.080209.

Moreno, Ana I., Jesús Rey-Rocha, Sally Burgess, Irene López-Navarro, and Itesh Sachdev. 2012. "Spanish Researchers' Perceived Difficulty Writing Research Articles for English-Medium Journals: The Impact of Proficiency in English Versus Publication Experience." *Ibérica* 24: 157–83. http://eprints.rclis.org/29319/1/4_13_24_Moreno.pdf.

Morris, David, and David Cudworth. 2018. "Having a Critical Friend: Further Anecdotal Tales in Pursuit of the Elusive Doctorate." *BERA Blog.* August 17, 2018. https://www.bera.ac.uk/blog/having-a-critical-friend-further-anecdotal-tales-in-pursuit-of-the-elusive-doctorate.

Morrison, Mike. 2019. "How to Create a Better Research Poster in Less Time (Including Templates)." https://www.youtube.com/watch?v=1RwJbhkCA58.

Muller, Nadine. 2012. "Editing Essay Collections & Special Journal Issues." *Dr. Nadine Muller* (blog). November 30, 2012. http://nadinemuller.org/guides-to-academia/editing-publications/.

Murray, Rowena. 2009. *Writing for Academic Journals*. Maidenhead, UK: Open University Press.

Murray, Rowena, and Sarah Moore. 2006. *The Handbook of Academic Writing: A Fresh Approach*. Maidenhead, UK: Open University Press/McGraw Hill.

Naidoo, Rajani. 2018. "World-Class Systems Rather than World-Class Universities." *University World News*. April 20, 2018. https://www.universityworldnews.com/post.php?story=20180417162622337.

Neumann, Ruth. 2001. "Disciplinary Differences and University Teaching." *Studies in Higher Education* 26 (2): 135–46. https://doi.org/10.1080/03075070120052071.

Neumann, Ruth, Sharon Parry, and Tony Becher. 2002. "Teaching and Learning in Their Disciplinary Contexts: A Conceptual Analysis." *Studies in Higher Education* 27 (4): 405–17. https://doi.org/10.1080/0307507022000011525.

Nevin, Ann, Jacqueline Thousand, and Richard Villa. 2011. "Working with Coauthors." In *The Handbook of Scholarly Writing and Publishing*, edited by Tonette S. Rocco and Timothy Gary Hatcher, 274–92. San Francisco: Jossey-Bass.

Newman, Isadore, and Carole Newman. 2011. "Increasing the Likelihood of Publishing Quantitative Manuscripts." In *The Handbook of Scholarly Writing and Publishing*, edited by Tonette S. Rocco and Timothy Gary Hatcher, 179–90. San Francisco: Jossey-Bass.

Newman, Isadore, David Newman, and Carole Newman. 2011. "Writing Research Articles Using Mixed Methods." In *The Handbook of Scholarly Writing and Publishing*, edited by Tonette S. Rocco and Timothy Gary Hatcher, 191–208. San Francisco: Jossey-Bass.

Newport, Cal. 2016. *Deep Work: Rules for Focused Success in a Distracted World*. London: Piatkus.

Nicolazzo, Z. 2017. "Imagining a Trans★ Epistemology: What Liberation Thinks Like in Postsecondary Education." *Urban Education*. https://doi.org/10.1177/0042085917697203.

Noble, Keith Allan. 1989. "Publish or Perish: What 23 Journal Editors Have to Say." *Studies in Higher Education* 14 (1): 97–102. https://doi.org/10.1080/03075078912331377642.

Noble, Safiya Umoja. 2018. *Algorithms of Oppression: How Search Engines Reinforce Racism*. New York: New York University Press.

Norton, Lin. 2009. *Action Research in Teaching and Learning: A Practical Guide to Conducting Pedagogical Research in Universities*. London: Routledge.

Nottingham, Anitra. 2014. "Making Effective Slides." Presentation at ANU, July 3, 2014. https://www.slideshare.net/AnitraNottingham/presentation-in-the-room.

Orsini-Jones, Marina. 2013. "Inquiry-Led Academic and Professional Development in Year 1 with Tailor-Made Assessment Tasks." In *Engaging Students in Active, Inquiry-based and Effective Learning*, edited by Jon Guest and Elwyn Lloyd, 1–11. Coventry: Faculty of Business, Environment and Society, Coventry University.

Özek, Yvonne Hultman, Gudrun Edgren, and Katarina Jandér. 2012. "Implementing the Critical Friend Method for Peer Feedback among Teaching Librarians in an Academic Setting." *Evidence Based Library and Information Practice* 7 (4): 68–81. https://doi.org/10.18438/B81C8W.

Pace, David. n.d. *Decoding the Ivory Tower* (blog). Accessed October 15, 2019. http://decodingtheivorytower.net.

Palgrave Macmillan. n.d. "Editing an Essay Collection." Accessed October 15, 2019. https://www.palgrave.com/gp/book-authors/your-career/mid-career-scholars-hub/editing-an-essay-collection/7487710.

Pasquini, Laura. 2016. "#AcWriSummer for #AcWri Accountability Summer 2016." *techKNOWtools*. https://techknowtools.com/2016/06/08/acwrisummer-for-acwri-accountability-summer-2016/.

Patriotta, Gerardo. 2017. "Crafting Papers for Publication: Novelty and Convention in Academic Writing." *Journal of Management Studies* 54 (5): 747–59. https://doi.org/10.1111/joms.12280.

Patriotta, Gerardo. 2016. "Cities of Noise: Sensemaking, Sensemakers and Organized Worlds." *Academy of Management Review* 41: 557–70. https://doi.org/10.5465/amr.2015.0357.

Pelger, Susanne, and Maria Larsson. 2018. "Advancement Towards the Scholarship of Teaching and Learning through the Writing of Teaching Portfolios." *International Journal for Academic Development*, 23 (3): 179–91. https://doi.org/10.1080/1360144X.2018.1435417.

Pells, Rachael. 2018. "Research Intelligence: How to Handle Rejection." *Times Higher Education.* November 8, 2018. https://www.timeshighereducation.com/news/research-intelligence-how-handle-rejection.

Pennsylvania State University. 2005. *Designing Communications for a Poster Fair.* http://www.personal.psu.edu/drs18/postershow/.

Perry, David. 2015. "Three Rules of Academic Blogging." *The Chronicle in Higher Education.* November 11, 2015. https://www.chronicle.com/article/3-Rules-of-Academic-Blogging/234139.

Peseta, Tai. 2018. "Keynotes: Starting Conferences with a Bang or a Whimper?" *Conference Inference.* June 4, 2018. https://conferenceinference.wordpress.com/2018/06/04/guest-post-by-tai-peseta-keynotes-starting-conferences-with-a-bang-or-a-whimper/.

Phillips, Louise Gwenneth, and Tracey Bunda. 2018. *Research Through, With and As Storying: Research Through, With and As Storying.* Sydney: Routledge.

Pilkington, Ruth. 2017. *Use of Dialogue for Fellowship.* York, UK: Higher Education Academy. https://www.advance-he.ac.uk/knowledge-hub/use-dialogue-fellowship.

Piwowar, Heather, Jason Priem, Vincen Larivière, Juan Pablo Alperin, Lisa Matthias, Bree Norlander, Ashley Farley, Jevin West, and Stefanie Haustein. 2018. "The State of OA: A Large-Scale Analysis of the Prevalence and Impact of Open Access Articles." *PeerJ* 6: e4375. https://doi.org/10.7717/peerj.4375.

Poole, Gary. 2013. "Square One: What Is Research?" In *The Scholarship of Teaching and Learning In and Across the Disciplines*, edited by Kathleen McKinney, 135–51. Bloomington, IN: Indiana University Press.

Popovic, Celia, ed. 2018. *Learning from Academic Conferences.* Leiden, Netherlands: Brill.

Popovic, Celia, and Alice Cassidy. 2018. "Engendering Learning by Engaging Potential Participants through Conference Focus and Format." In *Learning from Academic Conferences*, edited by Celia Popovic, 93–109. Leiden, Netherlands: Brill.

Porter, Stanley. 2010. *Inking the Deal: A Guide for Successful Academic Publishing.* Waco, TX: Baylor University Press.

Potter, Jackie, and Rebecca Turner, eds. 2018. *Doing a Good Job Well—Being Recognised as an Experienced, Professional Teacher in HE.* London: SEDA.

Potter, Michael K., and Erica Kustra. 2011. "The Relationship Between Scholarly Teaching and SoTL: Models, Distinctions, and Clarifications." *International Journal for the Scholarship of Teaching and Learning* 5 (1): Article 23. https://doi.org/10.20429/ijsotl.2011.050123.

Pritchard, Jane, Gina Wisker, and Jacqueline Potter. 2018. "Engaging in the Scholarship of Teaching and Learning as Part of Continuing Professional Development." In *Doing a Good Job Well—Being Recognised as an Experienced, Professional Teacher in HE,* edited by Jackie Potter and Rebecca Turner, 17–21. London: SEDA.

Purcell, Nigel, and John Lea. 2015. "Conclusion: Raising the Profile of Learning and Teaching, Being Reflective, Scholarly, and Becoming a Fellow of the Higher Education Academy." In *Enhancing Learning and Teaching in Higher Education: Engaging with the Dimensions of Practice,* edited by John Lea, 198–213. Maidenhead, UK: Open University Press.

Purdue Online Writing Lab. n,d. "Active Versus Passive Voice." Accessed October 15, 2019. https://owl.purdue.edu/owl/general_writing/academic_writing/active_and_passive_voice/active_versus_passive_voice.html.

Quintero, Elizabeth P. 2018. "Foreword: Through Storying, May We Never Be Still." In *Research Through, With and as Storying,* edited by Louise Gwenneth Phillips and Tracey Bunda, viii–x. Sydney: Routledge.

Race, Philip. 2014. *The Lecturer's Toolkit: A Practical Guide to Assessment, Learning and Teaching.* London: Routledge.

Ravn, Ib. 2007. "The Learning Conference." *Journal of European Industrial Training* 31 (3): 212–22. https://doi.org/10.1108/03090590710739287.

Ravn, Ib, and Steen Elsborg. 2007. "Creating Learning at Conferences Through Participant Involvement." Paper presented at the

Academy of Management Annual Meeting, August 3-8, 2007, Philadelphia, US. https://docsbay.net/creating-learning-at-conferences-through-participant-involvement.

REF2021 (Research Excellence Framework). 2019. *Guidance on Submissions 2019/01*. Bristol, UK: REF. https://www.ref.ac.uk/publications/guidance-on-submissions-201901/.

Rehm, Markus. 2013. "Dubious conference invitations. Just spam, or do these meetings actually take place?" Question posted on ResearchGate. July 9, 2013. https://www.researchgate.net/post/Dubious_conference_invitations_Just_spam_or_do_these_meetings_actually_take_place.

Reio, Thomas, and Ward Davis. 2005. "Age and Gender Differences in Self-Directed Learning Readiness: A Developmental Perspective." *International Journal of Self-Directed Learning* 2 (1): 40–49. https://www.sdlglobal.com/journals.

Review of Educational Research. n.d. "Aims and Scope." Accessed on May 13, 2020. https://us.sagepub.com/en-us/nam/journal/review-educational-research#aims-and-scope.

Richlin, Laurie. 2001. "Scholarly Teaching and the Scholarship of Teaching." In *The Scholarship of Teaching, New Directions in Teaching and Learning*, edited by Carolin Kreber, 57–68. San Francisco: Jossey Bass.

Ridley, Diana R. 2012. *The Literature Review: A Step-by-Step Guide for Students*. London: SAGE.

Robbins, Susan. 2016. "Finding Your Voice as an Academic Writer (and Writing Clearly)." *Journal of Social Work Education* 52 (2): 133–35. https://doi.org/10.1080/10437797.2016.1151267.

Roberts, David. 2018. *The Ultimate Guide to Visual Lectures*. Amazon Kindle.

Robinson, Jennifer Meta. 2018. "The SoTL Conference: Learning while Professing." In *SoTL in Action: Illuminating Critical Moments of Practice*, edited by Nancy Chick, 143–50. Sterling VA: Stylus.

Robinson-Self, Phil. 2018. "'In-house' Journals and the Scholarship of Teaching and Learning—Thoughts from a Discipline that Is

Not a Discipline." *Innovations in Practice* 12 (1): 21–33. https://doi.org/10.24377/LJMU.iip.vol12iss1article209.

Rocco, Tonette S. 2011. "Reasons to Write, Writing Opportunities, and Other Considerations." In *The Handbook of Scholarly Writing and Publishing*, edited by Tonette S. Rocco and Timothy Gary Hatcher, 3–12. San Francisco: Jossey-Bass.

Rocco, Tonette S., and Timothy Gary Hatcher, eds. 2011. *The Handbook of Scholarly Writing and Publishing*. San Francisco: Jossey-Bass.

Rocco, Tonette, and Plakhotnik, Maria. 2011. "Increasing the Odds of Publishing a Qualitative Manuscript." In *The Handbook of Scholarly Writing and Publishing*, edited by Tonette S. Rocco and Timothy Gary Hatcher, 3–12. San Francisco: Jossey-Bass.

Rockquemore, Kerry Ann, and Tracey Laszloffy. 2008. *The Black Academic's Guide to Winning Tenure—Without Losing Your Soul*. Boulder, CO: Lynne Rienner Publishers.

Rodrigues, Velany. 2013. "How to Write an Effective Title and Abstract and Choose Appropriate Keywords." In *Manuscript Writing Stage*, edited by Editage Insights. https://www.editage.com/insights/how-to-write-an-effective-title-and-abstract-and-choose-appropriate-keywords.

Rose, Michael E., and Willem H. Boshoff. 2017. "The Peer-Review System for Academic Papers Is Badly in Need of Repair." *The Conversation*. February 26, 2017. https://theconversation.com/the-peer-review-system-for-academic-papers-is-badly-in-need-of-repair-72669.

Rowe, Nicholas. 2018. "'When You Get What You Want, But Not What You Need': The Motivations, Affordances and Shortcomings of Attending Academic/Scientific Conferences." *International Journal of Research in Education and Science* 4 (2): 714–29. https://www.ijres.net/index.php/ijres/article/view/368.

Rowe, Nicholas. 2017. *Academic & Scientific Poster Presentation: A Modern Comprehensive Guide*. Cham, Switzerland: Springer Nature.

Rowe, Nicholas, and Dragan Ilic. 2015. "Rethinking Poster Presentations at Large Scale Scientific Meetings–Is It Time for the

Format to Evolve?" *FEBS Journal* 282 (19): 3661–68. https://doi.org/10.1111/febs.13383.

Rowell, Chris. 2019. *Social Media in Higher Education: Case Studies, Reflections and Analysis.* Cambridge, UK: Open Book Publisher. https://www.openbookpublishers.com/product/945.

Roxå, Torgny, and Katarina Mårtensson. 2015. "Microcultures and Informal Learning: A Heuristic Guiding Analysis of Conditions for Informal Learning in Local Higher Education Workplaces." *International Journal for Academic Development* 20 (2): 193–205. https://doi.org/10.1080/1360144X.2015.1029929.

Rubin, Mark, Nida Denson, Sue Kilpatrick, Kelly E. Matthews, Tom Stehlik, and David Zyngier. 2014. "'I Am Working-Class' Subjective Self-Definition as a Missing Measure of Social Class and Socioeconomic Status in Higher Education Research." *Educational Researcher* 43 (4): 196–200. https://doi.org/10.3102/0013189X14528373.

Ruitenberg, Claudia. 2005. "Deconstructing the Experience of the Local: Toward a Radical Pedagogy of Place." In *Philosophy of Education Yearbook*, edited by Kenneth R. Howe, 212–20. Urbana, IL: Philosophy of Education Society.

Rushforth, Alex, and Sarah de Rijcke. 2016. "Accounting for Impact? How the Impact Factor Is Shaping Research and What this Means for Knowledge Production." *LSE Impact Blog.* March 7, 2016. https://blogs.lse.ac.uk/impactofsocialsciences/2016/03/07/accounting-for-impact-journal-impact-factor-research-knowledge-production/.

Sadler, D. Royce. 2006. *Up the Publication Road: A Guide to Publishing in Scholarly Journals for Academics, Researchers, and Graduate Students.* Milperra: HERDSA Guide.

Sadler, D. Royce. 1999. *Managing Your Academic Career: Strategies for Success.* Sydney: Allen & Unwin.

Salomone, Paul R. 1993. "Trade Secrets for Crafting a Conceptual Article." *Journal of Counseling & Development* 72: 73–76. https://doi.org/10.1002/j.1556-6676.1993.tb02280.x.

Salter, Anastasia. 2018. "5 Tips for Would-Be Academic Book Authors." *The Chronicle of Higher Education.* ProfHacker. April 12, 2018.

Salter, Anastasia. 2016. "Open Thread Wednesday: Solutions for Tracking Projects." *The Chronicle of Higher Education*. ProfHacker. October 19, 2016.

Scales, Peter. 2017. *An Introduction to Learning and Teaching in Higher Education: Supporting Fellowship*. Maidenhead, UK: Open University Press.

Schön, Donald A. 1987. *Educating the Reflective Practitioner*. San Francisco: Jossey-Bass.

Schönwetter, Dieter J., Laura Sokal, Marcia Friesen, and K. Lynn Taylor. 2002. "Teaching Philosophies Reconsidered: A Conceptual Model for the Development and Evaluation of Teaching Philosophy Statements." *International Journal for Academic Development* 7 (1): 83–97. http://dx.doi.org/10.1080/13601440210156501.

Schwartz, Peter, and Graham Webb. 1993. *Case Studies on Teaching in Higher Education. Teaching and Learning in Higher Education*. London: Kogan Page.

Seppala, Nina, and Charlotte Smith. 2019. "Teaching Awards in Higher Education: A Qualitative Study of Motivation and Outcomes." *Studies in Higher Education*. https://doi.org/10.1080/03075079.2019.1593349.

Shaikh, Aijaz A. 2016. "7 Steps to Publishing in a Scientific Journal." *Elsevier Connect*. April 4, 2016. https://www.elsevier.com/connect/7-steps-to-publishing-in-a-scientific-journal.

Shanahan, Jenny Olin, Elizabeth Ackley-Holbrook, Eric Hall, Kearsley Stewart, and Helen Walkington. 2015. "Ten Salient Practices of Undergraduate Research Mentors: A Review of the Literature." *Mentoring & Tutoring: Partnership in Learning* 23 (5): 359–76. https://doi.org/10.1080/13611267.2015.1126162.

Sheffield Hallam University. 2016. *Developing a Personal Publication Strategy*. Sheffield, UK: Sheffield Hallam University. https://www.shu.ac.uk/~/media/home/research/files/ethics/developing-a-personal-publication-strategy.pdf.

Shulman, Lee. 2004. "Professing the Liberal Arts." In *Teaching as Community Property: Essays on Higher Education,* edited by Pat Hutchings, 12–31. San Francisco: Jossey-Bass.

Shulman, Lee. 1993. "Teaching as Community Property." *Change: The Magazine of Higher Learning* 26 (6): 6–7. https://doi.org/10.108 0/00091383.1993.9938465.

Silva, Angélica M., and Roberto Limongi. 2019. "Writing to Learn Increases Long-Term Memory Consolidation: A Mental-Chronometry and Computational-Modeling Study of 'Epistemic Writing.'" *Journal of Writing Research 11* (1): 211–43. https://doi.org/10.17239/jowr-2019.11.01.07.

Silvia, Paul. J. 2018. *How to Write a Lot: A Practical Guide to Productive Academic Writing.* Washington, DC: APA Life Tools.

Simmons, Nicola, Earle Abrahamson, Jessica M. Deshler, Barbara Kensington-Miller, Karen Manarin, Sue Morón-García, Carolyn Oliver, and Joanna Renc-Roe. 2013. "Conflicts and Configurations in a Liminal Space: SoTL Scholars' Identity Development." *Teaching & Learning Inquiry* 1 (2): 9–21. https://doi.org/10.20343/teachlearninqu.1.2.9.

Simmons, Nicola, and Ann Singh. 2019. *Critical Collaborative Communities: Academic Writing Partnerships, Groups, and Retreats.* Boston: Brill.

Sium, Aman, and Eric Ritskes. 2013. "Speaking Truth to Power: Indigenous Storytelling as an Act of Living Resistance." *Decolonization: Indigeneity, Education & Society* 2: I–X. https://jps.library.utoronto.ca/index.php/des/article/view/19626.

Skallerup Bessette, Lee. 2017. "Getting Started on Academic Twitter v2.0." *The Chronicle of Higher Education.* ProfHacker. January 24, 2017.

Skallerup Bessette, Lee. 2016. "How Twitter Changed My Life." *The Chronicle of Higher Education.* ProfHacker. October 11, 2016.

Skelton, Alan. 1997. "Conferences, Conferences, Conferences?" *Teaching in Higher Education* 2 (1): 69–72. https://doi.org/10.1080/1356251970020106.

Smailes, Gary. 2010. "The BubbleCow Guide to Academic Book Pitching: Part I." *PhD2Published.* September 1, 2010. http://www.phd2published.com/2010/09/01/the-bubblecow-guide-to-academic-book-pitching-part-1/.

Smart, Fiona, Mandy Asghar, Laurie-Ann Campbell, and Mark Huxham. 2019. "Electing to Speak: Professional Dialogue in the Context of Fellowship of the Higher Education Academy." *International Journal for Academic Development* 24 (3): 232–45. https://doi.org/10.1080/1360144X.2019.1585356.

Smart, Stuart, and Tony Heynen. 2019. "What We Learned by Trusting Students to Come Up with Ideas." The University of Queensland Institute for Teaching and Learning Innovation (blog). March 27, 2019. https://itali.uq.edu.au/blog/2019/03/blog-post-%E2%80%93-what-we-learned-trusting-students-come-ideas.

Smith, Chris. 2019. "6 Insights into Being a Productive and Happy Academic Author." *LSE Impact Blog.* March 7, 2019. https://blogs.lse.ac.uk/impactofsocialsciences/2019/03/07/6-insights-into-being-a-productive-and-happy-academic-author/.

Smith, Susan. 2015. *PhD by Published Work: A Practical Guide for Success.* London: Palgrave.

Soliman, Izabel. 2008. "Notes on Publishing in *HERD.*" *HERDSA News* 30 (2): 18–19. http://www.herdsa.org.au/sites/default/files/HERDSANews20083002.pdf.

SRHE (Society for Research into Higher Education). 2019. "International Research Conference 2019: Call for Papers." https://www.srhe.ac.uk/conference2019/downloads/arc/Call_for_papers_SRHE_ARC_2019.pdf.

Stevens, Danielle D. 2019. *Write More, Publish More, Stress Less: Five Key Principles for a Creative and Sustainable Scholarly Practice.* Sterling VA: Stylus.

Strawson, Hannah, Sue Habeshaw, Trevor Habeshaw, and Graham Gibbs. 2012. *53 Interesting Things to Do in Your Seminars and Tutorials.* Sydney: Allen & Unwin.

Sutherland, Kathryn, Isabella Lenihan-Ikin, and Charlotte Rushforth. 2019. "Valuing Students as Partners." In *Engaging Student Voices in Higher Education,* edited by Simon Lygo-Baker, Ian M. Kinchin, and Naomi E. Winstone, 37–54. Cham, Switzerland: Palgrave Macmillan. https://link.springer.com/chapter/10.1007/978-3-030-20824-0_3.

Swanwick, Tim, Kirsty Forrest, and Bridget C. O'Brien. 2018. *Understanding Medical Education: Evidence, Theory, and Practice*. London: Wiley-Blackwell.

Sword, Helen. 2017a. *Air & Light & Time & Space: How Successful Academics Write*. Boston: Harvard University Press.

Sword, Helen. 2017b. "Writing to the Heights and from the Heart." Plenary address at ISSOTL Conference (Calgary, Alberta), October 14, 2017. https://www.youtube.com/watch?v=52WT2YlxpI0.

Sword, Helen. 2016. "'Write Every Day!': A Mantra Dismantled." *International Journal for Academic Development* 21 (4): 312–22. https://doi.org/10.1080/1360144X.2016.1210153.

Sword, Helen. 2012. *Stylish Academic Writing*. Boston: Harvard University Press.

Sword, Helen. 2009. "Writing Higher Education Differently: A Manifesto on Style." *Studies in Higher Education* 34 (3): 319–36. https://doi.org/10.1080/03075070802597101.

Tabachnick, Barbara G., Linda S. Fidell, and Jodie B. Ullman. 2007. *Using Multivariate Statistics*. Boston, MA: Pearson.

Taylor, Peter G., Hitendra Pillay, and John A. Clarke. 2004. "Exploring Student Adaptation to New Learning Environments: Some Unexpected Outcomes." *International Journal of Learning Technology* 1 (1): 100–10. https://doi.org/10.1504/IJLT.2004.003684.

Taylor & Francis. n.d. "A Researcher's Guide to Search Engine Optimization." Accessed June 9, 2020. https://authorservices.taylorandfrancis.com/a-researchers-guide-to-seo/.

Taylor & Francis. n.d. "Video Abstracts." Accessed May 13, 2020. https://authorservices.taylorandfrancis.com/video-abstracts/.

Terras, Melissa. 2012. "Is Blogging and Tweeting about Research Papers Worth It? The Verdict." *Melissa Terras* (blog). April 3, 2012. https://melissaterras.org/2012/04/03/is-blogging-and-tweeting-about-research-papers-worth-it-the-verdict/.

Textbook and Academic Authors Association. 2015. "8 Reasons Why Academics Should Be on Social Media." *Blog on Textbook and Academic Writing*. February 24, 2015. https://blog.taaonline.net/2015/02/8-reasons-why-academics-should-be-on-social-media/.

Thesis Whisperer. 2018. "How to Run a Blog for 8 Years and Not Go Insane." *Thesis Whisperer* (blog). March 21, 2018. https://thesiswhisperer.com/2018/03/21/the-academic-blog-a-long-haul-flight/.

Thomson, Pat. 2019a. "Addressing 'the Gap' in the Field." *Patter* (blog). March 11, 2019. https://patthomson.net/2019/03/11/addressing-the-gap-in-the-field/.

Thomson, Pat. 2019b. "Introductions: Establishing Significance." *Patter.* April 1, 2019. https://patthomson.net/2019/04/01/write-a-compelling-introduction/.

Thomson, Pat 2019c. "2019 Was ..." *Patter* (blog). December 30, 2019. https://patthomson.net/2019/12/30/2019-was/.

Thomson, Pat. 2019d. "Choosing Images for Slideshows." *Patter* (blog). February 18, 2019. https://patthomson.net/2019/02/18/choosing-images-for-slideshows/.

Thomson, Pat. 2019e. "Make a Poster then Write Your Paper." *Patter* (blog). May 6, 2019. https://patthomson.net/2019/05/06/using-a-poster-to-write-a-paper/.

Thomson, Pat. 2019f. "Writing Targets—Word Count, Time Spent, or Chunks?" *Patter* (blog). June 3, 2019. https://patthomson.net/2019/06/03/writing-targets-word-counts-time-spent-or-chunks.

Thomson, Pat. 2019g "Tiny Texts—Small Is Powerful." *Patter* (blog). February 11, 2019. https://patthomson.net/2019/02/11/tiny-texts-if-not-beautiful%e2%80%8b-small-is-pretty-darn%e2%80%8b-useful/.

Thomson, Pat. 2019h. "Revise and Resubmit." *Patter* (blog). March 25, 2019. https://patthomson.net/2019/03/25/revise-and-resubmit/.

Thomson, Pat. 2017a. "Internationalising a Journal Article." *Patter* (blog). October 9, 2017. https://patthomson.net/2017/10/09/internationalising-a-journal-article/.

Thomson, Pat. 2017b. "Choosing a Conference." *Patter* (blog). September 4, 2017. https://patthomson.net/2017/09/04/choosing-a-conference/.

Thomson, Pat. 2016a. "Paper, Thesis and Book Titles— Think 'Key Words' and 'the Point'." *Patter* (blog).

February 18, 2016. https://patthomson.net/2016/02/18/paper-thesis-and-book-titles-think-key-words-and-the-point/.

Thomson, Pat. 2016b. "Text Work/Identity Work Online: Writing for Social Media." In *Publishing and the Academic World: Passion, Purpose and Possible Futures*, edited by Ciaran Sugrue and Sefika Mertkan, 100–15. London: Routledge.

Thomson, Pat. 2016c. "Seven Reasons Why Blogging Can Make You a Better Academic Writer." *Times Higher Education*. January 2, 2016. https://www.timeshighereducation.com/blog/seven-reasons-why-blogging-can-make-you-better-academic-writer.

Thomson, Pat. 2015. "Text Work/Identity Work." *Patter* (blog). September 9, 2015. https://patthomson.net/2015/09/09/text-workidentity-work/.

Thomson, Pat. 2014. "My Academic Writing Pipeline." *Patter* (blog). May 19, 2014. https://patthomson.net/2014/05/19/my-academic-writing-pipeline/.

Thomson, Pat. 2013a. "Why Write Book Chapters." *Patter* (blog). June 17, 2013. https://patthomson.net/2013/06/17/on-writing-book-chapters/.

Thomson, Pat. 2013b. "Three Reasons Why Editing a Book Is a Good Idea." *Patter* (blog). December 2, 2013. https://patthomson.net/2013/12/02/three-reasons-why-editing-a-book-is-a-good-idea/.

Thomson, Pat. 2013c. "Two Big Hassles in Editing a Book, and What You Can Do about Them." *Patter* (blog). December 9, 2013. https://patthomson.net/2013/12/09/two-big-hassles-in-editing-a-book-and-what-you-can-do-about-them/.

Thomson, Pat. 2012. "Conclusions Mis-en-place. Christmas Present Six." *Patter* (blog). December 19, 2012. https://patthomson.net/2012/12/19/conclusion-mise-en-place-christmas-present-six/.

Thomson, Pat. n.d. "Giving a Conference Paper?" Curated list of blog posts created on Wakelet. Accessed May 13, 2020. https://wakelet.com/wake/0799a8fd-84c0-44d5-94ec-f05e2de43332.

Thomson, Pat, and Barbara Kamler. 2016. *Detox Your Writing: Strategies for Doctoral Researchers*. London: Routledge.

Thomson, Pat, and Barbara Kamler. 2013. *Writing for Peer Reviewed Journals.* London: Routledge.

Tight, Malcolm. 2018a. "Tracking the Scholarship of Teaching and Learning." *Policy Reviews in Higher Education* 2 (1): 61–78. https://doi.org/10.1080/23322969.2017.1390690.

Tight, Malcolm. 2018b. "Higher Education Journals: Their Characteristics and Contribution." *Higher Education Research & Development* 37 (3): 607–19. https://doi.org/10.1080/07294360.2017.1389858.

Tight, Malcolm 2017. *Understanding Case Study Research: Small Scale Research with Meaning.* London: SAGE.

Tight, Malcolm. 2008. "Higher Education Research as Tribe, Territory and/or Community: A Co-citation Analysis." *Higher Education* 55 (5): 593–605. https://doi.org/10.1007/s10734-007-9077-1.

Toor, Rachel. 2013. "How to Write a Good Book Proposal, the Sequel." *The Chronicle of Higher Education.* October 8, 2013. https://www.chronicle.com/article/How-to-Write-a-Good-Book/142183.

Torosyan, Roben, and Alison Cook Sather. 2018. "Balancing Direction and Response: Four Dimensions of Transformative Facilitation in Educational Development." *To Improve the Academy* 37 (2): 188–206. https://doi.org/10.1002/tia2.20082.

Torraco, Richard J. 2005. "Writing Integrative Literature Reviews: Guidelines and Examples." *Human Resource Development Review* 4 (3): 356–67. https://doi.org/10.1177/1534484305278283.

Townsend, Michael A. 1983. "Titular Colonicity and Scholarship: New Zealand Research and Scholarly Impact." *New Zealand Journal of Psychology* 12 (1): 41–3. https://www.psychology.org.nz/journal-archive/NZJP-Vol121-1983-7-Townsend.pdf.

Trede, Franziska, Rob Macklin, and Donna Bridges. 2012. "Professional Identity Development: A Review of the Higher Education Literature." *Studies in Higher Education* 37 (3): 365–84. https://doi.org/10.1080/03075079.2010.521237.

Trigwell, Keith, and Susan Shale. 2004. "Student Learning and the Scholarship of University Teaching." *Studies in Higher Education* 29 (4): 523–36. https://doi.org/10.1080/0307507042000236407.

Tscharntke, Teja, Michael E. Hochberg, Tatyana A. Rand, Vincent H. Resh, and Jochen Krauss. 2007. "Author Sequence and Credit for Contributions in Multiauthored Publications." *PLoS Biology* 5 (1): e18. https://doi.org/10.1371/journal.pbio.0050018.

Turner, Rebecca, Tony Brown, and Andrew Edwards-Jones. 2014. "'Writing My First Academic Article Feels Like Dancing Around Naked': Research Development for Higher Education Lecturers Working in Further Education Colleges." *International Journal for Academic Development* 19 (2): 87–98. https://doi.org/10.1080/1360144X.2013.792729.

University of Birmingham. 2015. "A Short Guide to Reflective Writing." Birmingham: Academic Skills Centre, Library Services, University of Birmingham. https://intranet.birmingham.ac.uk/as/libraryservices/library/skills/asc/documents/public/Short-Guide-Reflective-Writing.pdf.

University of Bristol. n.d. "Networking: An Online Resource for Researchers." Accessed April 28, 2020. http://www.bristol.ac.uk/staffdevelopment/academic/researchstaffhub/opportunities/networking/.

University of Hong Kong. 2019. "TP21: The Teaching Portfolio as Evidence of Reflective Teaching in International Higher Education." Center for the Enhancement of Teaching and Learning. https://www.cetl.hku.hk/TP21/.

University of Manchester. 2018. "Faculty of Humanities: Personal Research Expectations Plan." http://documents.manchester.ac.uk/DocuInfo.aspx?DocID=32883.

University of Queensland. 2019. UQ Policy and Procedures Library. "5.70.17 Criteria for Academic Performance." https://ppl.app.uq.edu.au/content/5.70.17-criteria-academic-performance.

University of Queensland Institute for Teaching and Learning Innovation. "News." https://itali.uq.edu.au/news.

Van Lankveld, Thea, Judith Schoonenboom, Monique Volman, Gerda Croiset, and Jos Beishuizen. 2017. "Developing a Teacher Identity in the University Context: A Systematic Review of the Literature."

Higher Education Research & Development 36 (2): 325–42. https://doi.org/10.1080/07294360.2016.1208154.

Vande Pol, Natalie. 2019. "The Evolution of Academic Posters: From Poster 1.0 to Better Poster 2.0 to Hybrid Poster 1.5." *BEACON* (blog). September 1, 2019. https://www3.beacon-center.org/blog/2019/09/01/the-evolution-of-academic-posters-from-poster-1-0-to-better-poster-2-0-to-hybrid-poster-1-5/.

Vardi, Iris, and Robyn Quin. 2011. "Promotion and the Scholarship of Teaching and Learning." *Higher Education Research & Development* 30 (1): 39–49. https://doi.org/10.1080/07294360.2011.536971.

Varsavsky, Cristina, Kelly E. Matthews, and Yvonne Hodgson. 2014. "Perceptions of Science Graduating Students on their Learning Gains." *International Journal of Science Education* 36 (6): 929–51. https://doi.org/10.1080/09500693.2013.830795.

Vuong, Ocean. 2019. *On Earth We're Briefly Gorgeous*. London: Jonathan Cape.

Walker, Sharon. 2015. "Literature Reviews: Generative and Transformative Textual Conversations." *Forum: Qualitative Social Research* 16 (3): Article 5. http://dx.doi.org/10.17169/fqs-16.3.2291.

Watts, Richard E. 2011. "Developing a Conceptual Article for Publication in Counseling Journals." *Journal of Counseling & Development* 89: 308–12. https://doi.org/10.1002/j.1556-6678.2011.tb00094.x.

Weaver, Debbi, Diane Robbie, and Alex Radloff. 2014. "Demystifying the Publication Process—A Structured Writing Program to Facilitate Dissemination of Teaching and Learning Scholarship." *International Journal for Academic Development* 19 (3): 212–25. https://doi.org/10.1080/1360144X.2013.805692.

Weller, Ann. 2001. *Editorial Peer Review: Its Strengths and Weaknesses*. Medford, NJ: Information Today Inc.

Weller, Paul J. 2007. "Writing and Editing Books." In *The Complete Guide to Medical Writing*, edited by Mark C. Stuart, 389–405. London: Pharmaceutical Press. https://www.pharmpress.com/files/docs/cgmw_sample_chapter.pdf.

Weller, Saranne. 2011. "New Lecturers' Accounts of Reading Higher Education Research." *Studies in Continuing Education* 33 (1): 93–106. https://doi.org/10.1080/0158037X.2010.516744.

Weston, Cynthia, and Julie Timmermans. 2007. "Developing a Teaching Portfolio: How to Document Your Pedagogical Profile." *University Affairs.* June 4, 2007. https://www. universityaffairs.ca/career-advice/career-advice-article/ developing-a-teaching-profile/.

White, Caroline. 2004. *The COPE Report 2003.* London: BMJ Books. https://publicationethics.org/annualreport/2003.

Wijaya Mulya, Teguh. 2018. "Contesting the Neoliberalisation of Higher Education through Student–Faculty Partnership." *International Journal for Academic Development* 24 (1): 86–90. https:// doi.org/10.1080/1360144X.2018.1520110.

Wijaya Mulya, Teguh, and Anindito Aditomo. 2020. "Democratic Partnership with Academically Disadvantaged Students in an Undergraduate Academic Writing Course at University of Surabaya, Indonesia." In *Students as Partners and Change Agents in Learning and Teaching in Higher Education*, edited by Mick Healey, 61. Howden, UK: Healey HE Consultants. https://www.mickhealey.co.uk/ download/students-as-change-agents-handout-2.

Wildhagen, Tina, and Dionna Jenkins. 2020. "The Will to Collaborate across Difference: Mining Difference as a Rich Resource in a Student-Faculty Pedagogical Partnership." In *Building Courage, Confidence, and Capacity in Learning and Teaching through Student-Faculty Partnership: Stories from across Contexts and Arenas of Practice*, edited by Alison Cook-Sather and Chanelle Wilson. Lanham, MD: Lexington Books.

Willison, John. 2009. "A Handbook for Research Skill Development and Assessment in the Curriculum." The University of Adelaide. https://www.adelaide.edu.au/melt/ university-learning#research-skill-development-handbook.

Wilmot, Kirstin. 2018. "Designing Writing Groups to Support Postgraduate Students' Academic Writing: A Case Study from a South African University." *Innovations in Education and Teaching*

International 55 (3): 257–65. https://doi.org/10.1080/14703297 .2016.1238775.

Wilson, Mary. 2018. "Learning in Public: Providing a Keynote." In *Learning from Academic Conferences,* edited by Celia Popovic, 79–90. Leiden, Netherlands: Brill.

Winter, Jennie, Rebecca Turner, Lucy Spowart, and Pauline Kneale. 2018. "Planning Future CPD. What Comes Next?" In *Doing a Good Job Well—Being Recognised as an Experienced, Professional Teacher in HE,* edited by Jackie Potter and Rebecca Turner, 33–46. London: SEDA.

Witman, Paul D., and Laurie Richlin. 2007. "The Status of the Scholarship of Teaching and Learning in the Discipline." *International Journal for the Scholarship of Teaching and Learning* 1 (1): 14. https://doi.org/10.20429/ijsotl.2007.010114.

Wood, Danielle. 2017. "Yes, You're Entitled to Your Opinion—but It Helps if You're a Man." *The Conversation.* November 17, 2016. http://theconversation.com/yes-youre-entitled-to-your-opinion-but-it-helps-if-youre-a-man-68916.

Writing Across the Curriculum Clearinghouse. n.d. "What Is Writing to Learn?" Accessed October 15, 2019. https://wac.colostate.edu/resources/wac/intro/wtl/.

Wymer, Kathryn, Carolyn J. Fulford, Nia Baskerville, and Marisha Washington. 2012. "Necessity and the Unexpected: SoTL Student-Faculty Collaboration in Writing Program Research." *International Journal for the Scholarship of Teaching and Learning* 6 (1): Article 20. https://doi.org/10.20429/ijsotl.2012.060120.

Wynkoop, Paul. 2018. "My Transformation as a Partner and a Learner." *Teaching and Learning Together in Higher Education* 23. https://repository.brynmawr.edu/tlthe/vol1/iss23/4.

Yahlnaaw / Aaron Grant. 2019. "T'aats'iigang – Stuffing a Jar Full." *International Journal for Students as Partners* 3 (2): 6–10. https://doi.org/10.15173/ijsap.v3i2.4081.

Yancey, Kathleen Blake. 1998. "Reflection in the Writing Classroom." Logan, UT: Utah State University Press. https://digitalcommons.usu.edu/usupress_pubs/120.

Yin, Robert. 2018. *Case Study Research and Applications: Design and Methods.* Thousand Oaks, NY: SAGE.

Yosso, Tara J. 2005. "Whose Culture Has Capital? A Critical Race Theory Discussion of Community Cultural Wealth." *Race Ethnicity and Education* 8 (1): 69–91. https://doi.org/10.1080/13613320 52000341006.

Yosso, Tara J., Laurence Parker, Daniel G. Solórzano, and Marvin Lynn. 2004. "From Jim Crow to Affirmative Action and Back Again: A Critical Race Discussion of Racialized Rationales and Access to Higher Education." *Review of Research in Education* 28: 1–25. http://www.jstor.org/stable/3568134.

Zinnser, William. 1998. *On Writing Well: The Class Guide to Writing Nonfiction.* New York: HarperPerennial.

Zinsser, William. 1988. *Writing to Learn: How to Write—and Think—Clearly about any Subject at All.* New York: HarperPerennial.

INDEX

V

W

Printed in Great Britain
by Amazon